CW01510990

A Palace For Our Kings

The history & archaeology of a Mediaeval royal palace
in the heart of Sherwood Forest

By James Wright

With Foreword by Jonathan Foyle

To Helen

Published by Triskele Publishing 2016

www.triskelepublishing.com

A CIP catalogue record for this book is available from the British Library
ISBN 978-0-9954715-0-4

Printed and bound in Great Britain by
Intype Libra Ltd

*This book is dedicated to the memory of
Robert de Clipstone,
who stood up for the rights of his community*

James Wright is a Senior Archaeologist at the Museum of London Archaeology. Formerly he has worked as a conservation stonemason. His previous publications include a book on the *Castles of Nottinghamshire* and several journal articles relating to castles and palaces. Alongside fieldwork at Mediaeval buildings such as the Tower of London, Knole, the Palace of Westminster and Southwark Cathedral he has researched the history and archaeology of Kings Clipstone for over twelve years.

Jonathan Foyle has contributed the foreword to the book. He is a broadcaster, journalist and historic buildings consultant with a background in heritage conservation, research and curating buildings such as Hampton Court. He is Visiting Professor in Conservation at the University of Lincoln and has authored monographs on the cathedrals at Lichfield, Lincoln and Canterbury.

Contents

Foreword by Jonathan Foyle

Royal palaces exert a constant fascination, from wide-eyed children to the squinting scrutiny of archaeologists and historians. As a former buildings curator at Hampton Court and communicator of historic architecture through various media, I can testify to the public appetite for the stories they embody. Palaces are the arenas of faces familiar from lavishly-attired portraits, but they are also places of mystery with a beguiling capacity to retain many of their secrets. This may be due to a lack of documentation by which to vicariously imagine famous events, or an absence of the visual arts so crucial to reading an environment, but more commonly still, the problem is a lack of existence. Many of the great palaces built prior to the civil war are simply gone. Westminster, the greatest of all English medieval palaces and the exemplar by which to compare others across the country, is but a fragment of its former self. Some of the state apartments of Westminster burned in 1512 whereupon it was abandoned as a principal residence, and it was then turned into the seat of parliament in 1547, its vivid decorations broken or whitewashed. It famously avoided being blown up in 1605, but became much fitted-out with joinery – galleries, benches and panelling – that burned ferociously in 1834 after which the complex was largely pulled down and built over.

Today, the name 'Palace of Westminster' rings on, without any royal resident. And this is typical of English medieval royal palaces, having long suffered from being from ill-defined. The etymology of 'palace' comes from 'Palatium'– the Palatine Hill, though English palaces never bore a relationship to Rome except for an echo of imperialistic presence, and the occasional misattribution to Julius Caesar as their builder.

Having swapped emperors for kings, we might ask whether these 'palaces' must have been places from which to administer power. Were they all major residences to service a full court, or could some be minor affairs along progress routes to shelter a few hangers-on? Are smaller royal residences less palatial than bishops' palaces? When does a great castle or a hunting lodge become a palace – when contemporaries describe it so, according to those records that just happen to survive? Why do we not speak of 'Windsor Palace', if being a major royal residence is its primary claim? Without resolving these issues of status, studies of medieval palaces have suffered because such common – and often lazy – labels as 'King John's Hunting Lodge' hardly demand attention. King John seems to have hunted as routinely as Elizabeth I is supposed to have been holed up for the night in our high streets.

Thus it was for Clipstone in Nottinghamshire, a great royal house traditionally labelled as 'King John's Palace' but in the twentieth century described as a hunting lodge. And yet, as Howard Colvin described from the evidence of fourteenth-century documents, it would be a hunting lodge with a Great Gateway, Great Chapel, Great Hall, Great Chamber, King's Kitchen, Queen's Hall, Queen's Kitchen, Chapel adjacent the King's Chamber, lodgings for many leading courtiers, a stable for 200 horses and much besides. The cause for confusion is undoubtedly the disparity between documentation and visible remains, because like the great royal forest-palace of Clarendon in Wiltshire, just a few rubble walls remain to tease us into guessing how the very substantial ranges of buildings at Clipstone once represented a magnificent architectural ensemble. Even a basic understanding of its scale leads us naturally ask how medieval audiences perceived this palatial residence, which witnessed important assemblies as well as the pursuit of pleasure in one of the most renowned of royal forests.

Over the last decade or so, the authors' reassessment of the importance of Clipstone has led to significant discoveries. Through documentary analyses, revising the evidence of old archaeological excavations with new explorations, and offering a better analysis of the historical context, they help us to fill in the picture – and as importantly perhaps, guide us to ask the right questions. From the wide-eyed to the scrutineer, this book is warmly commended to any whose curiosity is aimed at better understanding that most enthralling era, which we have again labelled imprecisely: 'The High Middle Ages'.

Jonathan Foyle

Preface

Clipstone has played a very large part in my life. My archaeological interest in the site has now lasted for one third of my lifespan. The first encounter with King John's Palace was aged thirteen when I saw a very dramatic and highly captivating photograph of the building at a Nottingham tourist attraction. Many years later I saw the ruin shimmering enigmatically in the mist whilst I was camped in the meadow on the opposite side of the valley after a concert at Sherwood Pines. Eventually I visited the site whilst making an assessment of Mediaeval castles and great houses in Nottinghamshire. Three things struck me in the raw sunshine of that bitterly cold February afternoon: firstly, that the landowners, Mickie and Martin Bradley, had a strong-willed determination and infectious enthusiasm for the site far beyond anything that I had ever encountered in custodians of an ancient monument before; secondly, that the long centuries had not been kind to the building and it was now in a critical condition; thirdly, that the archaeological and historical potential had been vastly underestimated and underappreciated.

Many researchers have come before the publication of this book. Initially the antiquarians Thoroton and Grose, then travellers such as Palmer and Crowquill, and the eye of architectural historians Pevsner and Colvin. These were followed by, a gamut of archaeologists beginning in 1956 with Philip Rahtz and later scholars such as David Crook. Immediately after the turn of the millennium the local community produced a wonderful and deeply absorbing social history of Clipstone spanning one thousand years of narrative. Despite all of this work there has always been a lingering belief, widely held by residents, students, local authorities, researchers and tourists, that King John's Palace was never anything more than an insignificant hunting lodge in an obscure village in Sherwood Forest. This belief, more than any other, served to relegate the site to a minor footnote in history and led to the tragically poor state of repair that I found King John's Palace to be in. I am proud to say that in 2009 I was able to work with a team of archaeologists, planning officers, structural engineers, architects and stonemasons to conserve the building and leave it in the best shape that it has been in during the modern era. Part of the success of the conservation project was being able to draw on the previous research to present a new analysis of the site as a major royal Mediaeval palace in the heart of Sherwood Forest. Without studying the history of King John's Palace in detail the true significance of the building, and the enormous palatial complex of which it was once part, would have remained hidden. Without the willpower that such an understanding of the structure instilled, the remnants of King John's Palace may not be with us today.

All architecture has a unique historical background which helps to explain its existence and manner of use. Buildings are intrinsically linked to their times and the people that lived with them. Examples abound, from the castles built as a military and symbolic representation of the Norman Conquest to the walls of Southampton built in reaction to a raid by the French during the Hundred Years War. In the following century the Wars of the Roses were writ large across English architecture as Archbishop Bourchier continued his building project at Knole only during periods when the Yorkists were ascendant. Brick crenellations were added to the walls of London in 1477 after the siege by the Bastard of Fauconberg, and construction of Lord Hastings' castle at Kirby Muxloe came to a halt after Richard III peremptorily ordered his execution. These, of course, are structures effected by violent episodes. Chapels, churches, monasteries and cathedrals have left us with a physical reminder of both the piety and the fear of purgatory that underpinned the Mediaeval period. Manor houses, mills, barns and cottages speak of the agricultural economy and social history. Meanwhile, palaces were constructed as expressions of lavish wealth and status coupled with a level of power that rested easy as there was no necessity for the defensive fortification of residence. They were the venues for major events enacted on a national or international scale. Not only are we left with the built environment of the great houses, but landscape archaeology enables a wider vision of a managed countryside which reflected the romantic aesthetics of the age. Such sites were both effected by, and provided the location for, national and international events. Researching palaces leads towards an understanding of the full breadth of history as well as the minutiae of a site-based study. Clipstone was such a site and this book looks at its wider historical and architectural significance as much as the minutiae of its documentary and archaeological record. The story of Clipstone is as much informed by the national historical picture as by the regional one, and this background helps to explain the construction, use and decline of the palace.

The writing of this book has been fundamentally underpinned by a multi-disciplinary approach. I was tutored at the University of Nottingham by the great buildings archaeologist Dr Philip Dixon who instilled a mantra within me *'to always use all of the tools in the toolkit'* as a mechanism for reaching a more complete understanding of a site. Consequently my approach to the study of the palace at Clipstone has taken into account the techniques and interrogation of field and buildings archaeology, remote sensing, map regression, art and architectural history, landscape survey, documentary history, travelogues, historiography, nature conservation, oral history, etymology and consultation of a wide-ranging amount of secondary sources. My appreciation of the site was brought about by five sets of texts which have proved absolutely indispensable to my research. The first were the works of the earliest person to look at Mediaeval Clipstone in great depth – an amateur historian from Nottingham called Alfred Stapleton who laboured to produce a chronological account of the site in 1890; and the local community who published their own account of the settlement in 2002. Secondly, the published works of John Steane, Graham Keevill and especially Tom Beaumont James who have studied and excavated many Mediaeval palaces across England and provided the background context through which the significance of Clipstone could be finally realised. Professor James' project at Clarendon in Wiltshire has proved to be of greatest impact because the story of that great palace in many respects mirrors that of Clipstone. Thirdly, the great Middle English poem by an anonymous Midlands author *Sir Gawain and the Green Knight* which, despite the fantastical narrative, has proved itself time and again to be firmly rooted in the reality of life in the late fourteenth century. Fourthly, William Senior's estate map of Clipstone created in 1630 for the Earl of Newcastle, which has been generously provided by a private collection for use in this study (Plates 8, 9 and 11A). This extraordinarily accurate and very beautiful map is reproduced in the illustrations section and shows what is essentially a frozen Mediaeval landscape at the cusp of the changes which took place in the later seventeenth century and is therefore of prime value in reconstructing the landscape created and experienced by the Plantagenets. Finally, the translations of original building accounts from the second half of the fourteenth century by my old friend and colleague Richard Reeves have led to a far deeper understanding of the ground plan, buildings, materials, tradesmen, wages and construction of the palace than has ever been possible before. Much of the information gleaned from Reeves' translation work is published and interpreted in this book for the very first time.

James Wright, February 2016, South Norwood

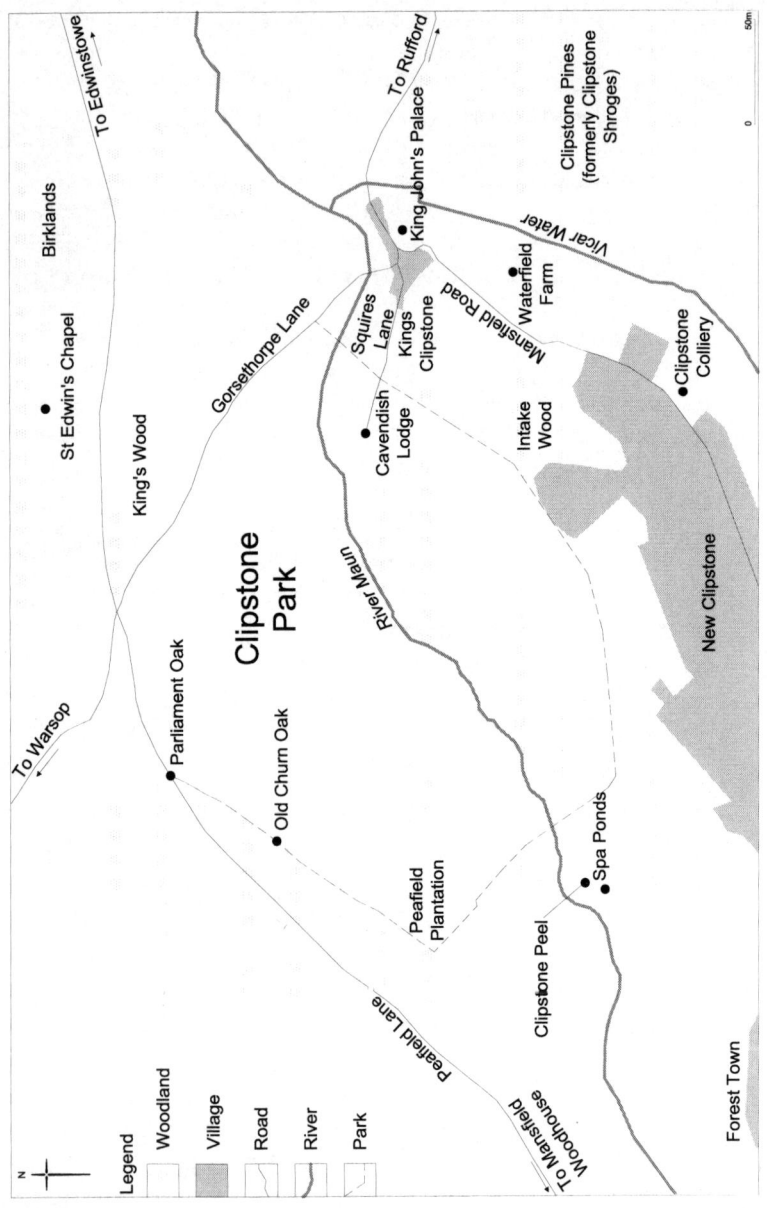

Figure 1: Map of the parish of King's Clipstone

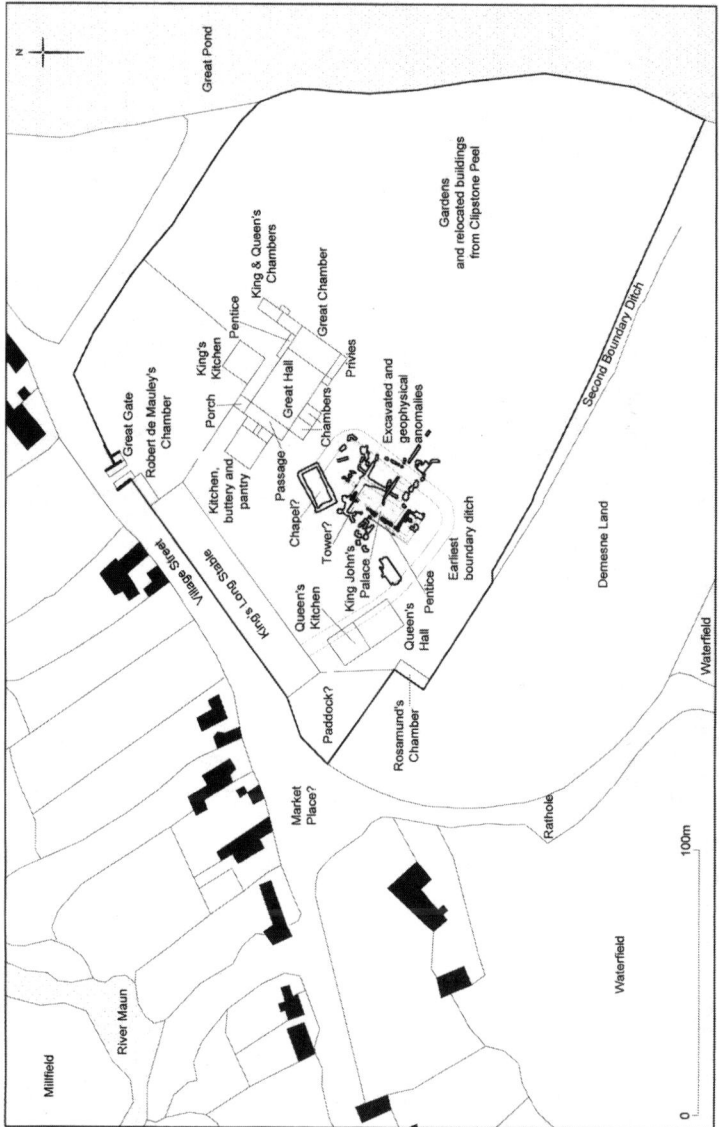

Figure 2: Composite map of the ground plan of the King's Houses, Clipstone in the fourteenth century (See Appendix 3 for detailed information on the construction of this figure)

Introduction

'This ruin stands on the forest, and was a palace for our kings'
~ John Throsby's edition of Robert Thoroton's *The Antiquities of*
Nottinghamshire, 1790 ~

On a low hill overlooking the confluence of the River Maun and the Vicar Water, amidst the gently rolling landscape of Sherwood Forest, stands an unassuming, roofless and ruined stone building (Plate 1 A). Sited just below the brow of the hill, it stands in splendid isolation in the eleven grassy acres of Castlefield. The building is made of local stone and is rectangular in shape, minus its south-eastern wall, and is approximately twenty-five by ten metres in dimension. To the west and north, the brick and pantile village of Kings Clipstone winds along Mansfield Road (Figure 1). Off to the south, beyond the fields of Waterfield Farm, the stark headstocks of the sadly dilapidated colliery at New Clipstone command the horizon. All around is woodland, mostly Forestry Commission coniferous plantation, but the occasional stand of deciduous trees can be made out. The western views are encircled by Peafield Plantation, off to the east is Sherwood Pines, to the north the looming mass of Birklands with the skyline broken by the majestic stone spire of St Mary's parish church two miles away in Edwinstowe.

The building has been known as King John's Palace since at least 1774 when John Chapman annotated his map of Nottinghamshire. In truth it was constructed over twenty years before King John came to the throne and was originally built as a hall for the great Angevin king Henry II during the late 1170s. At this time Henry was at the height of his powers and effectively ruled an empire that stretched from the Pyrenees to the Scottish borders.

After standing in Castlefield for the best part of 850 years the combined forces of history, opportune stone robbery, weather and utterly necessary, yet ugly, structural underpinning have had a dramatic effect upon King John's Palace. Without a thorough programme of conservation carried out in 2009 the building, which was in a very critical state, may not even be standing today. The three walls are mostly formed of a randomly coursed, rubble core of magnesian limestone, with all but a handful of the facing stones cut by highly trained Mediaeval stonemasons have been robbed away. Dramatic masonry overhangs and soaring pinnacles characterise the appearance of what was once a prime piece of architectural design. Yet there is still the impression of eroded buttresses, two openings, the suggestion of a first floor level, and a vaulted niche. There are hints at former glory.

The theatrical remoteness of King John's Palace in the twenty-first century belies the fact that it was once only one of many buildings in a palatial complex known as the King's Houses which sprawled across seven and a half acres of ground. The site was one of the very largest royal residences ever to have graced England during the Mediaeval period. Piercing a great wall encircling the site was a gatehouse tower which allowed access from the village street into a wide courtyard full of buildings such as the huge stable block capable of holding two hundred horses, a timber-framed chamber on a groundwall of stone built to accommodate the household knights and a chapel containing a chantry dedicated to the memory of Henry II with great glazed windows and decorated with elaborate sculpture. Dominating the view was a lofty great hall with a central hearth. The hall, which was filled with trestle tables and benches, served as the beating heart of the palace around which the daily rhythms of the royal court centred. It was connected by a passage to a kitchen with attached buttery and pantry for the storage for beer and bread which were so necessary for feeding the vast royal retinue that may have numbered in excess of five hundred souls. Beyond the upper end of the hall were the royal quarters. Separate suites were built for king and queen that incorporated chapels, chambers, wardrobes, privies, halls and kitchens that were lavishly appointed and kept warm by fireplaces set beneath great chimneys.

From the royal chambers the occupants would have been able to see neatly maintained gardens on the lower slopes of the hill and, to the east, a vast lake created by damming the Vicar Water. Rising up on the opposite slopes of the valley was an enormous rabbit warren beneath the vast Clipstone Wood. The village, newly styled *Clipston Regis*, was surrounded by its open fields worked by the tenant farmers. Their simple timber houses had long and narrow strips of land, reaching down the River Maun, within which they grew herbs and vegetables. Perhaps they also kept animals there too. Mills took advantage of Clipstone Dam and ground flour for the people. Further out to the west, south-east, and north-east were areas of deliberately cleared grassland, known as launds. Beyond them was yet more woodland. Far and away the best view lay to the west. From the upper rooms of the palace there was a view of the vast enclosed deer park whose timber pale fence ran for over seven miles in circumference. Within it was more high ground which dropped down steeply into the valley of the River Maun, the entire enclosed landscape cloaked in oak and birch woodland interspersed with open areas of heather and gorse – and teeming with fallow deer.

On a cold, wet and windy winter's morning this may all seem like a fanciful notion as one peers out across a damp muddy field at the rain dripping off the eroded masonry of the ruin. Many have scoffed at the idea that this was ever more than a simple hunting lodge. However the historical documents speak confidently of the presence of eight Plantagenet monarchs here within what was a very sumptuous palace. Across sixty years archaeologists have laboured within Castlefield and beyond. Slowly the lifestyle of these kings has come to light. The outlines of buildings buried for over five hundred years have been rediscovered along with beautifully carved stonework, painted glass from the windows, pottery that once sat on the tables in front of the household, clasps from illuminated books handwritten by monks, strap-ends from belts which once wrapped around fine clothing, seals belonging to knights, pendants from their horse harness, and coins with the very faces of the kings who stayed here upon them.

For over two hundred years Clipstone was the favoured residence of the Plantagenets in their great royal forest of Sherwood. Not only did they hunt deer in the park, but they held tournaments, hanged criminals, listened to choral music, drank copious quantities of wine, conceived a prince, built a fortress, met envoys from the pope and held parliament. This great assembly of the people reminds us that it was not just the monarchs who graced this landscape, but with them came their queens, children, dukes, earls, bishops, knights, clerks, stewards, chaplains, poets, foresters, messengers and farmers. The ordinary man has had as much of an impact upon Clipstone as have the kings. This is not just the story of a palace in the high Mediaeval period, but it is the tale of how the landscape came to look the way it does today. It is the story of kings, and also of dukes, farmers, archaeologists and the community that live, work and study here in the twenty-first century.

Chapter One

The King's Houses

'Clipstone Palace, of which some venerable ruins remain, consisting of several fragments of massive walls'
~ William White, 1832, *History, Gazetter and Directory of the County of Nottingham* ~

Defining the Palace

Nine years ago I was writing a book about the castles of Nottinghamshire. In order to establish which buildings I could and could not discuss within its pages I used the excellent definition of that class of monument as described by the great architectural historian Reginald Allen Brown: *'the private fortress and residence of a lord.'*[1] This wonderful classification is suitably elastic and allows for sites as diverse as Newark Castle, Lowdham Mound and Halloughton Manor House to be part of the same study. The site of the King's Houses at Clipstone received only a peripheral mention within the book as it was never a fortified site. During the early years of the fourteenth century a defensive peel was established by Edward II, three miles to the south-west of King John's Palace, and this played a greater part in the study. Crucially, the King's Houses did not enjoy such attention because the site belonged to an altogether different class of monument. It was a palace.

Put simply a palace is *'a large and impressive building forming the official residence of a ruler, pope, archbishop, etc.'*[2] This is again a pleasingly malleable definition which enables structures as widely varied in style, date and purpose as Blenheim in Oxfordshire, Knole in Kent, and Southwell in Nottinghamshire to be considered in the same class. Blenheim is, of course, the early eighteenth century mansion designed by John Vanburgh for the Duke of Marlborough (ironically on the site of the Mediaeval royal palace of Woodstock). Knole is a late Mediaeval great house variably occupied by a lord treasurer, archbishops, the monarchy and for the last four hundred years the

Sackville family. Southwell is a much smaller site adjacent to the minster church which provided accommodation for the incumbent bishops from the fourteenth century. Some castles, such as the Tower of London, can also be considered to be palatial based on the range and architectural elaboration of their facilities. However, it is generally a principle that palaces remain unfortified.

Many of the buildings found at manor houses such as the fifteenth century lord treasurer, Ralph Cromwell's property at South Wingfield, Derbyshire may also be found at a palace – the gatehouse, hall, kitchen, chapel and private chambers. However the sheer scale of a palace lifts it to an entirely different level. South Wingfield is a big site and must always be considered as a great house, but it was nowhere close in scale to the royal palaces at Clarendon and Clipstone both of which stretched to seven and a half acres of enclosed land. Whilst South Wingfield had a sizeable hall, Clipstone had three – the communal great hall and individual private halls for both king and queen. Equally, with great size came fabulously lavish decoration, as the powerfully competitive owners of palaces attempted to outshine their peers through architectural elaboration and innovation. Palaces heralded the high status of the individuals who commissioned them.

Roman and Carolingian Origins of Palaces

The word 'palace' derives from the Palatine Hill in Rome where the Emperor Augustus established a vast and grand residence in the first century BC.[3] Such Roman palaces proved to be a lasting influence on European architecture throughout the Mediaeval period. In particular the palace at Constantinople was a sprawling complex whose impact passed directly down to the Carolingian world of the late eighth century in northern France and Germany. Charlemagne's principle residence at Aachen symbolically became the centre of the Holy Roman Empire and as such was based on Roman notions of splendour and consciously reused Roman building materials in the design of his new structures.[4]

The persistent invasions of the empire by Vikings, Magyars and Moors led to the development of proto-castles. Some of these early structures, such as Mayenne (built in the Pays de Loire, France c 900), were again deliberately based on Roman designs. The tenth century residences of Henry I and Otto II drifted towards the east of the empire. There were fortified sites such as Tilleda near Kelbra, Germany, but the palace at Madgeburg on the Elbe River was in total contrast and owed a great deal to the model of Aachen. At Aachen, and also at the new site at Goslar, Germany (which was built in c 1050), the power of the state was buttressed by proximity to major religious complexes. This was a common phenomenon throughout Mediaeval Europe.[5] In late Saxon England Edward the Confessor located the palace of Westminster adjacent to his new minster church. The double height chapel at Aachen may have acted as a powerful influence on later Medieval designs, in particular that of Sainte-Chappelle, Paris (begun in 1239), which was itself a direct inspiration for many of Henry III's chapels, especially that of St Stephen, Westminster.[6]

The early Mediaeval Germanic feasting halls owe their origin to communal living based on the war band, and this was combined in function with the Roman audience chamber such as the early fourth century Konstantinbasilika at Trier constructed for the Emperor Constantine. Charlemagne's hall at Aachen was begun in 794 and, although it was based architecturally on Trier, combined Germanic and Roman utility which in turn influenced Edward the Confessor and later William II's eleventh century great hall at Westminster. So we can therefore see a linear pattern of influence from Trier to Aachen to Westminster and beyond to the provincial halls at sites like Clipstone. The design of gatehouses such as the one mentioned in mid-fourteenth century records at Clipstone also harked back to the Roman models, which themselves probably lay with triumphal arches that could still be seen and used at English towns like the Newport Arch in Lincoln. As with their Roman predecessors Mediaeval gatehouses fulfilled the four functions of regulation of traffic, security, accommodation (there was a chamber above the great gateway at Clipstone), and as a symbolic statement of power.[7]

Rome impacted all aspects of Mediaeval life from the use of Latin as the language of literature and record, to Roman law codes which underpinned European society, and of course Roman Christianity emanating from the Vatican was all pervasive.[8] Small wonder then that the most powerful in society such as the kings who built, remodelled, hunted and lived at Clipstone were under the spell of Rome when they commissioned a palace there. King John's Palace was constructed on the principals of Roman architecture based on the round-headed arch.

Plantagenet Palaces

The English kings had a variable number of palatial residences over time. Henry II and Richard owned 23, John increased this stock to 29. The number of palatial residences had fallen to around 20 by the reign of John's grandson, Edward I (1239–1307), who was perhaps more concerned with fortifications as a result of his military ambitions in the Holy Land, France, Wales and Scotland. By 1485 there were only 8 regularly used palaces in England, none of none of which were located further north than Oxfordshire.[9] Clipstone was maintained as a royal residence from at least 1164 until the mid-fifteenth century. It was part of the regular itineraries of the kings until 1396 after which, although it was never visited and was often granted for periods of time to loyal retainers, the monarchy continued to pay for its maintenance and even constructed new buildings there as late as the 1440s.

The feudal economy of the earlier Mediaeval period was based on tenant farmers working the land for their lord in return for food and a place to live. This was coupled with an avid enthusiasm amongst the aristocracy for hunting, which led to a preference for royal houses being located at rural sites in this earlier period.[10] This preference for the open countryside could also be linked to political events. For example, in 1264 rebellious Londoners destroyed the manor of Isleworth belonging to Richard of Cornwall, brother of Henry III as part of an outward show of support for Simon de Montfort.[11] This urban civil unrest led Edward I to significantly strengthen the defences at the Tower of London during the early years of his reign.[12] The king's houses were therefore carefully chosen to be outside of towns, yet still related spatially to major urban centres with which they had to maintain a connection despite the turbulence of the citizenry. Consequently, Henry II built a hall at Wigford on the outskirts of Lincoln, Clarendon was intervisible with Old Sarum (later Salisbury), and Woodstock was in proximity to Oxford.[13] It follows that Clipstone was close to royal sites at Mansfield, Darlton and Nottingham. Nottingham latter incorporated the vast complex located on Castle Rock which acted as fortress, residence and centre of regional governmental. There was inevitably some overlap between the residential and administrative functions of Nottingham Castle and the palace at Clipstone – both were designed to '*impart powerful messages of control and dominance*'[14] although the former had a defensive quality akin to the Tower of London and Windsor Castle, which the latter did not. Palaces were able to take advantage of the open landscape and inevitably sprawled across a greater area of ground as the need for defence management did not demand a confined enclave be adopted.

A further reason for the location of sites such as Clarendon, Woodstock and Clipstone being located in in rural areas was so that the monarchy could take advantage of the proximity of the great game reserves created in the royal forests such as that of Sherwood. Forests were not necessarily endless stretches of woodland; they were usually a mixture of trees, open ground and cultivated land in lightly populated regions of poor quality soils which provided a habitat for the deer and other beasts of the chase. The forest was a legal definition, associated with Forest Law. Perhaps one third of England was under this law during the twelfth century. The law was intended to protect the beasts of the chase and to encourage their welfare so that they would thrive and enable the kings to have vast stocks to hunt. In the forests red, fallow and roe deer plus the wild boar could be hunted only by the king. Lesser animals such as hares, rabbits, foxes, badgers and wildcats could be hunted by others only under royal licence of free warren. However the protection of the beasts necessitated the careful control of the animals' habitats, and this greatly impacted upon the life of the peasant farmers. Regulation controlled the cutting of timber for building or firewood. The clearing of woodland for agriculture was severely limited. Woodland pasture for pigs, known as pannage, required the payment of a fine and could only be enacted under close supervision – unless the deer were fawning, in which case pannage was entirely prohibited. Carts had to be kept on the highways and could not be taken into the woodlands. Dogs had to have the claws on their forefeet trimmed (known as 'lawed'), and it was strictly forbidden for the people to carry bows and arrows. The draconian law effected lands which were actively occupied and farmed. The law was not simply for land set aside for royal use. Although parts of the forest were made up of royal demesne, much was held by other lords whose rights were circumscribed rather than extinguished. Essentially, Forest Law was additional to the ordinary government and law of the land.[15] There was a very definite correlation between afforestation and the location of royal palaces. As the area under Forest Law increased so did the number of royal residences. Henry II tightened his control on the forests in the later 1170s, so we see not only the appearance of Clipstone in Sherwood, but also of Feckenham in Worcestershire, Wakefield in Yorkshire and a further five other houses.[16] Hunting deer and other animals within the forests provided for the feast, and venison was the food of social prestige. Hunting was also a mechanism for training in horsemanship and martial feats for the wars. Demonstrations of courage and fitness for war also acted as bonding experiences, cementing social and political relationships between neighbours and allies.[17] These multifunctional aspects of the hunt were exploited at Clipstone by Richard I who opted to meet William the Lion, King of Scotland, there in 1194. Edward II timed many of his lengthy stays at the King's Houses to perfectly compliment certain hunting seasons of particular species of deer. Richard II made his first visit to Clipstone Park directly after resolving a political crisis, probably as a way to unwind with the pleasures of the chase.

Certain general statements can be made about what Plantagenet palaces looked like, and it is clear that Clipstone was entirely typical. Hilltop sites were often favoured, although they were essentially unfortified. Undefended sites were a feature of the English experience as, despite semi-regular tensions and short outbreaks of civil war, on the whole the king was safe in England. This contrasts with the French monarchy of the time, who had to resort to heavily protected castles and towns especially during the fourteenth and fifteenth centuries. The fact that lightly enclosed palaces were a feature of the royal built environment is testament to the effective power and control that the English monarchy exercised during the Mediaeval period.[18] Despite this relative security, a society which was based on militarism and the retention of power needed to make certain architectural statements in its buildings – towers were a big part of this. Therefore it is common to find that, although the palaces might be surrounded by ditches and walls pierced by an impressive looking crenelated gate tower, their purpose was more symbolic than effective. Ranges of buildings, rather than curtain walls, often acted as the perimeter of a palace. The boundary wall at Clipstone was only half a metre thick and there is evidence of a Mediaeval splayed window at ground floor level facing directly onto the village street in the gatehouse.[19]

Despite the design of palaces not being intended to cope with a serious siege, there were certain security considerations that needed to be made. For long periods of time the monarch would not be present at all. Henry III reigned for 65 years 5 months and 16 days, yet we only know for certain that he spent a total of four days at Clipstone, despite ordering expensive programmes of building work during the 1230s, 40s and 50s. The palace would not have been left unattended during these periods of absence. Keepers such as Roger de Essex, Earner Engayne and Robert le Vavassur were charged with monitoring the site for the monarch. The enclosure of a palace was necessary to deter brigands. As law and order declined during the early years of the fourteenth century the numbers of semi-fortified sites grew to a peak during the reign of Edward II.[20] Many Nottinghamshire barons, such as Sampson de Strelley and Nicholas de Canteloupe, fortified their manor houses as much to protect their families and possessions from organised gangs active in the East Midlands (such as the rampaging Folville and Cotterill families) as to aggrandise themselves through high status architecture.[21] Edward II was sufficiently insecure that he felt obliged to construct a fortified peel at Clipstone in 1316 to cope with the threat posed by his troublesome cousin Thomas of Lancaster. The peel was actually used by the local people as a refuge during disturbances in the area in 1317–18.[22]

Within the enclosure of the palace the buildings had a very diverse layout. This remained the case until the fashion for symmetrical courtyards took over in the later Medieval period. This fashion was exemplified by Thomas Bourchier's three courtyards at Knole and Henry VII's development of Hampton Court. The term 'palace' was rarely applied by contemporaries to describe such grand buildings. Gerald of Wales wrote that Bishop Henry of Blois built '*palatia sumptuosissima*' (sumptuous palaces) and William Fitzstephen noted that the Tower of London was '*arx palatina*' (fortified palace).[23] In the building accounts of the time royal residences were most commonly referred to as '*domus regia*' (King's Houses) which is a term that accurately represents the '*incoherently and irregularly laid out*'[24] chaotic asymmetry of multiple buildings linked together by pentices[25]. On the approach to a Mediaeval palace the overall appearance must have been one of a densely packed settlement with a confusion of differing building heights, orientations, and rooflines.

The hall was at the epicentre of the Mediaeval palace. It was a multifunctional space that could be used for feasting, entertainment, and as a courthouse. Many lower status people would have used it as a sleeping space. Mediaeval palace halls were spaces that could be used as an art gallery, with windows deliberately placed high enough so that tapestries could be hung against the walls beneath them. That art, and the architecture which encased it, acted as a potent symbol of the cultured nature, aesthetics, learning and power of the lord who presided there. The design feature of lower and upper ends of the hall engendered the extreme forms of social hierarchy. During feasts the location in which a person sat was directly indicative of their social status, so that the closer to the lord that they were seated the more important the person. This highly ritualised society was almost completely dominated by men, and the presence of women in the hall was a great rarity. The ceremony of the feast was emphasised by the great honour of serving the lord. Carving the meat was ritualised and very skilful (reminiscent of the butchery of the hunt), so that only a trusted and very high status retainer would be engaged for such service. It was certainly not a menial task to serve food at the high table. The location of this table at the upper end of the hall was usually characterised by a raised dais, the proximity to a source of heating, greater provision of lighting and immediate accessibility to the private quarters beyond. Despite the rigors of such a status-conscious society, the hall was viewed as engendering a sense of community beneath that lordship. In the thirteenth century Bishop Grosseteste advised the Countess of Lincoln to always '*be seated at the middle of the high table, that your presence as lord or lady may appear only to all... constrain yourself to eat in the hall before your people for this shall bring great benefit and honour to you.*'. A century later Langland made a complaint about nobles no longer regularly using great halls in preference for private dining in their chambers: '*for when the lord and lady eat elsewhere every day of the week, their hall is a sorry deserted place.*'[26]

The kitchens that provided the great feasts of the nobility were detached to avoid fire, smells, heat, smoke, and steam. These kitchens were usually a single storey to allow air circulation through louvres in their roof structures to create adequate ventilation. Sanitary provisions were basic. Pits were employed to receive any wastage and garderobes deposited human waste into a variety of places including the sea, lakes and moats, but most commonly into cesspits which would have to be routinely cleared out by one of the lowliest of household servants – the gongfermour (literally meaning 'privy farmer').

The separate ranges of buildings were linked by lean-to timber-framed passageways known as pentices and, as much of the palace infrastructure was constructed from timber, outbreaks of fire were frequent. This meant repairs had to be made ad hoc, often in advance of royal visits. These visits would then create wear and tear on the buildings which would lead to further necessary repairs. Such constant use of residences meant that for much of the time they would have appeared as a building site, and it is clear why the ground plan of a palace was essentially a fluid affair which led to a chaotic asymmetry.

Chapels provided for the spiritual life of the palaces. There would have been at least one at every residence, but like Clipstone (which had a communal chapel, chapels for king and queen as well as a more remote chapel on the edge of the park served by the chaplain from the palace) multiple chapels were entirely normal. Winchester Castle also had four chapels and their proliferation can be explained by the need for private devotion alongside the presence of multiple royal households present at a residence at once, coupled with the sacred and removed nature of Mediaeval kingship.[27] Aside from the more regimented services of the day, joyful rituals took place in the chapel. Examples include the wedding of Roger Beauchamp and Sybil Patteshull in 1337 at Clipstone, which was witnessed by Edward III and Philippa of Hainault.[28]

Private chambers were often added piecemeal. The original conception at Clipstone seems to have consisted of merely a chapel, hall and chambers which were later enclosed within a courtyard.[29] Separate royal suites of rooms and chapels were a characteristic of only the larger houses or fully developed castles,[30] and do not seem to have been added at Clipstone until the mid-thirteenth century when Henry III upgraded the existing accommodation to provide for Queen Eleanor.

The Itinerant Household

Medieval kingship was largely itinerant and the king rarely stayed in one place for more than a few days. John was one of the more mobile monarchs and made 150 moves per year on average, whereas his son Henry III averaged 80 locations a year until after 1250 when his health began to decline and this slipped to just 22 in 1271. The martial kings Edward I and Edward III were also notably mobile, the latter managing to travel a total of 65 miles between the morning of 18 May and the afternoon of the following day in 1360.[31] A reason for this continual cycle of gruelling and relentless progress was the establishment and continuation of power through the living presence of the monarch. This entailed a display of power through a demonstration of unencumbered travel. In the Norman and early Angevin period this would be punctuated by crown-wearing ceremonies as status events, laying claim to property, warfare and the conference of honours, charters and justice[32] – '*royal itinerary dramatized in concrete terms the fact that the king was ruling.*'[33]

Although Edward II was capable of travelling at speed his reign was marked by very lengthy spells in single locations. He spent a total of 62 days at Clipstone between 29 October 1315 and 25 January 1316; the following winter a similar pattern was followed when Edward was again at Clipstone for thirty days between 9 December 1316 and 17 January 1317. There are undoubtedly political reasons for such unusually lengthy visitations bound up with ongoing strain placed on his relationship with Thomas of Lancaster who was also present in the Midlands during this time. The pressures placed on food provision were clearly more than could be coped with locally, as foragers were sent out into Lincolnshire in 1316. The previous year an astonishing 1,700 fish had been consumed by the royal household during the Christmas period from the stocks at Clipstone.[34]

It was the size of the permanent household (*domus*) and extended household (*familia*) that created so many mouths to feed, and that led to the necessity to keep moving. In the early twelfth century the domus was a relatively small number, around 150. This number increased significantly later in the period.[35] There were in excess of 200 people listed in Edward I's entourage for 1306, whereas Edward III travelled with a retinue of some 350–450 souls. Alongside the king, queen and members of the royal family, the following could include officers of the household, chaplains, surgeons, messengers, porters, trumpeters, valets, grooms, sumpters, huntsmen and a dizzying array of servants with very specific tasks such as looking after the books, the wardrobe and the kitchens.[36] The inventory of Edward III's daughter Joan in 1348 gives us an idea of just what all of those servants and staff members were required to transport: furnishings for a chapel and hall (including hangings decorated with parrots and roses), hangings for two beds, two chairs, three ceremonial saddles, a large amount of equipment for the kitchen, buttery and pantry including a supply of expensively prized spices.[37] Given that Joan was merely a princess and would have had a reduced household, much smaller than the king's, it is somewhat mesmerising to consider just how many people carrying such large amounts of goods must have been present at Clipstone.

Members of the royal family had their own manors, so when travelling individually they probably took their own households to those rather than to the kingly sites.[38] Estates were developed to provide for specific branches of the royal family and in this way individual households were able to become economically independent.[39] Isabella of France was gifted the manor of Eltham, the Black Prince favoured his residence at Kennington. Portchester was placed in the ownership of various queens, as was the Queen's Bower at Bolderford in the New Forest. In 1235 the Tower of London was used by Henry III's sister Isabella for an extended period of time. The picture that emerges indicates that although the preference was for dispersed households, the nature of family and political life necessitated that those households must have converged. Edward III's son Lionel of Antwerp had a chamber kept for him at Clipstone in the 1340s pointing to his presence in Sherwood Forest. Eleanor of Castile was specifically granted and acquired manors for her own use which hints that royals did not use the king's residences unless they were travelling with him (as she was when at Clipstone during her final year in 1290).[40]

Court Life

In 1177 Henry II's lord treasurer, and future Bishop of London, Richard Fitzneal wrote a text entitled *Dialogus de Scaccario* (Dialogue of the Exchequer) in which he stated that: '*The forests are also the sanctuaries of Kings and their chief delight. Thither they repair to hunt, their cares laid aside the while, in order to refresh themselves by a short respite. There, renouncing the arduous but natural turmoil of the court, they breathe the pure air of freedom for a little space.*' This indicates that, as Fitzneal saw it, the principle reason for monarchs to visit their rural palaces was for relaxation and so that they could go hunting. As we have already seen this perhaps casts a rather single-minded purpose across the venture because Fitzneal, as treasurer, must have been aware that Henry II conducted the day-to-day business of the court from the palaces in his forests. Henry issued a charter to the order of the Lazarites from Clipstone in August 1181, and we know that his next definite visit occurred in 1185 when he issued more charters to Thurgarton Priory, Nottinghamshire and Barlings Abbey, Lincolnshire. As befits a monarch Henry was also in some very august company when he sent out these documents, as they were witnessed by the Bishop of Durham and Earl of Arundel amongst others.[41] Analysis of the documents relating to Clipstone demonstrate that the kings were extremely business-minded when they were at the palace. In 1290 Edward I paid 200 marks to merchants in Pistoia in Italy, in 1307 Edward II ordered that the former treasurer Walter de Langton's land and possessions be seized, and in 1345 Edward III ordered 51,000 florins to be delivered to the Earls of Lancaster and Pembroke.[42]

We mostly know the whereabouts of Mediaeval monarchs from the writs that they issued as they travelled about the land. It is almost certain that we are missing many of these documents and that some days they simply were not dispensed. In 1338 Edward III was in Hertford on 8th January but his whereabouts are then not known until he reappeared on the 11th some 130 miles to the north at Blyth, Nottinghamshire.[43] It is entirely possible that Clipstone was visited en route, but as no writs were issued during this three-day period we can simply never know where he actually was.

Palaces were intended to impress the king's subjects with a display of their power and might through symbolic architecture, and the list of magnates and high-ranking churchmen who were present at Clipstone throughout the period of its use reflects this. At John's first visit to the King's Houses in March 1200 the Earl of Essex, Sherriff of Nottingham, Archdeacon of Wells and Archdeacon of Cleveland were also present. Palaces were also constructed to shine on the international stage. Richard I staged his diplomatic meeting with his ally William the Lion of Scotland at Clipstone in 1194 and in January 1317 Edward II received the papal envoy Amenenus de Pelagrua.[44]

One purpose of a palace was as a location for feasting, and an important aspect of banqueting was the consumption of wine. A contemporary chronicler known to us only as the Monk of Evesham recorded that Richard II was keen on '*staying up half the night, and at other times right through until the morning drinking.*'[45] Wine was only available to the very highest levels of society and along with venison was consumed in virtually unlimited quantity.[46] We have many references to the transport of wine to and from Clipstone. John ordered two tuns of wine to be moved from Nottingham to Clipstone on 28 September 1205. Two years later, on 28 July 1207, he demanded that three tuns of 'Wascon' and one tun of 'Mussac' wine were transported to the palace, and on 12 October the same year three dolia (around 624 gallons in total) of wine were sent to the King's Houses.[47] John's son Henry III was perhaps not as thirsty as his father when he ordered the Sheriff of Nottingham to sell all of his wines stored at Clipstone in August 1249.[48] However on the feast of St Edmund in 1244 the combined households of Henry III and Bishop William Ralegh consumed five tuns of wine whilst at Winchester.[49] This was also the period where supplies of wine increased at Clarendon leading to the doubling in size of the cavernous partially vaulted cellar.[50]

Household entertainments were varied. Music was a much favoured pastime at residences under Henry III.[51] At Clipstone we only really know about music during the reign of his grandson Edward II when a female chorus recruited from Bilsthorpe performed in front of Queen Isabella.[52] Pursuits such as chess, dice, music and acrobats were popular under Edward I[53] and Christmas masques took place at the residences under Edward III.[54] During the later fourteenth century we have evidence that courtiers enjoyed reading aloud from texts to one another, and the two book clasps discovered in Castlefield in 2011 point towards expensive hand-written texts being present at Clipstone.[55]

Palaces were used in a remarkably elastic fashion by the monarchs. Their purposes varied according to a wide variety of circumstances not just from king to king but even within individual reigns. The personal preferences of a king might lead to a combination of reasons to visit a particular palace which may have involved sport, recreation, councils, parliaments, building campaigns, impressing magnates and dignitaries, retreating from plague, or as a resting point on a longer journey. Significantly it is only the great castles and palaces that bore witness to major political enactments. Whereas Clarendon or Clipstone witnessed key assemblies, smaller sites such as Ludgershall, Wiltshire hosted none of the pivotal life-events of the Plantagenets.[56]

We shall discuss the great Mediaeval pursuits of hunting and jousting in some detail below, but now it is time to say something of the early history of Clipstone so that we can better understand the landscape that existed by the mid-twelfth century when Henry II began to develop the King's Houses.

Chapter Two

Early History of Clipstone

'*Then he sent his men over all England into every shire and had them find out how many hundred hides there were in the shire, or what land and cattle the king himself had in the country, or what dues he ought to have in 12 months from the shire*'
~ Anglo-Saxon Chronicle on the Domesday Survey ~

Prehistory

By the time of the Domesday Survey of 1086 the landscape of Clipstone had already been intensively occupied and managed for several millennia. Small numbers of flints dating from the Mesolithic (c 8000–4000 BC) to the Bronze Age (c 2000–700BC) have been uncovered during excavation within Castlefield.[57] Bronze Age metalwork has also been recovered from within the parish – a spearhead and an arrowhead – and there is also a suspected ring ditch in the vicinity of New Clipstone which is assumed to be a ploughed out round barrow associated with the high status cremation funerary rites of the period.[58] The Bronze Age marked the beginning of a technological revolution in metalworking which helped to solidify and build upon the agricultural advances made during the Neolithic period (c 4000–2000BC). From c 1800BC circular houses began to appear as part of structured individual farmsteads or small family groupings as the landscape was intensively farmed and divided with boundaries leading to widespread deforestation.[59]

Romano-British Farmers

Agricultural land-use continued into the late Iron Age and Romano-British period and a number of cropmarks recorded from aerial photography in the northern quarter of Clipstone parish represent rectilinear field systems associated with small stock enclosures and perhaps domestic sites. Typologically, and from their orientation, it is assumed that these were part of the brickwork plan field system from the late Iron Age which stretches across the Sherwood sandstones.[60] The small interlocking fields were a common feature of the British Iron Age agrarian landscape, and their use was not seriously interrupted by the coming of the Roman empire. As in more remote areas the villa system of farming had a more limited impact.[61] Despite this, the adjacent parish of Mansfield Woodhouse to the west of Clipstone contains a suspected Roman road, Leeming Lane, with an associated marching camp at Roman Bank. Further to the north-west a small villa site was exposed in 1780 by the antiquarian Major Hayman Rooke.[62]

Pottery of the Romano-British period is known from Castlefield, some of it from sealed archaeological contexts such as a small ditch[63] and the charcoal-rich fill of a pit[64] which both yielded locally-made greyware sherds similar to those manufactured at Gateford, Nottinghamshire in the first and second centuries.[65] Nearby, finds of several contemporary copper alloy brooches,[66] a very worn Roman coin which had been reused as a pendent,[67] a lead spindle whorl,[68] a small coin hoard[69] and a mid-third century coin have been discovered.[70] Meanwhile several Roman fragments of tegula and imbrex from a tile roof have been recovered from the topsoil[71] indicating that structures of a reasonable status Romano-British farmstead were probably once located within the vicinity of Castlefield.

Early Mediaeval

There is a strong local tradition which links Edwinstowe and Clipstone to the death of King Edwin of Northumbria at the battle of Hatfield. Edwin died in 633 in conflict with the combined forces of Penda of Mercia and Cadwallon ap Cadfan of Gwynedd. Edwin was later canonised as he was considered to be a Christian martyr fighting against the pagan Penda. Ironically this was not a war of religion, Penda's ally Cadwallon was actually a Christian himself, but instead had everything to do with territorial ambition. The precise location of the battle is not fully understood, but placename evidence and the discovery of a large number of skeletons during the 1950s in an apparent mass-grave beneath foundations of the north wall of the twelfth century church at Cuckney, six miles to the north-west of Clipstone, has led to speculation that it may have taken place close by. Traditional stories persist that, prior to his burial at Whitby, the slain king was interred at nearby Edwinstowe[72] and it is possible that King John's 1205 foundation of St Edwin's Chapel in Birklands may have been related to this.

The settlement of Clipstone came into being during the Early Mediaeval period, although the first historical reference to Clipstone was not until the Domesday Book when it was mentioned as 'Clipestune'.[73] Subsequent written sources used the forms Clipestone, Clippeston and Clipiston. The name means 'Klyppr's Farm' with the derivation of the first element being from an Old Scandinavian personal name 'Klyppr', and the second element from the Anglo-Saxon word for farm or hamlet 'tun'.[74] The placename is a relative of what has come to be called a Grimston Hybrid whereby a combination of an Old Scandinavian personal name and an Anglo-Saxon word were spliced together, indicating that the name must have been given after the Danish incursions into the East Midlands during the mid-ninth century. Clipstone is essentially a name that is indicative of the blending of the two cultures within the Danelaw. Clipstone was part of the administrative district known as the Wapentake of Bassetlaw and nearby is the possible meeting place at Thynghowe. The site was identified by map regression and placename evidence – 'thyng' denoting a gathering and 'howe' a mound. An enclosure encircles the hilltop which is located at the parish boundary between Edwinstowe and Warsop.[75] Significantly, only Clipstone parish divided Thynghowe from the boundary between the Wapentakes of Broxtowe and Bassetlaw.

The settlement pattern within the manor of Clipstone probably began to nucleate during the mid-ninth century as farmers had begun to exhaust the easier soils which were possible to plough individually and needed to come together in a co-operative effort to share resources of oxen to pull their ploughs through more difficult soils. There may have been some lordly coercion towards nucleation and the beginning of the Mediaeval open field system as landowners sought to maximise crop harvests and demanded a communal effort rather than relying on the lower-yielding independence of the Middle Saxon period.[76] Consequently the late Iron Age or Romano-British brickwork fields to the north of the parish may have become waste due to the infertility of the land and the open field system developed around the conjunction of the River Maun and Vicar Water. Aelfric of Cerne Abbas' written dialogue gives an accurate impression of rural life around the year

1000 as it must have been experienced across the land in the late Saxon period: '*Every day at the crack of dawn I have to drive the oxen out to the field and yoke them to the plough. I would never dare to scive at home, no matter how bad the winter weather: I'm too frightened of my landlord for that. No, once I've yoked the oxen and fastened the share and coulter to the plough, I must plough a full acre or more every day...My lad drives the oxen with his goad: he's hoarse today because it's so cold and he's been doing all that shouting...I've got to fill all the oxen's bins with hay, give them water, muck them out...It's hard work all right, sir, because I am not free.*'[77] Late Saxon shelly-ware pottery was recorded during fieldwalking of Castlefield in 1991[78] and it is likely that these represent a background scatter of material associated with the nightsoil manuring of the open fields. There is also tantalising evidence of ditches cut in the south-east quadrant of Castlefield which were earlier than the Mediaeval palace boundary ditch and may contain Saxo-Norman era pottery in the upper fill.[79] Potentially these are part of the Saxon land management of Clipstone, but further work is required before this interpretation is confirmed.

Subsequent to the Anglo-Saxon re-conquest of Mercia in 910 it is feasible that Clipstone was part of the "Sciryuda" referred to in 958.[80] The name means 'Shire Wood' and it may have been a precursor to what became Sherwood. The earliest reference to the county within which Clipstone is located – Nottinghamshire – also occurs during this period, when the Anglo-Saxon chronicle recorded that in 1016 Cnut led a raiding part through the county.[81]

Later in the eleventh century the Domesday Survey tells us that Clipstone was in the hands of two Saxon lords in 1066, Osbern and Wulfsi, and that the value of the manor was set at 60 shillings.[82] Ownership of the lordship was in two pairs of hands, and although there were not two distinct manors there may have been multiple centres of settlement. Landscape analysis has hinted that these may have been located along Squires Lane to the west and around the area of the later Mediaeval water mills on the River Maun to the north-east. Following the establishment of the twelfth century palace the present village probably conjoined between the earlier nuclei directly to the north of Mansfield Road with the River Maun to the rear of the properties[83].

Wulfsi was a fairly major landholder in west Nottinghamshire, and especially in Bassetlaw, owning estates at Blyth, Cuckney, Hodsock, Greasley, Hockerton, Carlton-on-Trent, Marnham and the lost villages of Roolton and

Sutton Passeys. The name Wulfsi derives from a much older Saxon form of the name originally spelled Ulfsig meaning 'victory-wolf.' Eventually Wulfsi became Wulsi and finally by the late Mediaeval period was a well-known surname – Wolsey. The latter name made especially famous by Henry VIII's Lord Chancellor and Archbishop of York – Cardinal Thomas Wolsey (1473–1530). It is not certain whether Wulfsi survived the Norman Conquest of 1066, however it is somewhat significant that a landowner and tenant with the same name is connected to two manors in a similar part of the county in 1086 – West Drayton and Strelley. It is entirely possible that this represents a much diminished estate of a disenfranchised pre-Conquest landholder or possibly one of his relatives.

Domesday

The 1086 Domesday Survey preceded a considerable round of taxation which was probably needed to pay the Norman King William I's soldiers involved in armed conflicts created by tensions with France, Brittany, Wales, Scotland and Denmark. This was compounded by turbulent times created by the ever-present threat of revolt in England, a land that had been ravaged by '*war, hunger and pestilence*' exacerbated by bad weather and crop failure. The survey seemed to have three functions – an assessment of the local contributions that could be made to the nationwide tax levy known as the king's geld; a survey of the feudal land and revenue held by the king's tenants who were his military hierarchy at a time of potential crisis; and finally, it recorded the enormous changes in land ownership during the past twenty years since the Conquest and established the means to finally settle legal disputes over that ownership. Questions asked by the surveyors included the name of the estate, its past and present owners, the numbers of ploughs, the population and landscape details such as woods, meadows, pasture and mills. Finally the inevitable valuation – how much was the manor worth in 1066 versus the assessment in 1086.[84] Clipstone dropped in value by 20s, a fact possibly related to the reprisals against rebels in the North and Midlands. The commissioners went to each shire court to hear the testimonies of local juries regarding the king's possessions and the pre-existing Anglo-Saxon local government bureaucracy was effectively utilised as the mechanism for gathering the data.[85]

The translated text of the Domesday reference for Clipstone reads very simply:

Land of Roger of Bully
Bassetlaw Wapentake
In Clipstone [Clipestvne] *Osbern and Wulfsi had 1 carucate of land taxable. Land for 2 ploughs. Roger has 1 ½ ploughs in lordship and 12 villagers and 3 smallholders who have 3 ½ ploughs. 1 mill, 3 shillings; woodland pasture in places, 1 league long and 1 wide. Value before 1066, 60 shillings; now 40 shillings*

The agricultural nature of the feudal economy is confirmed through the discussion of how much ploughland was in lordship – a carucate, for example, was the Danish equivalent of the Saxon hide which amounted to the total area of land that could be ploughed by eight oxen – this of course varied across the country according to the nature of the soils.[86] Domesday described Clipstone's woodland as suitable for pasture, and the later enclosure of the deer park eventually directly affected that resource. The men of Mansfield must have once enjoyed this common right as in 1200 they discussed the payment of fifteen marks with King John to have the pasture returned to the way it was before Henry II's enclosure. Apparently the fee was never paid,[87] perhaps it was simply too expensive for the commoners to consider.

The total population of a Domesday manor is usually calculated as a multiple of between four and five times the number of tenants stated in the survey to account for the presence of women and children who were not assessed[88] which puts Clipstone's inhabitants at between 60 to 70 individuals. The High Forest area of Sherwood was characterised by very low population density in 1086, amounting to an average of less than 2.5 individuals per square mile. Nationally the numbers of smallholders accounted for 10–25% of the population. These were the highest class of peasants who were not bound to an estate and who had the right to sell their land despite being bound through services or rents to their lord. One fifth of the population of Clipstone was smallholders, a low percentage in a region where more than 40.6% of the population were in this class.[89] More commonly called 'sokemen', the smallholders had become well established by the period of the Danish Five

Boroughs in the East Midlands although their numbers decreased after the Conquest. The reason for this proliferation of sokemen is debatable. It may be regional and related to the establishment of the Danelaw, however it is simply not possible to say whether these conditions might have pre-existed the Viking incursions and may be much older and related to a Middle Saxon society which was inherited by the Danes untouched by the influence of Wessex. The area of land held by the sokemen of the eastern counties was relatively small and, in truth, despite a level of independence their economic position was less than that of the un-free villeins (tenant farmers) of southern England.[90]

The lordship of the manor was held by Roger de Bully who was one of the principle Norman landowners in England, a group that numbered perhaps only 180 men whose income was estimated to be in excess of £100 per year. Roger was born c 1038 and came from Bully in Upper Normandy (known as Buslei c 1060). He was one of the veterans of the Hastings campaign which had won William the Bastard, Duke of Normandy, the crown of England in 1066. De Bully was related to the Counts of Eu and therefore to William; he was also a member of the family of Roger de Montgomery, Earl of Shrewsbury and Arundel, a man linked to other top-ranking Normans including Odo of Bayeux, the half-brother of William. Given such powerful connections it is not surprising that Roger de Bully was granted 163 estates in Nottinghamshire, Derbyshire and south Yorkshire following the Conquest, of which Clipstone was one of eighteen manors that he kept as part of his own private demesne land. Roger and his wife Muriel granted the tithe of one carucate of land at Clipstone to the monks of Blyth when they founded a priory there in 1088.[91] De Bully died c 1098–9 and his son passed away without heirs in 1102. At this point the lordship of Clipstone seems to have reverted to the Crown thus setting the scene for the development of the royal residence in the manor.

Sherwood Forest

The presence of Sherwood Forest was a key reason for the monarchy's interest in Clipstone. Forest Law was introduced by the Normans to a land that was not used to such restrictions. Although there was a concept of the ownership of woodlands and the animals within them during the Saxon period, if those animals strayed into another man's wood he was free to hunt them. Deer were not the preserve of the monarchy alone. The Norman idea of a forest set aside for the enjoyment of the king alone comes from the laws of Charlemagne and northern France.[92] The forests provided an important source of produce for the crown so that venison was eaten or deer sent as gifts to aristocrats and churchmen, the trees provided necessary building materials for residences and charcoal was produced to fuel the smelting and smithing of iron.[93] The forests also proved to be an economic asset through heavy fines levied for transgressions, and as a result were held onto with determination by a succession of very strong kings.[94]

The development of Forest Law in Nottinghamshire followed a nationwide pattern. In the mid-twelfth century Henry I added to the forest stock[95] and the county north and west of the Trent was afforested, although this may have been the case right back into the reign of William I. There was a discernible slip in the control and administration of the forests during the years of King Stephen's troubled reign, This was rectified and then probably increased under Henry II.[96] Forests were such a symbol of royal power and authority that Henry II reneged upon his wartime promise to reform the Forest Law. After the total victory over his rivals in 1174 Henry II he retrospectively punished all those who had recently infringed upon the forest. The law therefore became a stringent political tool and a survey of the forests in 1175 was carried out in person by the king.[97] Richard I took the lands of Southwell Minster out of the forest in 1189, but it was partly the tension caused by the extents of the forests that contributed to the outbreak of civil war between John and his barons.[98]

Magna Carta attempted to redress the balance but had no great effect, despite reissues in 1216 and 1217.[99] The Charter of the Forest in 1217 agreed to the removal of all land added to the forest by Henry II except that in royal demesne, but it was not until Henry III came of age that he ordered the enquiry of 1227 which fixed the extent of Sherwood so that the east of Nottinghamshire ceased to be forest.[100] Nationally the changes to Forest Law took almost a century to implement, exacerbated by Henry's policy of essentially ignoring the Charter of the Forest and relying on an aggressive use of Chief Justices to line his coffers with fines. Nothing was firmly resolved during Edward I's reign, but a weak Edward II began to show some concessions at the 1316 Lincoln parliament, and these were consolidated by Roger Mortimer's failure to stop the slippage.[101] The boundaries and laws pertaining to Sherwood, and by extension Clipstone, were essentially fixed by 1227 and confirmed by future perambulations. These boundaries were the River Meden in the north, the King's Highway (followed roughly by the course of the modern A614) and the Dover Beck in the east, the River Trent in the south, and the River Leen to the west.

Within Sherwood Forest, Clipstone sat in the area of the High Forest stretching between Bestwood Park in the south to Budby and the River Meden in the north. Within this region were a number of royal woodlands such as Forsworn Wood, No Man's Wood, Lyndhurst and the hays of Birklands and Bilhaugh. The word 'hay' referred to the enclosure hedge which ran around the woodlands. Additionally, most manors contained their own stretches of woodland including nearby *Maunsefelde Wode* and *Wodhowse Wode*. The church also held woodlands within the forest – those owned by the Abbot of Rufford lay immediately adjacent to Clipstone Shrogges. Interspersed between the woods were wide areas of characteristic heathland known from the Viking word 'ling' and surviving in placenames such as Hardwick Linge as late as Richard Banks' 1609 Crown Survey of Sherwood Forest. This landscape of woods and heathland was incapable of supporting a high density of population due to the poor quality of the local soils, however it provided the perfect habitat for deer. It was also eminently suitable for the *par force des chiens* technique of hunting the native red and roe deer across the landscape and an ideal location for the creation of a deer park within which to protect the imported fallow deer.[102]

The penalties that could be imposed upon the local population at Clipstone for poaching the king's deer, or even for cutting down the trees upon which the animals relied for their habitat, were severe. In the eleventh century the Anglo-Saxon Chronicle railed against William I: '*so that whosoever slew a hart, or a hind, should be deprived of his eyesight.*' In the twelfth century John of Salisbury pointed out that '*the punishment prescribed is confiscation of goods or loss of life and limb.*' Magna Carta demanded that '*all evil customs connected with forests…and their wardens shall immediately be inquired into… and shall be utterly abolished by them so as never to be restored.*' Although the 1217 Charter of the Forest removed the death penalty for poaching there were still a severe punishments for transgression: '*No man from henceforth shall lose either life or limb for killing our deer; but if any man shall be taken and convicted for taking our venison, he shall make a grievous fine if he hath anything whereof, and if he hath nothing to lose, he shall be imprisoned a year and a day.'*

Before we move on to look at exactly when, how and why Henry II established his palace and deer park in Sherwood Forest it is worth noting that the Forest Law was so unpopular and controversial that even his own treasurer Richard Fitzneal wrote disapprovingly of it in the *Dialogus de Scaccario*: '*The Forest has its own laws based, it is said, not on the common law of the realm, but on the arbitrary decision of the ruler; so that what is done in accordance with the law is not called "just" without qualification but just according to forest law.'*[103]

Chapter Three

Development of the Park and Palace:
1164–1199

'He is a great, indeed the greatest of monarchs for he has no superior of
whom he stands in awe, nor subject who may resist him.'
~ Arnulf, Bishop of Lisieux on Henry II ~

The first indication of a royal residence at Clipstone occurred in 1164 when
£20 was spent on works at the manor.[104] This was a reasonable sum of money,
spent either on the initial construction of a fairly insignificant hunting lodge
or on repairs to a larger structure whose origins are unclear. Prior to this the
principle lodging in the region had been at Mansfield, where a sum of 40s was
spent in 1130 to prepare Henry I's chamber.[105] Thirty-four years later his
grandson Henry II was perhaps considering the first royal visit to Clipstone as
he ordered £4 12s 6d to be paid for a tun of wine to be transported up from
London.[106] The modest lodgings in Sherwood were clearly appreciated as a
further 46s 8d was spent on the houses again in 1170–1 and 43s and 20s was
spent on honey in 1171–2 from the enclosed woodland known as the hays of
Clipstone,[107] which might just possibly have been a precursor to the park.
Clipstone therefore became a hunting lodge with links to other nearby royal
residences in the region at Nottingham and Darlton, in the same way that the
Norman kings developed Clarendon as a lodge related to neighbouring Old
Sarum in Wiltshire.[108] Crucially this development of the lodge at Clipstone
came at a time during the mid-twelfth century when there was a positive
explosion of secular building projects across England.[109]

Physical evidence of this early use of the site by the monarchy is very
elusive. John Steane queried whether there might be a timber hunting lodge
beneath the ruin of King John's Palace.[110] Philip Rahtz found evidence of an
earlier off-set foundation on a different orientation to the extant building which
may relate to a structure earlier than Henry II's hall of the 1170s.[111] These early

hunting lodges tended to be relatively ephemeral and small in scale. Rahtz's excavations at another site associated with King John at Writtle, Essex showed that the lodge commissioned there in 1211 by Henry II's youngest son was merely 0.8 acres in area and contained a single range consisting of chapel, hall and kitchen which was accessed across a moat from a gatehouse.[112] The origins of Clipstone may have been equally modest.

The year after the first mention of the King's Houses, the manor of Clipstone was stocked for 44s by Robert Fitzralph, the Sheriff of Nottingham, with six oxen, ten cows, ten sows, ten beehives and twelve sheep. The following year the manor rendered 100s which was paid into the treasury.[113] It is possible that this represents the royal demesne land being stocked as part of a deliberate attempt to enlarge the yield of the manor due to an increased interest and presence at the residence. 1164 may very well be the first year of royal activity at Clipstone.

During the mid-fourteenth century a catalogue of buildings at the King's Houses which were ordered to be repaired by Edward III include a tantalising mention of 'Rosamund's Chamber' at Clipstone amongst a list of suites belonging to king, queen, princes, bishops, earls and lords.[114] It has so far been impossible to find a connection to anyone linked to the household by the name of Rosamund during this period. There has been speculation whether or not this might be a reference to Rosamund Clifford the mistress of Henry II.[115] Rosamund's affair with Henry began around 1173 and lasted until her death at Godstow Priory, Oxfordshire in 1176. This potentially places the building of the chamber after the beginnings of the hunting lodge and prior to the development of the palace buildings in 1177–8. Forty year old Henry was certainly smitten enough with seventeen year old Rosamund to construct the Moorish-style water gardens for her, known as Rosamund's Bower at Everswell near the palace of Woodstock, Oxfordshire[116] and the propensity to retain the name of former occupants real or imagined to structures is a widespread phenomenon. It may be that if the fourteenth century chamber was not named after an obscure member of Edward III's court, then there may have been a folk memory attached to one of the early buildings at Clipstone which associated it with the love affair between Henry II and Rosamund. The link could have been prompted by the publication of the French Chronicle of London c 1345 which included the earliest version of the story of the affair and appeared just three years before the reference to Rosamund's Chamber at

Clipstone. Intriguingly, alongside some repair details relating to a lead guttering and timber-framed garderobe, the location of the chamber is given as being on the line of the south-western palace boundary ditch.[117] The ditch was probably established in the mid-thirteenth century under Henry III and therefore outside of the much smaller enclosure created under Henry II. Consequently Rosamund's Chamber, like Rosamund's Bower in Oxfordshire, may have stood at a distance from the twelfth century King's Houses which could be indicative of it being an earlier structure.

St Mary's Guildhall, Lincoln

The design of a mid-twelfth century building constructed for Henry II on the outskirts of Lincoln had a remarkable impact on the architecture of Clipstone. During the Christmas of 1157, seven years before the beginnings of the lodge at Clipstone, Henry II attended a very curious ritual known as a 'crown-wearing' in the suburb of Wigford, a mile to the south of Lincoln Cathedral. The location of this event has a particular resonance for the architectural history of King John's Palace. Such ceremonies were popular under William I but had died out during Stephen's reign. Henry was a young man, aged just 24, and until 1154 he had been simply the Duke of Anjou (hence the family-grouping name 'Angevin') prior to taking the throne of England after the death of Stephen whose reign had been plagued by civil war. It is possible to see why the new king may have found a revival of the demonstration of majesty especially favoured by his Norman ancestors appealing. Crown-wearings had been held at the feasts of Christmas, Easter and Whitsun under William usually at the palaces of Winchester, Westminster or Gloucester. Henry briefly revived the tradition that is best described in the words of David Stocker: *'Crown-wearing, of course, was not the mere appearance of the king wearing the diadem at a church service: it was a sequence of elaborate ceremonies and feasts at which the king was formally seen at the head of his baronage, who were set alongside him in order of precedence. Furthermore the king was also seen crowned by the populace as a whole during processions which, if we are right...may have progressed from Wigford to the Cathedral.'*[118] Roger of Hoveden recorded that a *hospicium* (a hall built specifically to stage an entertainment or event) was constructed for Henry II at Wigford, and royal accounts rendered show that the building was completed immediately before

Henry attended the property at Christmas 1157. This building is now known as St Mary's Guildhall.[119]

Fronting onto the High Street at Wigford is the West Range of St Mary's Guildhall. It is a five-bay rectangular building constructed in a light honey-coloured Lincolnshire limestone and measures approximately 20 by 6.5 metres internally. The structure has been remodelled on several occasions (the southern third of the building was rebuilt on its own footprint in the late Mediaeval or Early Modern period). It has 1.3 metre wide walls sitting on a foundation 2 metres thick. The three northernmost bays are original although they have been reduced in height by approximately 3 metres. Originally the building was two storeys in height and consisted of a wide gateway at ground floor flanked by two chambers with a single hall at first floor accessed by a newel stair in the north-east corner. The central gate has a hood moulding featuring a chamfered flat band into which are incised carvings of nine-petalled flowers around a central boss. The gate is further elaborated by flanking shallow buttresses and above there is a sculpted string course supporting two carved human heads which bear similarity to contemporary work at Lincoln Cathedral. Originally the gateway was vaulted and had timber screens to the north and south. The ground floor chambers were also vaulted with two unequal sized bays each. A buttress in the centre of the northern bay carried a first floor chimney and there is evidence internally for the fireplace. The remains of four first floor two-light windows survive with chevron ornamentation similar to work recorded at Winchester Cathedral, and there is evidence for shutters and window-seats within the hall. There is also elaborate blind arcading still in situ within the north elevation of the hall. A timber floor was laid over the vault below. The original wall plates from the twelfth century roof structure are still in situ.[120]

The size of the hall at Wigford is much more substantial than local domestic halls, such as the Jew's House and 46–47 Steep Hill in Lincoln, and must be considered to be part of a very special class of twelfth century hall architecture. Given the royal patronage and the relationship to the high status activity associated with a crown-wearing ceremony it is little wonder that there is an elaboration and scale when compared to other halls. Comparable structures are halls at Sherbourne Castle, Dorset, Framlingham Castle, Suffolk, or Wolvesey Palace, Hampshire. The similarity to Framlingham may be deliberate as it was constructed by Henry II's architectural and political rivals the Bigod family.[121] The significance of St Mary's Guildhall is that it was itself the architectural model for King John's Palace which was constructed twenty years later and twenty-seven miles to the west of the Wigford hospicium by a newly victorious Henry II.

The Avegins at War

Henry II's quarrel with his eldest son – Henry the Young King – began during the early months of 1173. The Young King had been crowned aged just fifteen whilst his own father was still alive and very much in power. This was a ceremony particular to the Capetian dynasty of France and was a mechanism to groom a successor for power. However, the Young King felt aggrieved that he had no lands assigned to him despite being a crowned monarch in his own right. The Young King's household was selected and paid for by his father who deliberately kept him short of money in an attempt to restrain the excesses of a *'charming, vain, idle spendthrift'*. The argument was encouraged by Henry II's great rival King Philip II of France, but was even more dangerously supported by a wide range of barons in England and Normandy, William the Lion of Scotland and members of Henry II's own family – most notoriously his sons Richard and Geoffrey and his consort Eleanor of Aquitane (Plate 2).[122] This disagreement spilled over into an open war in May 1173, fought on both sides of the English Channel, and rumbled on until King Henry's comprehensive victory sealed at the treaty of Montluis on 30 September 1174.[123]

Henry was utterly triumphant and now at the all-powerful pinnacle of his rulership. He may have been magnanimous in victory towards his sons as he took their grievances seriously so that lands, castles and financial allowances were granted to them, however he was also determined that a strong statement of his power needed to be made. The Scottish king William the Lion was forced to do homage as Henry's liegeman in December 1174, and was imprisoned until 1177 and afterwards held in sway by sanctions. The Earls of Chester and Leicester also remained in prison until January 1177. Queen Eleanor spent much of the rest of her marriage to Henry under close guard. The King re-imposed Forest Law as a very high priority in 1175–6 and actively pursued and retrospectively fined those who had infringed the law. Not only was this a very clear statement of the reassertion of royal authority, but it provided an impressive amount of revenue with which to refill the royal treasury after the expenses of war. At the same time as the renewal of Forest Law, Henry took possession of all English castles throughout 1176–7 and reshuffled their custodians.[124] This intense interest in the physical symbols of power – the forests and the castles – showed Henry's concern to demonstrate his all-powerful status through interventions in both the hunting reserves and the built environment.

Henry was now unrivalled as the most powerful ruler in Europe. France was humbled. Treaties were signed with the Irish in 1175 and the Welsh in 1177. Envoys were received from the Holy Roman Emperor, Constantinople, Rheims, Savoy and Flanders. At the end of 1176 Henry began to style himself as *'king of the English, duke of the Normans, duke of the Aquitanians, and count of the Angevins'.*[125] This was precisely the moment that major construction work began at Clipstone, and in the regnal year 1176–7, for the first time ever, Henry spent more on unfortified residences than on castles[126]. The period leading up to the development of the King's Houses deep in Sherwood Forest was therefore marked by a revived monarchy determined to flex power by developing a major residence within a royal forest. The fact that the centrepiece of this palace was modelled on a building constructed twenty years previous specifically for a crown-wearing shortly after the cessation of a war at the beginning of Henry's reign cannot have been accidental.

Construction Begins

The very bland lists of royal accounts show us that in the second half of the 1170s Henry II spent slightly over £500 on his manor at Clipstone. This is a very significant expenditure during a period when the most powerful baron in the early thirteenth century, Roger de Lacy, received an annual income of just £800.[127] The initial building season of 1176–7 concentrated on the astonishing £210 spent on constructing a vivarium (notionally a fishpond, but in reality an enormous lake). The following regnal year of 1177–8 saw a further £20 of work on the vivarium but also the same sum spent on building a chapel, and £36 6s 8d on a house. A sum of £65 spent during the period 1178–9 was split between Nottingham Castle and Clipstone. We shall never fully understand how it was divided but more was probably spent on the house and chapel. Additionally £10 12s 6d was spent on enclosing the park and a further £126 on the vivarium. At this point we start to hear about Henry Leech, Reginald de St Maria, Adam de Mortain and William fil Walkelin who were the individuals responsible for overseeing the quarriers, sawyers, carters, stonemasons and carpenters working on the construction project. A reference to a payment made to Hugo de St Mauro of £4 15s 3d for horses and beasts for the king's use may also be an oblique reference to a royal visit. Henry was clearly keen to monitor progress on the site for which he was investing so much money. Construction wound down during 1179–80 with the completion of the deer park for £30, and a note that William fil Walkelin was still in charge of the works. Given Henry's dedicated interest in the control of both the castles and the forests in the years after his victory over his many political enemies, it is absolutely no shock that the first clearly documented royal visit to the King's Houses at Clipstone took place in August 1181, less than a year after the completion of works.[128]

King John's Palace

The extant building standing on a north-east to south-west orientation within Castlefield is a rectangular building constructed from locally sourced magnesian limestones, known as Linby, Mansfield Red and Mansfield White, quarried within a twelve mile radius of the palace (Plate 1 B). There is also a small percentage of carboniferous sandstone from Stanton Moor, Derbyshire, quarried approximately twenty-five miles to the west. Internally the ruin measures approximately 19.8 by 7.3 metres, dimensions which are favourably comparable to St Mary's Guildhall. The measurements are gauged from robber trenches, wall foundations and buried ashlar recorded by Philip Rahtz.[129] As at Wigford the building was at least two storeys in height and, approximately 2.4 metres up the interior longitudinal elevation, and there are fragmentary remains of ten beam slots to carry an upper floor. This floor level is also represented by a ledge let into the profile of the north-east wall. The narrowed profile of the wall also matches up with four coursed ashlar stones, one of a handful of indicators of the original face of the wall at first floor level. The varied profile of the north-west elevation may reflect a line of first floor windows, the ledges of which are approximately 3.5 metres above ground. There is no direct evidence that blind arcading was featured to mark the high end of the building, but similar examples at Wigford and Bishop's Waltham make it a distinct possibility.[130]

The north-west elevation has three openings at ground level. The most northerly was underpinned with pre-cast masonry in 1991 due to structural concerns. Rahtz found evidence of a blocked opening at the north-west corner of the ruin which, although interpreted as a window,[131] may have originally been a door like that at St Mary's Guildhall. The interpretation as a door was made during Richard Sheppard's 1991 evaluation.[132] A matching narrow doorway was clearly depicted to the south in a very accurate antiquarian engraving published by Francis Grose in 1772.[133] This door was shown as a semi-circular Romanesque doorway complete with its voussoirs. A southern doorway was postulated by Stocker at Lincoln.[134] The central opening of the wall was photographed in 1956[135] when a coherent arch was still visible and it is still framed by the remains of two buttresses in a manner identical to the Wigford hospicium. The south-west elevation features a return wall to the west and a niche with a segmental arch barrel vault to the east. Rahtz confirmed that two small rooms stood to the south-west[136] and it was found that the more westerly of these had a floor of rubble stone laid in pale yellow mortar.[137] These structures vary from the scheme at Wigford, but were integral to the design of the building and have an unknown function.

Alongside the architectural similarities between King John's Palace and St Mary's Guildhall, suggesting a comparable mid twelfth century date for both, there is a wealth of corroborative evidence present. Rahtz recorded several post-holes, pits and beams slots during his excavation which yielded late twelfth to early thirteenth century pottery. He also uncovered a wonderfully evocative twelfth century Romanesque stone carving of a mythical beast's head (Plate 3 A).[138] The muzzle of the beast has two rows of serrated teeth bared in a growl of anger or warning whilst its huge eyes protrude forward in a hungry and alarming manner. Perhaps this disquieting sculpture once loomed out over the string course above the central door at Clipstone just like the more sedate human faces peered out at Wigford. The forest setting may have demanded a more visceral motif than that of the suburban hall. Rahtz recorded further Romanesque stonework including a possible plant vase plus the foot and corresponding drapery of a figure sculpture.[139] More recently the current landowners uncovered a chevron ornamented voussoir, probably from a window whose original dimension was two metres in width and similar in character to examples produced in the Winchester region. Additionally, in the garden of Maun Cottage (built on the site of the palace gateway) lie seven chamfered voussoirs with recessed roundels of a very similar character to those found over the gate arch at St Mary's Guildhall (Plate 3 B). There is certainly strong architectural evidence for Henry II's late twelfth century construction at Clipstone.

To all intents and purposes, although Clipstone is much degraded, in the second half of the twelfth century King John's Palace was the twin of St Mary's Guildhall and must be interpreted as a high status hall with chambers constructed along the same principles as the hospicium of twenty years earlier. It is eminently plausible that Henry II was attempting to reassert the political statement of power made during his crown-wearing at Wigford through identical architecture built in the aftermath of the treaty of Montluis. Henry II's vast landholdings coupled with much travelling and an enormous income led to a king who was conversant with the latest styles in architecture.[140] French halls of the twelfth and thirteenth centuries (such as those belonging to Palais Royal and Archbishop of Paris) were always on an upper floor and, unlike the single storey English halls of the 13th to 16th centuries, had no screens passages or open hearths.[141] The newel stair was introduced to England by the Normans and was the chief method of communication between floors in stone buildings. Very practically they take up very little space, allow doors to be placed on all sides of their circumference and can be lit easily by relatively small openings.[142] An intramural newel provided a means of access in the north-east corner at Wigford and, although it is undated, a fragment of a newel post complete with a mason's banker mark was excavated at Clipstone in 2011[143] demonstrating that such architectural features were present on site. Both Wigford and Clipstone may therefore be designed alongside Continental principles gleaned from Henry's experience in Europe.

Frustratingly, Rahtz himself argued that the ruin dated to the period of Edward I. His evidence was based on the discovery of a single sherd of pottery which he found sealed in the lowest of six surviving floor levels within the interior of the ruin. This was very tentatively assigned a thirteenth century date, yet Rahtz was himself very unsure on the dating of the pottery and actually wrote *'a sherd of ? 13th century date'* in his article for the Thoroton Society.[144] A re-evaluation of the pottery assemblage from all of the excavations at Clipstone is underway and has so far discovered that some of the identification and dating of fabrics has been in error. It is also worth noting that if Rahtz was correct in his identification of the pottery it may even be possible that the floors were inserted after a wholesale removal of earlier deposits.

Despite this dating inaccuracy, Rahtz made some other very useful observations about the archaeology of the ruin. Of the six successive floor levels, the lowest of was made of clay and had an associated hearth in the north-east corner. Curiously he also reported the presence of three square foundations which were interpreted as bases for columns and part of a stone column was discovered in the demolition rubble.[145] This is considered intriguing as the building has no evidence of vaulting and the first floor was supported by ten transverse timber beams. Perhaps the width of the building daunted its builders, who feared that the oak beams might sag under tensile stress, so a longitudinal bridging beam was supported on three piers. Equally, and perhaps more likely, given that the middle pier would have blocked clear access to the central doorway, these may have been added during a remodelling of the building. As the lowest floor level seems to be contemporary with the piers this may be evidence of a very significant remodelling of the building. In the two centuries following the Norman Conquest builders rarely left the span of a building unsupported and even structures which were originally a single span might later be remodelled to include aisle posts such as the insertion of mid-thirteenth century piers within the mid-twelfth century East Hall at Wolvesey Palace, Hampshire.[146]

A room measuring twelve by twenty-four feet (7.32 metres) was excavated by Rahtz to the north-west of the ruin. The relationship is unclear however the room would have been accessed from the north-west door and may therefore have been built up against the pre-existing hall. The substantial foundations of this building were observed to a depth of at least two metres by a ground penetrating radar survey[147] suggesting a very considerable structure, perhaps a tower or large forebuilding. A narrow passageway, which may be an external pentice also ran parallel with the entire north-west elevation.[148] This may have provided a sheltered communication between the ruin, the room to the north-west and the two chambers to the south-west and was probably also a later addition.

Henry and Richard

Henry II was back at Clipstone again in February 1185 during a period of time where he had much on his mind due to the recent offer made to him by Patriarch Heraclius of the throne of Jerusalem. The leper king Baldwin IV was nearing the end of his life and his heir was but a small boy. A great military leader was needed at this turbulent time in the Holy Land which was seriously threatened by the forces of Saladin. Henry was ever pragmatic, and whilst he was out hunting with the chronicler Gerald of Wales he told the latter: '*If the patriarch or anyone else comes to us, it is because they are seeking their own advantage rather than ours.*'[149] Henry was certainly a great lover of the hunt. Gerald himself tells us that '*he was addicted to the chase beyond measure, at the crack of dawn he was off on horseback, traversing the wilderness, plunging into woods.*' William of Newburgh adopted a slightly more judgmental tone when he reported that '*He delighted in the pleasure of hunting as much as his grandfather and more than was right.*'[150]

The visit of 1185 sparked a new phase of building work at the palace when Henry ordered that the court of Clipstone should be enclosed (presumably by a wall or palisade around the complex) at a cost of 60s with the project overseen by the keeper of the manor Humphrey de Bussei and Tom de London.[151] This enclosure was potentially the D-shaped enclosure ditch noted by Rahtz which swung down to the south-east from the Tin Tabernacle, curved right around the ruin and headed back up to the north-west in the direction of Mansfield Road. The extent of the ditch was confirmed through ground penetrating radar in 2015.[152] A section across this ditch in 1956 to the south-east of the ruin found that it contained twelfth and thirteenth century pottery and was capped by stone rubble; and to the south-west another trench across the feature found that after natural silting it had been deliberately backfilled and levelled with initially redeposited natural soil with thirteenth or fourteenth century pottery followed by stone chippings.[153] The ditch was cut through made-ground of uncertain date,[154] demonstrating that there had already been a great deal of prior landscaping at the site by the time it was constructed. Rahtz found a structure consisting of a stone wall foundation in association with a beam slot and post hole relating to this boundary ditch to the west of the ruin[155] and this was confirmed by the ground penetrating radar survey in 2011.[156]

The final accounts relating to Clipstone under Henry II relate to alterations made to the infrastructure of the wider landscape in 1186–7. Seven years on from its completion the park pale was in need of repairs.[157] The enormous expense spent on the vivarium during the 1170s is possibly explained by the

1180s reference to 50s being spent on breaking up one fishpond and carrying the fish to a second.[158] An extensive aquatic environment had been constructed based on the relatively small River Maun and Vicar Water, clearly their resources had been maximised by the Angevins. The lake and dam still visible on the estate map drawn by William Senior in 1630 probably originated during this period.

Given how little time Richard I spent in England during his reign, it is encouraging to find that he not only visited but also thoroughly enjoyed Clipstone during 1194. This was the year in which the Lionheart, who had been imprisoned and ransomed during his return from the Crusades, was released from his captivity. His brother John and Philip of France had encouraged Richard's captors by offering the Holy Roman Emperor either 150,000 marks for possession of the king, 100,000 marks to actually keep him under lock and key until Michaelmas 1194 or £1000 a month on an ongoing basis.[159] John had a great deal of reason for wanting Richard kept in prison as he had attempted to make a power-grab and England was essentially in a state of civil war – John's forces in the midlands had been driven back to the castles of Nottingham and Tickhill and were besieged by barons loyal to Richard.[160] Richard landed at Sandwich on 13 March and almost immediately Tickhill surrendered. Nottingham was briefly besieged and, after the taking of the outer bailey plus some peremptory hangings of the garrison, the castle capitulated on 27 March.[161]

At this point Richard seemed to be reacting to an agreed timetable because, only two days after the completion of the siege, he travelled the twenty miles north '*to see Clipston and the forests of Sherwood, which he had never seen before, and they pleased him greatly.*'[162] He immediately returned to Nottingham where he held a great council during which his brother John was ordered to present himself for trial within forty days. Present at this council was David, the brother of the William the Lion, who seems to have been acting as a fixer for the Scottish king as on 2 April Richard returned to Clipstone specifically to meet him.[163] We can therefore interpret Richard's forty mile round trip to Clipstone on 29 March as a prudent act to ensure that the facilities built by his father would be sufficient to meet his old ally. William had declared with Richard against Henry II in 1173, was captured at Alnwick and held in prison until 1177.[164] Henry then imposed fearful sanctions on William which were only removed after Richard came to the throne in 1189. Consequently when John attempted to recruit William to his cause in 1193 the Scot was in no mood to risk his throne and refused to become involved with his traitorous schemes.[165] William was perhaps also keen to meet with Richard as he had a claim to press over the ownership of Northumbria. Richard no doubt wanted to ensure that, after he returned to the Continent, his northern borders would be secure.[166] A half penny of William the Lion was found in Castlefield during recent excavations and, although it might relate to a slightly later issue than the 1194 meeting, it is tantalising evidence of the diplomatic relationship between England and Scotland in the latter days of the twelfth century.[167] Richard stayed for another day at Clipstone on 3 April[168] whilst William headed north to Worksop, where he presumably lodged at the castle or priory. Business was not over between them as they then progressed to Southwell the next day and stayed together more or less constantly until William headed north again on 22 April.[169] This period of closeness included a crown-wearing at Winchester on the 17 April in which the Scottish king carried a sword in the procession before Richard. This was the first crown-wearing since Henry II's ceremony at Wigford in 1157,[170] and it is thought-provoking that Richard and William first met at a building modelled on the location of that event.

Chapter Four

Politics and Palace Expansion:
1199–1307

'The singing masons building roofs of gold'
~ William Shakespeare, 1599, *Henry V* ~

John

One of England's most notorious kings, John, has already featured several times in the story of Clipstone. We have seen how he aggressively added to the residences owned by the monarchy, how he was particularly interested in the wine stocks at the palace and how he unsuccessfully attempted to assume power in Richard's absence. The point was also made about how John was perhaps the most mobile of all English monarchs, making an average of 150 moves per year on his itineraries. The pattern of John's use of Clipstone testifies to this speed as he spent only nine days there in total and over seven visits never stayed more than two nights.

John's reputation as a monarch is still a divisive point for historians, especially with the recent 800th anniversary commemoration of the signing of Magna Carta which has renewed these arguments. Essentially John was no worse than any other Mediaeval monarch. What is different in the case of John is that firstly he relied heavily upon, and then crucially alienated, high ranking churchmen as his advisors. The chroniclers of the day were monks and they have handed down a very skewed version of events as a result of John's arguments with the church. His impetuous nature led to personality clashes with many of his barons, often because of his inventively efficient measures to gather taxes. However John had inherited enormous debt from his father and brother who had ruled before him. Both Henry II and Richard have an inflated reputation in the chronicles. It should be remembered that both also died, as did John, fighting civil wars. Despite his loss of Normandy, John can still be seen as a capable soldier – he supported and encouraged the formation of a powerful navy which eventually won a resounding victory over the French off Dover. Even at the moment of his death John had successfully divided his enemies in Scotland from the barons in southern England. Consequently the reign of his son began with a strong foothold in the west and midlands under the powerful regency of William Marshall.[171]

John's troubles with the Church centred on his argument with Pope Innocent III over the choice of Stephen Langton as Archbishop of Canterbury. The king's refusal to accept this nomination and his adherence to John de Grey succeeding in the post led to an interdict being served on England between March 1208 and June 1214 during which time the spiritual life of the nation was deeply affected by the ban on church services. The refusal of John to back down led to his own excommunication which lasted two years starting in 1211. This must have deeply wounded John who was a relatively sincere and devout Christian. The religious life of Clipstone was enhanced when he endowed the chapel of St Edwin in 1205[172] which is known from cropmark evidence to have sat within a sub-trapezoidal enclosure to the south of the current memorial cross.[173] Building accounts from the mid-fourteenth century routinely refer to the '*chapel of St Edward in Birkland*' which is almost certainly the same building, although it is not absolutely clear whether there was a later rededication or if the name Edward was interchangeable with Edwin. Either way, these accounts reveal that the chapel was a substantial masonry structure as four carters were employed for twenty days to haul loads of stone for the five masons and two labourers who worked on the building for twenty-four days during the period 1360–3.[174] Later records show that it was roofed with Mansfield stone slates.[175] The early fourteenth century Survey of Birklands mentions 'Prestwich' in a location to the north-east of the chapel which is a placename meaning the priest's enclosure[176] and may relate to land put aside for the use of the chaplain. After the lifting of the interdict John made a payment in 1215 for the chaplain of Clipstone to say masses for his father in a chantry at Clipstone.[177] This chantry was clearly within the palace as in 1486 Richard Scoley was explicitly paid a stipend as chaplain of the chantry within the manor of Clipstone on top of his duties at the St Edwin's chapel.[178] The chantry would have taken the form of a separate altar within the main palace chapel at which masses would be said in memory of the deceased. Chantries were rare prior to the mid-fourteenth century, although there was an early foundation at nearby Lincoln Cathedral for Bishop Hugh c 1235.[179] The very oldest chantries date from the late twelfth century and one was founded by John himself at Lichfield Cathedral in April 1192 whilst he was still Count of Mortain.[180] John was a catalyst in the early use of chantries as they were still not commonly found in buildings at this period. The Clipstone chantry was also rare in that it was founded within a palace rather than a monastery, church or cathedral. It is ambiguous whether the chantry was still active from the survey of 1525, but if it was then it was certainly dissolved in 1545.

The period of the interdict marks a number of years where John's interest in Clipstone went cold. Aside from early visits in 1200, 1201 and the foundation of St Edwin's Chapel in 1205, John ordered repairs to the King's Houses in 1204, 1206, 1207 and in 1208–9 spent £42 on both house and pond.[181] With the exception of a single days visit in December 1210, the appeal of the palace was not resumed until further repairs were ordered in 1214 prior to a flurry of interest in 1215 which began with the order for masses to be said in the chantry, continued with payments to the keepers of the manor and culminated with two royal visits in March 1215.[182] John wrote a letter during the period of his journey through Nottinghamshire in late March 1215 to the Sheriff of Nottingham which affords us some detail on exactly what was involved in transporting his possessions as he travelled between Nottingham and Clipstone. There were four long carts each drawn by three or four horses which carried John's '*wardrobe, weapons, game and hunting equipment*', additionally two other horses bore food provisions.[183] We should not read too much into the king's apparent absence from Clipstone between 1210 and 1215. John continued his frenetic itineraries around his kingdom as usual, and was often at Nottingham, Southwell or Laxton and there are long periods of time when there is no indication of his location, particularly during the summer of 1211 and May 1212. It is entirely possible that he was present at Clipstone but the records just do not exist.

There is a persistent tradition[184] that it was whilst he was hunting at Clipstone that John heard of the revolt of the Welsh under Llewelyn the Great in August 1212 and consequently ordered twenty-eight hostages held at Nottingham Castle to be hanged. Flushed by his recent military success against the Irish, John had invaded Wales in May 1211 and penetrated as far as Bangor which he razed to the ground. The leader of the Welsh, Prince Llewelyn ap Iorweth of Gwynedd, was forced into signing a humiliating treaty acknowledging John as his overlord. However, in the summer of 1212 the king's enemy Pope Innocent III released the Welsh from their oaths against John as part of strategy to undermine the authority of the English monarch. The Welsh immediately began the systematic re-conquest of Gwynedd,[185] and when John heard of their actions on 14 August the chronicler Matthew Paris tells us that '*before he would eat meat, out of revenge for the incursions of the Welsh, he caused the twenty-eight lads, whom he had taken hostage the year before, to be hanged upon a gallows.*'[186] Paris was emphatic that John was at Nottingham Castle when he heard of the revolt. Neither is there any evidence that he was at Clipstone during this time. John was travelling north from Woodstock, Oxfordshire and was in Northamptonshire between 9 and 12 August, at Gunthorpe in Nottinghamshire on the 13th and Nottingham from 14 until 22 August when he moved on to Southwell, Laxton and Kingshaugh. Quite simply he was moving in the wrong direction to have been at Clipstone on 14 August when he heard of the Welsh uprising. Stapleton actually interrogated this data when he wrote his history of Clipstone in 1890 and stated that he could not find any evidence that the tradition went back further than the 1830 Nottinghamshire Directory, although he admitted that Major Hayman Rooke may have alluded to the story in 1799. Compelling a notion as it is that the angered John held an impromptu council beneath the canopy of the Parliament Oak on the north-western boundary of Clipstone Park, there is simply no historical evidence to back it up.

On the occasions that John was present at Clipstone it can be said with some certainty that he was attracted by the opportunities for the chase. In November 1200 and December 1210 he visited during the deer hunting seasons of red hind, fallow and roe does.[187] Puzzlingly John's five other visits to Clipstone occurred during the closed fawning season in March. Perhaps this is merely coincidental, but it does seem odd that a king so renowned for the hunt would choose to visit a palace with a huge deer park when it was irregular to use the amenity. John loved hunting so much that the poet Bertran de Born explicitly blamed it for his downfall:

> *He loves better playing and hunting,*
> *Brachets, greyhounds and hawks,*
> *And repose, wherefore he loses his property,*
> *And his fief escapes out of his hand.*[188]

John was cognisant of the criticisms levelled at him for his all-consuming passion for hunting as, in a fit of atonement, he arranged for one hundred paupers to be fed at his expense at Newcastle in 1209 after he hunted on the Feast of St Mary Magdalen.[189] Again in 1212–13 he could not resist going hawking on the Feast of the Innocents and consequently gave alms of one penny and a banquet to fifty paupers for each for the seven cranes that his birds of prey had taken (a total of 350 people) at Ashwell, Cambridgeshire.[190] Given such regular penance for infringements on the sanctity of holy days it may be that John did not respect the closed season in his deer parks either.

John gave his name to King John's Palace, the ruin still standing in Castlefield, yet as we have seen it was really his father who commissioned the building. There are a great many buildings in England bearing John's name and the late eighteenth century antiquarian Francis Grose observed this when he noted that '*King John and the devil being the founders, to whom the vulgar impute most of the ancient buildings, mounds, or entrenchments, for which they cannot assign any other constructor.*'[191] It is fitting then that a contemporary of Grose, John Chapman, gives us the earliest known citation of the name King John's Palace on his 1774 map of Nottinghamshire. A century before Chapman, Dr Robert Thoroton referred to the site simply as the '*manor of Clipston*'[192] and it seems plausible that the attribution of the building to John occurred during the late seventeenth or eighteenth century.

A Child King

When John died, probably of dysentery, in October 1216 at Newark Castle he left behind a boy-king of barely nine years of age to reclaim a war-torn land with the assistance of his protector and regent William Marshall. It is somewhat surprising to discover that Henry III went on to hold the reins of power for the longest period of any English Mediaeval monarch. Henry did not assume his full regal powers until January 1227, so the work carried out at Clipstone during this early period of his tenure must be seen in the light of the regency. Repairs were made in 1219–20 on the dam, park pale and the King's Houses[193] including the refurbishment of the palisade around the compound.[194] The complex had been first enclosed in 1185 and it seems probable that the timbers had rotted during the subsequent thirty-five years and required replacement as part of what must have been a regular programme of work to any earth-fast structures.

More dramatic was an order given in the Henry's name on 7 February 1223 to take wood from the forest to repair the King's Chamber which had been damaged by fire.[195] This was reiterated on 6th May but it is clear that the work was never carried out as, over five years later, in September 1228 the keeper of the manor Brian de Lisle was ordered to hand over the money allocated to him for the repairs to the Sheriff of Nottingham so that he could organise the work.[195] Mediaeval buildings were, and still remain, vulnerable to fires due to the high volume of timber used in their framing, panelling and roof structures in combination with a preponderance of central hearths open to the roof where smoke would pass either through the thatching or via a hole or louvre.[197] Despite the introduction of chimneys during the Norman period, the open hearth had a lengthy use so that even in the fourteenth century the Bishop of Lincoln was happy to have one constructed over an earlier hearth at Lyddington, Leicestershire in a direct continuity of the open hearth tradition.[198] Burned stonework was recorded at Clipstone by Philip Rahtz,[199] and a layer interpreted as a burned timber resting directly on heat-affected sand was observed in 2011.[200] Although it cannot be stated confidently that either of these finds directly relate to the fire of 1223 they do go some way towards indicating that such fires occurred.

It was probably the damage caused in 1223 and the tardy repair work that led Henry and his household to stay at the nearby residence of Jordan Foliot at Grimston in November 1227. Foliot had been a supporter of King John from at least 1212 although he may have briefly followed his lord, John de Lacy, into rebellion in 1215. Despite this Henry III made three visits to Grimston between 1227–9 which may be considered unusual as the family were only of the middling sort. He clearly got on with the Foliots as in 1229 he gave a gift of deer for their newly enclosed park and in 1236 Richard Foliot was licenced by the king to inherit his lands prior to coming of age following the death of his father Jordan.[201] Richard Foliot served as a knight of the household from c 1247–60[202] and may well have been present with Henry during the early 1250s when he began to regularly use Clipstone after a great deal of building work had been completed.

Eventually the King's Chamber was entirely rebuilt, probably in timber, during 1233–4 by the master carpenter Robert de Hotot at a cost of £130. It was built complete with an undercroft and wardrobe below[203] indicating that the main room was a first floor chamber. This was the beginning of a great series of building projects conducted at Clipstone during Henry's reign and was probably the first to be undertaken in the flourishing Early English Gothic style which at the time was characterised by tall and narrow lancet windows or plate tracery. Few such chambers of the period still stand, perhaps the most analogous (albeit constructed in stone) would be the surviving first floor chamber block at Temple Manor, Strood, Kent which dates to c 1225–50.

Assassin at Woodstock

The St Albans chronicler Matthew Paris recounted that in September 1238 a very curious attempt was made on the life of Henry III whilst he was at his palace of Woodstock. During the day after the Nativity of St Mary (9 September) a clerk was admitted to the royal presence demanding that the king *'resign to me the kingdom, which you have unjustly usurped, and so long detained from me'* The clerk also hinted that he was a disenfranchised member of the royal family (perhaps one of the profligate John's bastards?). Rather naturally, the members of the household wanted to attack the man, whom they considered to be insane, however Henry advised mercy. Perhaps this was foolhardy as that night the clerk crept in through an unbarred window in the King's Chamber and began hunting for Henry through his apartments with a knife in hand. It was somewhat fortunate for the king that he was in the habit of sleeping with Queen Eleanor in her chambers as one of her maids, Margaret Biseth, caught sight of the would-be assassin and raised the alarm. In fear the man barricaded himself in a room but the door was broken down and the royal attendants captured and interrogated him. Paris goes on to record that Henry ordered his assailant to be taken to Coventry where he was drawn and quartered with his remains hung in a gibbet[204] – the very earliest example of this torturous execution in English history. In the short term Henry was clearly very rattled by the attempt on his life and security became paramount. The plain glazed windows in the privy chamber at his apartments at Westminster were fitted with iron bars in 1238,[205] as they were at Clarendon,[206] and bars were duly added to the windows of the King's Chamber at Clipstone in 1251.[207]

The extremely brutal ending to the clerk's life tells us that Henry was a man given a great shock that was determined to enact the bloodiest death that could be devised upon the assassin. However it also gives us a rare insight into the sleeping habits of king and queen because the account specifically states that he was asleep in Eleanor's chambers. Eleanor of Provence (c 1223–1291) was the daughter of Duke Raymond Berengar V and came from the Savoy region of southern France. Married to Henry in 1236 she was a genuine love match and his intellectual equal. She was influenced by sophisticated Savoyard architecture and lavish palatial designs, and together the royal couple embarked on a great programme of building work throughout their residences in England.

The Great Rebuilding

Henry III spent much of the year 1244 in ecclesiastical wrangles with the Pope and a brief failure of a war in France. During the summer he travelled north, originally intending to invade Scotland but alternatively a peace was renewed at the Treaty of Newcastle with Alexander II,[208] the son of William the Lion and husband of Henry's sister Joan. En route to the north the king stayed at Clipstone during July. This visit prompted an order to the Sheriff of Nottingham to select twenty-six tuns of wine from Boston to be delivered to Nottingham Castle, with six tuns then forwarded to Clipstone and Blyth.[209] This visit to the King's Houses was the first by Henry and it sparked off an extensive remodelling of a complex which had not been radically altered since construction during his grandfather's reign. On the very day of Henry's stay the Sheriff of Nottingham was ordered to build *'a fair great and becoming hall of wood, and a kitchen of wood, and a wardrobe for the queen's use.'*[210] The hall was still standing during the 1360s when its roof was repaired with thatch board and its clay and lime daub walls were pargetted.[211] Palaces often featured multiple halls such as the two at the royal castle of Old Sarum, one of which was used specifically for business dealings whilst the other was reserved for entertainments and feasts. This administrative versus domestic division can also be seen at Lincoln Bishop's Palace, whereas in the late Mediaeval period summer and winter halls were built at Caistor.[212] At Clipstone the multiple halls appear to have related to the provision of accommodation for separate households.

Henry seems to have been aware that the facilities at Clipstone were not up to the highest standard of the day. It is not even clear whether there was even a suite of apartments for the queen prior to 1244. Chambers were constructed for her at many of the king's houses and castles within a decade of marriage.[213]

By this period the total number of royal residences numbered over sixty properties which were often maintained and repaired immediately prior to the king's visits with especial diligence shown towards provision for the comfort of Eleanor.[214] The Liberate Rolls show Henry's voice and personality coming through very strongly and clearly usually in a very demanding, exacting and impatient manner;[215] for example his demand for glazing the king's garderobe window at Westminster '*so that chamber may not be so draughty as it has been.*'[216] The choice of words at Clipstone are more gentle – '*a fair great and becoming hall*' – which was perhaps reflective of the care felt by Henry in providing accommodation for Eleanor. This apparent care connects to a wider trend for subdivision of space as the Mediaeval period wore on so that private suites were constructed for individuals as the household community began to disperse away from the Early Mediaeval hall lifestyle (although the great hall continued to be used for lower status communal sleeping).[217] The queen's apartments were often sited adjacent to gardens, of which was particularly fond,[218] lying beneath the palace complex on the hillslope leading down to the lake to the east of the palace. The terraced gardens still survive directly below the queen's quarters at Clarendon where a gallery accessed by a newel stair was built in 1244 to allow views across them towards Cockey Down. Similar features are also known from Woodstock, Okehampton, Castle Rising and New Buckenham.[219]

All of the building in 1244 was of timber framed construction, including the kitchen which had clay and straw daub walls that were re-plastered during the mid-fourteenth century.[220] As we shall see Henry was very influenced by French architecture and Mediaeval kitchens in France tended to be circular and octagonal whereas English examples were rectilinear. Later Mediaeval examples in both England and France were built in stone and were usually an integral part of the service area beyond the lower end of the hall.[221] The thirteenth century timber kitchen at Clipstone may have been a separate building, isolated due to the threat of conflagration of the timber and plaster created by the multiple heat sources for cooking. The kitchen probably had tile floors and firebacks but would still have been vulnerable to catching fire.[222] Kitchens could be of impressively large sizes which should come as no surprise given the number of staff required to prepare elaborate feasts for the extensive household. The thirteenth century king's kitchen at Clarendon, constructed in the same year as the Queen's Kitchen at Clipstone, was to be '*every way within*

the walls forty feet' which corresponds neatly to the 12.8 metres of the western
kitchen located beyond the east end of the Great Hall[223] The most famous of
all Mediaeval kitchens is the early fourteenth century stone structure at
Glastonbury Abbey which reflects both English and French tastes as it has a
square plan supporting a polygonal roof. Kitchen equipment such as cauldron
legs are a common archaeological find on palace sites[224] and at Clipstone a
metal detector survey in 2012 turned up no fewer than three copper alloy
examples from the topsoil of Castlefield.[225]

Covered passageways known as pentices were added to keep food warm
when the food was taken between kitchen and hall or chamber such as the
pentices arrayed around the kitchen courtyard at Clarendon.[226] Pentices might
also have been required to link ancillary buildings related to the activities of
the kitchen including the standard buttery and pantry for storing ale and bread
respectively as well as more unusual structures such as the salsary or
'*herlebcheria*' (perhaps a scullery or slaughterhouse) at Clarendon.[227]
References to wells, brewhouses, bakehouses, cellars, barns and store rooms
are fleeting, none survive from Clipstone at all, but these necessary buildings
must have been present to keep the household supplied with necessary
provisions.[228] Reference was made to ale having been present in 1207 at
Clarendon, but as it could only be kept for a week or two it may have been
purchased off site and brought to the palace only when required in large
quantities,[229] otherwise the palace skeleton staff presumably made their own
home brews. Records from the 1360s confirm that a buttery[230] was present at
Clipstone so it clear that ale was consumed on the site. Quite where the vast
quantities of wine known to have been brought to the palace were kept remains
a mystery, as there is no physical or documentary evidence for a cellar like the
one at Clarendon.

Attention next turned to a Gothic replacement for Henry II's Romanesque
chapel. In 1246–7 a new chapel costing £26 13s 4d was commissioned. The
relatively low amount spent indicates that this may also have been timber
framed as were many other thirteenth century royal chapels.[231] Eighteen new
chapels were founded at royal residences under Henry and at least fifty
maintained at his residences in total.[232] Henry was undoubtedly very religious,
attending mass at least three times a day. John Steane has pointed out that he
may have sought religious absolution for the troubled nature of his reign often
caused by poor rulership.[233] Henry emulated his contemporary monarch, and

the eventual saint, Louis IX of France as a great chapel builder, and although the structure at Clipstone was relatively simple the double height Sainte Chapelle in Paris was a great influence on many of Henry's other chapels[234] especially St Stephen's at the palace of Westminster. The king was personally involved in financing building schemes at Westminster Abbey, Worcester and Gloucester cathedrals[235] and throughout the kingdom his reign was marked by a tremendous acceleration in building in the Gothic fashion which brought about many new stylistic and engineering changes that forever altered the face of English architecture.

More detail on the chapel is given as a result of Henry's next visit to Clipstone in December 1251 when an order went out to purchase '*a chalice, vestments, books and other necessary ornaments*' and to fit the chapel with wainscoting (wooden panelling). The king's comfort was also considered as the Sherriff of Nottingham was commanded to build a passageway between Henry's chamber and the chapel, and at the same time both the queen's chapel and the new chapel were glazed[236] – a reminder of Henry's testy order to install glazing at Westminster to reduce drafts. Window glass was at the forefront of style and taste when it was introduced during Henry's reign[237] and must have been widely utilised as most archaeological excavations in Castlefield have revealed both the glass quarries and their lead cames.[238] Due to its fragility glass was probably manufactured close to the site, whereas lead was brought in from the Peak District mines as it was to the much more distant Clarendon in the thirteenth century.[239]

Although the survival of the built environment in Castlefield is extremely patchy due to extensive robbing of the site during the late Mediaeval and nineteenth centuries (even ground penetrating radar surveys have failed to produce a coherent plan) there are still fragmentary glimpses of structures. The river cobble foundations of a two-cell rectangular building, with a southern porch added later, were partially excavated in 2011. Lying to the north, and on a slightly different orientation to King John's Palace, the foundations contained pottery from the mid-twelfth century.[240] This was tentatively interpreted by Channel 4's Time Team to be a chapel due to the presence of a figural sculpture fragment in a building with a two-cell arrangement (nave and chancel?) on a broadly east-west alignment. However Wessex Archaeology did not draw any firm conclusions in their final archaeological report of the programme's excavations.[241] Against the chapel interpretation is the relatively poor survival of the features coupled with a relative absence of corroborative artefacts; in its favour is the shape, size and orientation. The internal dimensions of the building foundations measure approximately 8 by 5 metres (the actual building would have been slightly larger assuming offset foundations) which compares favourably to Henry III's chapels at King's Cliffe or Eleanor's at Kempton and Havering which measured 9.1 metres in length by 3.65–4.2 in width.[242] The orientation of the structure is to the north of east, but as the historian and archaeologist Anne Sassin Allen has demonstrated in an exhaustive survey of Mediaeval Welsh ecclesiastical buildings this is actually entirely normal. Orientation was not linked to the position of true east, sunrise on patronal feast days, a chronological bias or magnetic declination; instead it was more likely to have been influenced by surrounding landscape features such as street patterns, pre-existing buildings and topographic landmarks.[243] It is worth noting that the building in question in Castlefield is orientated along the same axis as the palace boundary to the north-west and its easternmost gable would have pointed directly towards a return in the boundary of the palace enclosure where Dam Close met the Great Pond, as shown on an estate map made of Clipstone in 1766 (Plates 10 and 11B). The identification of the building is however still a moot point.

Wherever the chapel lay it would have been off limits to the villagers of Clipstone. There was no parochial status afforded to the chapels within palaces, even when located close to settlements. The main palace chapel was, in a sense, a public space for members of the household only. The parish church of Clipstone was St Mary's, located two miles to the north at the royal manor of Edwinstowe, so there was unlikely to have been any special consideration on the part of the monarchy towards building another place of worship for the local people – the royal focus was entirely on the spiritual provision for the royal household.

Multiple chapels were common to all royal residences. Along with the chapel already discussed we have heard mention of a chapel for the queen and in the next century there was a reference made to the king's chapel.[244] Private devotion was as important as communal – hence the proliferation of such buildings in the reign of Henry III – but these personal chapels need not have been grand spaces. Henry's chapel in the Wakefield Tower at the Tower of London was basically an enlarged window embrasure in the king's chamber although references to a timber screen and stained glass in 1238 hint at a degree of elaboration even within this confined space.[245]

The names of many of the chaplains at Clipstone survive in the record, principally during the fourteenth century – Henry de Wytheton, Robert Rotor and John Davy – who were usually paid 100s a year for their duties in the chapels and chantry. Reference to the continued use of a chantry indicates that it must have either been rebuilt or an existing structure incorporated within the new chapel. The chaplains usually served both the King's Houses and the chapel in Birklands, although towards the end of Henry III's reign two chaplains were appointed and the one at St Edwin's Chapel was listed as being called Walter. Spiritual matters were not always at the forefront of the chaplain's minds as in 1318 Nicholas de Nottingham was fined 1d for taking a load of branches from the king's woods. A fine of 1d was a harsh penalty which, as we shall see, was imposed at a time of very cold winters and great famine.

Henry visited Clipstone twice during the winter of 1251–2, once during December on his progress up to York (where he spent Christmas) and again in January on his return journey to the south.[246] The significance to the palace of these visits is similar to his stay in 1244 in that they acted as catalyst for building work as a result of the king's savvy eye for architecture. We have already heard how works were carried out on two of the Clipstone chapels in 1251, the other orders issued to the Sheriff of Nottingham give us our first inkling of the expansive nature of the palace by this time, and it is possible to start to understand the morphology and inter-relationships of the buildings. It is clear that construction had not been completed to Henry's liking, or had not been fully completed, in 1244 as a request was made again for a wardrobe in the queen's apartments which was to be accompanied by a privy chamber (garderobe) in her great chamber. The queen's wardrobe was listed as being immediately adjacent to the king's wardrobe as there was to be a double chimney which had a shared flue between the mantles of each suite, showing that the royal apartments of Henry and Eleanor must have been directly next to each other as they were at Clarendon. Back to back fireplaces were installed for economy. The earliest such arrangement is commonly said to be at the gatehouse for Windsor Manor in Bedfordshire built in 1394–6,[247] and consequently it may be that the example installed at Clipstone in 1251 was one of the very earliest of its kind.

The king's chamber was whitewashed, quite a job as the space was big enough to warrant two chimneys with a window between them. This window was subsequently blocked up and the remaining windows in Henry's chamber were installed with protective iron bars, a legacy of the attempt on his life at Woodstock thirteen years previous. The king also demanded en suite facilities as there were instructions given to break through the wall at the foot of his bed to make a garderobe. This privy probably emptied into a cess pit contained within an abutment that was emptied via an archway at its base by the unfortunate 'gong fermor' who was tasked with maintaining sanitary arrangements at the palace. The privy chambers of both Henry and Eleanor were glazed and the king's was roofed with timber shingles.[248] There is an irony that the king required the royal privies to be glazed so as to reduce the drafts experienced at Westminster yet he was also given to complaints '*since the privy chamber of our wardrobe at London is situated in an unsuitable place, wherefore it smells badly*'[249] – which could of course have been mitigated by better ventilation!

Sanitation was perhaps at the forefront of Henry's mind in 1251 as he also requested a new garderobe to be installed at the high end of the hall. At the opposite end a new chamber '*with a privy-chamber and other necessaries*' was constructed. The benches were removed from what was explicitly described as '*the new hall*'[250] indicating that Henry II's old hall, the standing ruin, was no longer in use as a hall or was no longer the principle hall in the complex. The fact that it has survived into the present day indicates that in the mid-thirteenth century a new function had been found as occurred at Clarendon in March 1244 when Henry III ordered that '*the old hall to be made into a chamber.*'[251] Sadly we do not have any record of when this new hall was constructed at Clipstone, although the late 1240s seems to be the most likely period. English halls of the period were single storey, heated by open hearths and had an entrance at the lower end which also accessed the screens passage, buttery, pantry and kitchen beyond. The dais at the high end would have been fitted with a canopy over the high table as a mark of power and status.[252] This was a very alien architectural tradition to that of Henry II's French-style hall of the 1170s, and it might even be argued that it represented a decline in sophistication and certainly a lack of economy in methods of heating. Building accounts from the reign of Edward III demonstrate that Henry III's hall was constructed on a stone groundwall with a timber framed superstructure, containing glazed windows, and supporting a shingle roof. Attached to the hall at the lower end was the porch, kitchen and two household chambers linked by a drainage gutter made of hollowed out tree trunks.[253] It is difficult to know what the roof structures of the palace buildings such as the great hall would have looked like. Most of the buildings at the palace were open to the rafters and as such may have had highly decorated timbers which were intended to be visible to make an aesthetic statement. In Nottinghamshire high status Mediaeval domestic buildings tended towards crown-post roofs such as the thirteenth century example at Annesley Hall or the Old White Hart, Newark which dated to 1313 and which is considered to be one of the finest that the Midlands has to offer.[254]

Beyond the high end of the hall was a great chamber within which was a '*small chimney*' that the king requested be removed.[255] This was probably a similar space to that immediately east of the Great Hall at Clarendon. It was common for the private chambers and more public hall to be divided by intermediate rooms which acted as a waiting lobby for visitors. This served a very practical function but was also related to security and the need to express power.[256] Henry's comfort in moving about the palace was maintained by the introduction of pentices '*from the entry of the king's chamber to the gable of the hall, and another passage to the new chapel.*'[257]

Finally, the sheriff was ordered to build '*a great gate*' above which was a chamber with yet another garderobe.[258] Physical evidence for the stone ground storey of the gatehouse still survives in situ (described below) but Edward's III's repairs to the gate in 1360–3 prove that its first floor was timber framed and pargetted. Additionally there was an order for four chains and hooks for the stout doorway to the upper chamber and the gravel surface of the gate portal was renewed.[259]

The High Sheriff of Nottinghamshire, Derbyshire and the Royal Forests in 1251 was Robert de Vavassur who perhaps had an intimate knowledge of the King's Houses as he had acted as steward there during the mid-1240s when he would have overseen the construction of the new chapel. Ten months later, in 1252, Henry sent out one of his characteristically terse writs to Robert insisting that he '*break without delay, the wall at the foot of the king's bed in the king's chamber at Clipston, and to make a certain privy chamber for the king's use.*'[260] Henry's orders of 1251 had not been followed as closely as he might have wished, and along with the seven year delay in constructing the queen's wardrobe on top of Brian de Lisle's slowness to repair the king's chamber in

1223 perhaps it is not so very surprising that the king often sounded so exasperated.

Analysis of Henry's orders to Vavassur enables a notional ground plan to be built up of the more high status areas of the King's Houses. The Great Hall had a chamber at one end and a garderobe at the other. The king was able to access the gable of the high end directly via a passage from his own apartments. Henry's whitewashed chamber with its barred windows was at first floor directly above his wardrobe and both storeys were heated by chimneys. Immediately next to the king's apartments were those of Eleanor of Provence which may have been the twin of Henry's as they also featured a ground floor wardrobe with a chamber and garderobe above. Although it is unclear exactly where the queen's chapel was sited (possibly within her own suite), the new palace chapel must have been close by to the hall and royal apartments as it was linked to them via a passageway. The picture that emerges is one that is very similar to the plan of Henry and Eleanor's remodelling of Clarendon Palace where the very grand wainscoted hall of c 1230 – measuring 31 by 15.9 metres and furnished simply with trestle tables, stools and benches[261] – granted access to a waiting chamber to the east. Beyond were Henry II's chambers, extensively remodelled by Henry III to include an elaborately painted and enlarged chapel above the Antioch chamber. Further to the east were the queen's chambers, again enlarged and highly decorated under Henry III.[262] The privies attached to the royal suites at Clarendon were all located on the north side of the buildings, away from the main courtyard and facing towards the terraced gardens.[263] It is therefore not unrealistic to suggest that the royal quarters at Clipstone lay on the eastern side of the complex facing out towards the gardens and lake beyond. Clarendon's planform can still be seen on the ground, however something of the lost grandeur of Clipstone under Henry III can be understood through a careful reading of his instructions to Robert de Vavassur.

Henry moved north in the summer of 1255 and his final visit to Clipstone, in August of that year, bore a kinship with his first visit as it was part of his itinerary as he rode north to assist his son-in-law Alexander III of Scotland. Still a minor, the young king's regency was marked by rivalry between the Earl of Menteith and Alan Durwurd, the Justiciar of Scotland. Durwurd's supporters had taken possession of Alexander hence Henry dashing north to attempt to settle matters.[264] Presumably the king was happy with the facilities of the palace as he did not recommend any further work to be carried out at the King's Houses, however he was about to enter a troubled phase in his reign which temporarily disrupted his passion for architecture.

Henry III's construction programme at Clipstone must be seen in context. Although it led to a substantial remodelling and expansion of the site, the king's spending there was not comparable to that of Westminster or Windsor, or even the mid-range costs at Clarendon and Woodstock.[265] It was an occasional site for Henry, which he visited only four times yet was still of importance to him as it warranted so much remodelling. The same scenario can be seen at the Tower of London which was also expanded during the reign to include '*new towers, chambers, a great hall, a kitchen and various other ancillary buildings*' however Henry spent relatively little time even at this great fortress-palace in his capital at London.[266]

Henry's spending on domestic architecture was prodigious. The restoration of Rochester Castle between 1217–37 cost in excess of £600, he spent £1000 at Corfe, the rebuilding of Clifford's Tower at York cost £2600, and in the 1240s and 1250s extensions at Dover Castle, including a new great hall, amounted to £7500. Guildford Palace saw additions including a new window flanked by Purbeck marble columns in the queen's apartments, coloured glass in the windows of the great hall which had walls painted with stories of Dives and Lazarus and a screen painted with story of St John and St Edward the Confessor. Meanwhile Henry's chambers were painted green and picked out with gold and silver stars. Widespread building work occurred at Nottingham, Deganwy, Dyserth, Montgomery, Grosmont, Whitecastle, Skenfrith, Chester, Beeston, Tattershall, Tickhill, Stogursey, Pickering, Pontefract, Newcastle, Sheffield, Kenilworth and Caerphilly. At Westminster expense was lavished upon the Queen's Chamber, Chapel and Painted Chamber. At Windsor refurbishments were carried out on the great hall in the outer bailey, the king's houses, houses in the moat and the great tower. New towers were constructed at the south-west end of middle and upper baileys, there were new walls and towers on north and south of lower bailey and a new wing of royal apartments and a chapel was built after Henry and Eleanor's marriage in 1236 with chambers and nurseries for their children Edward and Margaret. Much work occurred on the queen's apartments in the 1240s and 1250s which was then followed by the reconstruction of the royal chapel.[267]

Henry III spent in excess of £30,000 on buildings. As a child his guardian was Bishop Peter des Roches, a man with a passion for building who seems to have greatly inspired the impressionable young king. From 1236 Eleanor deepened his interest in architecture and there is a sense that Henry was often building to make his Savoyard queen feel at home.[268] However Henry and Eleanor's spending led to problems. The king's powerful brother-in-law, Simon de Montfort, never received the promised dowry after his marriage to the king's sister Eleanor. This led to a needling grudge which underlined de Montfort's dealings with the king and finally burst into rebellion. Despite Henry's parsimony over the dowry, which eventually led to such division in the kingdom relating to more widespread issues of democracy and representation, the lesson was simply not learned and personal spending on palaces soared again after the Baron's War.[269] Expenditure on the King's Houses at Clipstone was symptomatic of a very great problem.

Looking for Henry

The expansion, remodelling and repair of the site at Clipstone under Henry III continued throughout the reigns of the three monarchs who followed him and led to an increase in the total area of the site. The D-shaped boundary ditch excavated by Rahtz in 1956 contained pottery dated to the thirteenth or fourteenth centuries in its final backfill[270] and this may represent an expansion of the palace as Henry ordered the old boundary ditch to be filled in. A rectilinear area surrounding the ruin measuring 90 by 60 metres was traced via geophysical resistance survey and reflects the presence of demolition rubble from the buildings which once stood around King John's Palace.[271] Excavation has shown that this demolition rubble stretches to the south-east of the earlier ditch and there are glimpses of structure such as a robbed out foundation at least 1.9m wide and 0.94m deep. This suggests a very sizeable superstructure and was supported by a surviving masonry buttress over 1.8m wide which incorporated a piece of chamfered stonework in its makeup.[272] This is reminiscent of the reuse of Reigate Upper Greensand and Purbeck limestone from Henry III's building projects at the Tower of London during remodelling of the defences under Edward I.[273]

Within the area of the built environment of the King's Houses the material culture has often been found to be surprisingly poor. Rahtz blamed this on the very eroded nature of the site,[274] but James has pointed out that this is a feature common to the archaeology of most Mediaeval palaces[275] and even the great castle at Nottingham, which has been extensively excavated, has produced a relatively low assemblage in comparison to other types of sites in domestic occupation.[276] Pottery, one of the most commonly found of archaeological artefacts, was certainly used at palaces and Rahtz, Richard Sheppard in 1991 and Wessex Archaeology[277] have all recorded moderate amounts of fabrics at Clipstone. More recently a ceramic fragment was recovered showing a deer looking over its shoulder, as if being hunted, in a similar pose to that illustrated in manuscripts of the Mediaeval period.[278] Documentary accounts indicate that pottery was carried about during the itineraries of kings, magnates and clerics as can be seen from a reference in 1290 to a cart in the entourage of the Bishop of Hereford overturning and smashing a large amount of ceramics near Wantage, Oxfordshire.[279] Pottery was often preferred for serving up victuals as, unlike silver or pewter, it did not taint the taste of the food; although in the later Mediaeval period communal serving platters were used less as private dining became preferable. In this way food and dining became yet another method of social exclusion through the refinement of the palate.[280]

Preliminary findings from a reassessment of the entire pottery assemblage from Clipstone has shown that although there is evidence for fabrics from the mid-twelfth to mid-thirteenth centuries, it is the material from the later thirteenth and fourteenth centuries which is most common in the record. This certainly fits with the evidence from the documentary sources which indicates an expansion of the site facilities and visitations by the monarchy during that period. The main suppliers of pottery to the King's Houses came from an unusually wide range of areas including Nottingham, Derbyshire, Lincolnshire and south Yorkshire as well as imported material brought in from northern France[281] which complements evidence for wares imported from the Saintange region of France and Malagan Spain at Clarendon.[282]

Documentary evidence points towards the wholesale removal of large amounts of rubbish from palaces such as Wolvesy or Lincoln and five hundred cartloads of refuse was transported from Clarendon in the fifteenth century, perhaps as a response to the Black Death which was commonly thought to originate from rotting matter and to be carried on the air.[283] The itinerant nature of the royal household which stopped at residences for usually very limited periods of time may also explain the reduced assemblage and this may have been exacerbated by the giving of food to the poor as alms.[284] However the relatively modest quantity of pottery found can be linked to the basic reality that it was used less frequently at palaces because the dining vessels of aristocracy and royalty were more often made from expensive glass or metal. Glass vessels have only been recovered from two palaces[285] and metal wares are also rarely excavated, and are better known from documentary references or illustrations and from museum collections (where they are removed from their original context), however they were carefully transported along with the household due to their precious nature and use by the top levels of society.[286] In the kitchens three legged metal cauldrons were stood, suspended or placed on a range and used for stewing meat,[287] but the experience of most members of the household must have been the consumption of food and drinks from simple wooden or leather containers.

The 1251 building accounts mention the presence of the great gate with its chamber and privy for the first time. The decision to build this structure probably marks the nucleus of the expansion of the site beyond the Henry II's smaller enclosure. The location of this gate has been identified through a multidisciplinary approach. Placename evidence pointed to the presence of a late eighteenth century public house known as the Gate Inn. This Inn was run by landlord James Cutts at what is now a picturesque private dwelling known as Maun Cottage (Plate 4 A). The earlier name seems to be a folk memory of the palace gatehouse. Maun Cottage stands forward into Mansfield Road along with its neighbours Brammer Farmhouse and Arundel Cottage to the east creating a pinch point in the village street (Plate 4 B).[288] with a reduced width pavement that causes locals great danger from the dizzying speeds of motorists passing through the settlement. Historic mapping from 1766 reveals that Maun Cottage and Brammer Farmhouse are built to the north of an older property boundary running behind the cottages. This was the boundary wall of the King's Houses and can be clearly seen on the 1630 estate map of Clipstone. In precisely the same location of the contemporary Maun Cottage, William Senior drew the representation of a building with a strip of land to its rear. This is anomalous as it is one of only two properties intruding into what was then called Mannorgarth, containing the roofless representation of King John's Palace. The likelihood is that this was a house which had been developed by remodelling one of the original buildings from the palace.[289]

A standing building survey of three historic properties south of Mansfield Road has revealed the presence of significant quantities of in situ Mediaeval stonework. The magnesian limestone boundary wall runs east-west though both Brammer Farmhouse and Arundel Cottage and survives up to first floor height. It is possible to see how the post-Mediaeval brick cottages were first constructed immediately to the north of the palace enclosure creating the pinch-point in the village street. The Mediaeval wall was found to be 0.51 metres in thickness,[290] precisely the same dimension as the boundary wall at Henry III's favoured priory at Merton in south-west London.[291] The modern measurement is essentially meaningless yet when it is rendered in historic units it proves to be exactly twenty inches. This is a satisfying round number, however twenty inches also corresponds to five hands breadth, an important unit of measurement in a largely illiterate society (a hand is taken to be four inches and is still used when describing the height of a horse). It is tempting to picture the clerk of the works instructing the master masons at both Clipstone and Merton to build their walls to be five hands breadth thick.

Brammer Farmhouse also contained two walls orientated north south which were bonded into the boundary wall. Two of these walls extend to the south into the palace enclosure forming three sides of a structure that had a splayed door or window which looked out to the north through the boundary wall. The western wall also extended to the north of the enclosure boundary[292] and is mirrored by another stone wall in the east elevation of Maun Cottage.[293] These projecting walls may relate to either the portal of the great gate or the porter's lodge which would have monitored entry into the palace.

The clue provided by the presence of the surviving wall and gatehouse leading off the village street means that it is possible to view Mansfield Road as the boundary of the site to the north. The road curves around Castlefield to the south-west and enters a deep hollow way known locally as the Rathole. In the Mediaeval period this was how the local community accessed the arable Waterfield by skirting around the north-western corner of the palace. To the east of the gate, the boundary wall headed down to a green lane, shown on the 1766 map leading to Dam Close, which accessed the shore of the lake from Mansfield Road. A triangular piece of land known as the Croft to the north-east was in place at least as early as 1630 and survived into the early years of the twenty-first century when it was called The Kennels. It is unclear if the area was part of the palace enclosure or whether the King's Houses were bounded by Dam Close, but from this point the eastern boundary of the palace was the Great Pond.[294]

Geophysical surveys and several seasons of excavation have revealed the south-western boundary of the palace to have been a very substantial earthwork bank and ditch measuring between 5.8 and 6.2 metres in width and surviving to a depth of 1.13–1.31 metres. The feature can be traced on a south-east to north-west linear alignment from the earthworks of the lake for 160 metres before historic mapping shows that it dog-legged up towards Rathole. Pottery found in the lower half of the ditch and in the make-up of the bank dates from the later thirteenth to early fourteenth century and helps to give a date range of construction to a period similar to the documentary reference to the building of the great gate on the opposite side of the enclosure.[295]

The total area enclosed by the boundaries of the palace was at least 7.5 acres which is an extraordinarily large expanse of ground when considered in relation to the very biggest complexes, such as the 7.65 acre Clarendon or Eltham in south London. The entire enclosure would not have been covered by buildings, rather they would have sprawled in a rambling and asymmetrical manner around irregular shaped courtyards that may themselves have been subdivided by walls. The list of known buildings during this period is impressive: great gate, chapel, great hall, chamber at the low end of the hall, great chamber, king's chamber with wardrobe below, queen's chamber with corresponding wardrobe, chapel and kitchen. Additionally there were numerous privies, passageways and chimneys. The ancillary structures of the palace are less well understood at this period, but orders for repairs a century later under Edward III confirm their presence and we must therefore imagine barns, stables, granaries and kitchen amenities. Beyond the buildings were the gardens, lake and of course the deer park. It was during the reign of Henry III that the King's Houses truly came to deserve the appellation of palace, however the accommodation became even more lavish under his son Edward.

Edward I

The Pipe Rolls of Edward I reveal that Clipstone Park was assessed as being 1440 acres in dimension[296] which shows that it was of a near equivalent size to the survey published in 1630 where the park was itemised as being 1457 acres. This was a tremendous resource for a king well known to be a very keen hunter who employed fifty-three keepers in the 1280s, offered up a model of a sick falcon at a shrine to expedite its healing[297] and was renowned for making

POLITICS AND PALACE EXPANSION: 1199–1307

the kill of pursued stags himself with a sword.[298]

Edward visited Clipstone twice in 1279–80, during a three year period that was marked by a time of relative calm and prosperity in England with no major issues or crises facing the monarchy. In the years previous Edward had been involved in a major programme of castle-building as a measure to subdue the Welsh, a coinage irregularities sting against the Jews which netted £36,000, and a lengthy conference with Philip III of France in Amiens to settle issues in Gascony.[299] Now Edward was able to stage regular parliaments at Easter and again in the autumn of each year. This meant that he could personally handle any matters arising before they spiralled out of hand, such as reforming the see of Canterbury and a commission to investigate the legality of landownership. Crucially the king managed to maintain harmonious relationships with both church and magnates. Such peaceable days allowed a relative level of leisure enabling a slow progress in the summer and autumn of 1280 through the northern counties of England, which explains the presence of the king at Clipstone in August. Notably, many of the destinations on his itinerary during these three years involved stays at hunting reserves in the New Forest, Essex and Northamptonshire.[300] Significantly his visits to Clipstone occurred in late summer and early autumn during the hunting seasons of the red stag and the fallow buck.[301]

Edward's beloved queen, Eleanor of Castile, routinely joined her household with the king's during this period which can be seen as an Edwardian golden age of peace. The royal children Eleanor, Joan and Alfonso were also old enough to have accompanied their parents during these years, although their siblings Margaret and Mary were usually housed in the south at Windsor or Woodstock.[302] Although the future Edward II was not born until 1284, the visits with his father to Clipstone in 1290 and 1300 began in him a love for this area of Sherwood Forest as it certainly became a highly favoured residence during his own reign.

Edward I's grief at the death of his own father was remarked upon by the King of Sicily to have been very great. One effect of the old king's character may have been to instil a great love of architecture in his son which was also passed to Eleanor of Castile through the lavish quarters provided for her at Guildford in the years immediately after her marriage to Edward aged just ten.[303] This architectural education paid dividends as the visits to Clipstone led to an order for the redevelopment of the royal suites with chambers for the king and queen constructed at a cost of over £400.[304] The high cost of works in comparison to the construction of Henry III's chamber for just £130 indicates that the buildings were probably of stone; essentially this was an upgrade from the timber framing of forty-six years earlier. Details of repairs made to the King's Chamber during the reign of Edward III confirm the presence of a stone chimney and garderobe complete with buttresses and a lead roof. Also roofed in lead were the porch and private chapel, the latter was glazed and there is reference to a lead spout which may hint at the presence of a gargoyle. The chamber was accessed at first floor via an external stair which continued an architectural tradition at Clipstone begun by Henry III. The physical location of the king's apartments seems to have been maintained as the fourteenth century accounts also refer to the pentice connecting them to the Great Hall[305]

Like his father, Edward was very much influenced by the French style of architecture and Eleanor also brought the fashions of her native Spain.[306] It is noteworthy that the rebuilding at Clipstone occurred at precisely the same time that Edward and Eleanor were engaged in the construction of the highly romantic and continental style Gloriette at Leeds Castle, Kent which was built to contain their apartments surrounded by a dramatic aquatic landscape.[307] The legacy of the peaceful years 1278–81 was the production of some of England's greatest ever Mediaeval buildings. Sadly the apartments at Clipstone are long gone; perhaps the most similar surviving building to Edward and Eleanor's chambers in Sherwood is the double solar block at Ludlow Castle constructed by Peter de Genevill c 1283–92 and added to slightly later by Roger Mortimer c 1314.[308]

The Welsh Uprising and the Palace Stables

The easy days came to a juddering halt on 25 March 1282 when galloping messengers arrived from Wales to inform Edward that Dafydd ap Gruffydd and Rhys Wyndod were in armed rebellion, eventually to be joined by the reluctant Llewelyn, Prince of Gwynedd. Edward showed tremendous energy and resolve in mustering three armies with which he co-ordinated a campaign leading to the utter destruction of the independent Welsh state. Seven thousand troops gathered at Chester under Reginald de Grey, seventeen hundred men were at Dinefwr under Gilbert de Clare and six thousand more were under the direct command of Edward himself at Rhuddlan. Llewelyn died in battle at Cilmeri in December 1282 and the king remained in Wales until August 1283, shortly after the capture of Dafydd. In total the war cost somewhere in the region of £120,000,[309] and it is rather surprising that it was precisely during this period of intense and expensive conflict in Wales that Edward chose to spend an additional £104 8s 5d on a stable at Clipstone, far away from the front.[310] The stable was no ordinary structure as it was capable of holding two hundred horses and later documents illustrate its great size through the moniker of '*the King's Long Stable.*'[311]

Palace stables are mentioned frequently in contemporary documents but their physical remains are rarely found. The stone foundations of those at Goodrich Castle and at Minster Lovell survive, but only the Tythe Barn at Maidstone Palace, which started off life as the stable, still stands. Typically stables were timber framed and the vast size of the one at Clipstone must have necessitated this building material as a stone structure would have been prohibitively expensive. The building would have been well ventilated and lit, large and long enough to allow multiple animal standings, and well drained. Archaeologists may expect to find damage to floors by mettlesome animals and artefacts such as curry combs and horseshoes. Such buildings were invariably located close to the gatehouse[312] as hinted at in the late Mediaeval poem *Sir Gawain and the Green Knight*:

> *Then they yielded to their guest, yanked open the gate,*
> *And bidding them rise he rode across the bridge.*
> *He was assisted from the saddle by several men*
> *And the strongest amongst them stabled his steed.*[313]

The specific location of the King's Long Stable is given within the building accounts of the King's Houses dated 1348–9 as standing immediately adjacent to the keeper of the manor's chamber which in turn stood next to the Great Gate. It is apparent from other accounts in this document that this range of buildings lay to the west of the gate and lined the south of the village street.[314] The modern landscape rises away from the gate in this direction and it is possible that the Mediaeval ground level of the stable may have been stepped or terraced. Slightly later building accounts give detail on the appearance of the stable, which was certainly timber framed as the carpenter Thomas Gurneld was paid to lay new groundsills in 1394–5[315] and its walls were clay-daub that was plastered and pargetted with lime render. Internally there were the expected racks and mangers and its roof was covered with an astonishing 26,000 shingles and the ridge was broken by seven louvres.[316]

There must have already been a stable at Clipstone as the provision of accommodation for the king's horses, which were the mainstay of his itinerary transportation, was a matter of necessity. When Henry IV ordered a new stable at Clarendon in the early fifteenth century it was capable of holding between 85 to 120 horses, measured 45 by 8 metres, enclosed 360 square metres and may have replaced an earlier structure excavated in the 1930s which was less than half the size.[317] Even with the upgrading of the stables at Clarendon the sizable building must have been only half the dimension of the vast edifice constructed at Clipstone for Edward I. John Steane has speculated that it may have been intended to act as part of a royal stud farm,[318] however there is no evidence of future administrative documents such as those from Rayleigh, Neyland, Eastwood, Woodstock, Knoll[319] and Odiham.[320] More likely the stable was constructed at Clipstone during a period of time when Edward was focused entirely on the war effort against the Welsh uprising. This necessitated the movement of thousands of royal troops, a great many of them mounted. Although Clipstone was far from the epicentre of fighting household knights were being mobilised from across England and Clipstone may have acted as a convenient muster point in the north midlands. Equally, Edward himself needed to maintain his mobility with an increased wartime household all requiring accommodation for both their mounts and baggage animals. The king maintained horses at places as diverse as Macclesfield, Chertsey, St Albans and Braemore, Berwick and Norham so that his accounts are littered with references to '*collars, traces, girths, halters, saddles, cloths and covers, stirrups and harnesses.*'[321] The numbers of horses stabled by Edward steadily increased during the 1290s so that in May 1293 it was noted that the royal family kept 269 horses throughout their residences in England of which 34 specifically belonged to the king.[322] Even with the war over Edward required his houses to be able to cater for large numbers of visitors as in late 1283 he began to give thanks for his victory by visiting religious buildings in the Welsh Marches. Christmas was spent at Rhuddlan before he moved on to spend the early months of 1284 paying his respects at the shrines in Yorkshire and Lincolnshire.[323] It was on his way between Wales and the north of England that Edward once again visited Clipstone and probably made the first use of the long stable. Conveniently his three day stay coincided with the hunting seasons of the red hind, fallow doe and roe buck.[324]

The 1290 Parliament and the Death of a Queen

The ongoing enquiry into landownership was beginning to cause widespread disgruntlement during the late 1280s as it was proving to be very costly in lawyers and bribes for magnates to defend their perceived rights. Additionally *'a great many men who did not have charters lost, without recovery, liberties and free customs'*. Edward's lords were frustrated that after great personal expense during the war in Wales they were now being held to ransom for their own lands in the courts. Meanwhile Edward needed the potential income from the enquiry as he was deeply in debt to the tune of £110,000 after three years spent touring Gascony in some splendour, a province that could not financially support the king's vast retinue.[325] Moreover the queen was coming under increased criticism for profiting from debts run up by landowners beholden to their Jewish creditors – in 1278 she had obtained Leeds Castle from the strapped William Leybourne in return for clearing his outstanding financial liabilities.[326] Edward needed a solution to both problems and the scheme that he came up with was the very definition of Machiavellian.

As a holding manoeuvre the king allowed that the liberties of landowners could stand so long as they could be proven back to 1189 and he offered his chief opponent, Gilbert de Clare, Earl of Gloucester, his daughter Joan in marriage. Edward then moved to crush the remaining two thousand Jews still living in England. He had learned from the experience of Charles of Salerno

that he could take the moral high ground in this scheme by emphasising that the expulsion of the Jews would damage the royal coffers as he could no longer rely on their loans to top up income from taxation and from his estates. This gave him leverage to demand a grant of taxation. A second lavish marriage was held at Westminster between his daughter Margaret and John, heir to the duchy of Brabant. This provided the perfect opportunity for Edward to rally the magnates to his cause, which proved eminently successful – the lords would be rid of their own debts to the Jews and could therefore afford to help the king with his own. A tax was duly granted – £116,000 – the greatest sum of money ever collected in England during the Mediaeval period. Edward then declared that every member of the Jewish religion had to leave the realm before 1 November 1290.[327]

The relevancy of this financial chicanery, at the cost of the Jews, to Clipstone is that Edward was now entirely debt free and could once again consider returning to the Holy Land for the first time since he left his crusade in 1273–4. The Pope had offered a very generous £130,000 towards the costs of the war and Edward summoned his parliament to meet at Clipstone on 12 October 1290 specifically to discuss the arrangements of the new crusade which was due to leave England at midsummer 1293.[328] On 14 October, whilst at Clipstone, the king announced to the assembly that he planned to return to the Holy Land and a taxation of one tenth was granted by parliament to help to fund the venture.[329]

Edward seemed very financially minded during the early days of the gathering as he ordered payment to his servant Elias de Hanville for an arduous horseback journey into the north to bring jewels which had been taken into Scotland, from the wardrobe at Newcastle-upon-Tyne, back down to Clipstone. Perhaps these were to be used in the payments authorised to his Italian creditors including Lapus Bonchi and Gradus Pini.[330] Italians were even closer to Edward as he ordered a payment of £100 annually to Francis Accursius,[331] the son of a professor of law from Bologna. Accursius was the king's secretary from 1273 to 1281 and later acted as a legal advisor to Edward[332] so it is no great surprise that he was present at the parliament.

In total 251 pleas were heard at the Clipstone parliament[333] concerning a wide variety of matters. A claim was heard from the Abbot of Ramsey that he should receive money from fines imposed in the royal courts as had been agreed between his predecessors and the monarchy in the past. Edward ordered that by the next parliament this ancient right should once again be paid by the exchequer.[334] The family of the infant Hugh de Neville petitioned the king to annul what they saw to be an illegal marriage between their relative and the even younger daughter of Thomas Weyland. The marriage had been arranged by Weyland who was currently acting as Hugh's guardian. Weyland was formerly accused of corruption in the king's service and had been stripped of all his chattels, including the wardship of the young John. Even though Thomas Weyland was a disgraced royal servant, Edward still chose to uphold his case and the marriage was not annulled.[335] Also present at the parliament was Richard Foliot, who we previously encountered as one of Henry III's favoured household knights. He was still part of the royal retinue at Clipstone in 1290 when he was appointed keeper of Horstan Castle, Derbyshire.[336]

The king used the parliament to attempt to quell an ongoing dispute between the earls of Hereford and Gloucester. The latter, Edward's constant critic and new son in law, Gilbert de Clare, was claiming custody of the temporalities (secular income from church estates) during a vacancy in the see of Llandaff which was in turn challenged by his rival, Humphrey de Bohun. Effectively this had overspilled into a private war between the two Marcher lords with several raids carried out by Gloucester's men on de Bohun's town of Brecon. An exasperated Edward attempted to lay the matter to rest by claiming royal prerogative over the temporalities, however de Clare brought his grievances before the Clipstone parliament and on 2 November forced a decision in his favour. Meanwhile the king was careful not to incur the wrath of Hereford and granted him fifteen deer on 7 November – a perfect example of the monarchy using their hunting reserves to offer status gifts to powerful lords. Regardless, the belligerent Gloucester launched yet another attack on Brecon later in the month and the case rumbled on until February 1292 when Edward finally seized both earldoms and imposed heavy fines on his turbulent Marcher lords.[337]

The clerks of the Chancery must have been kept enormously busy churning out records of the parliament. Due to the huge numbers of delegates present at the King's Houses the available accommodation was stretched beyond capacity so that the clerks were forced to lodge three miles away at Warsop. Meanwhile we get our first ever reference to the placename '*Clipiston Regis*' (Kings Clipstone) as a result of a record made by the Queen's Remembrancer, Thomas de Merk.[338] The lengthy amount of time spent at Clipstone by such a swollen number of people inevitably led to a degree of wear and tear on the palace infrastructure, and similar to the aftermath of Richard I's meeting with William the Lion in 1194, this necessitated repairs to the houses, dam and weir amounting to £160.[339] A further largescale gathering at the palace was narrowly avoided at the end of the decade when Edward suggested to second wife Marguerite of France that they kept the Christmas feast at Clipstone. The wilful queen stated that she preferred St Albans, but eventually the feast was observed at Windsor.[340]

So why did Edward choose to hold parliament specifically at Clipstone in the autumn of 1290? Of the previous twenty-one parliaments held during his reign only two had been spent away from the administrative centres of London and Westminster – those in the Marcher lands at Gloucester in 1278 and Acton Burnell in 1283,[341] both of which occurred by necessity in the aftermath of the war in Wales. The choice of Clipstone was therefore highly unusual. Stapleton insisted that Edward was intending to head to Scotland to begin his claim to the throne and called parliament en route. However a petition lodged at the parliament regarding a land dispute on the Scottish borders shows that Edward was not overly concerned with matters north of the border and was not yet considering the imperialism that raised its head in the beginning of The Great Cause in 1291–2. The king simply dismissed the quarrel with the words '*let it wait until there is a king in Scotland.*'[342] In fact the English king was engaged in very positive and peaceful negotiations with the Scottish magnates to marry his son Edward to the deceased Alexander III's only remaining heir, his granddaughter, Margaret of Norway. Emissaries had been sent north in September to greet the returning queen-to-be after she landed on her journey from Scandinavia at Norway's territory of Orkney.[343] News of Margaret's untimely death on the islands reached the ears of Edward whilst the parliament was still sitting at Clipstone and shaped Anglo-Scottish politics for many years to come. However Scotland was not uppermost in Edward's mind when parliament was summoned.

Margaret of Norway's predicted arrival in Scotland was certainly not imminent and Edward was in no great hurry to meet her. Eleanor of Castile's biographer Sara Cockerill has pointed out that the decision to hold parliament at Clipstone was probably a reaction to the declining health of the queen. Edward and Eleanor's itinerary after the Brabant wedding at Westminster concentrated on the queen's estates in Buckinghamshire, Bedfordshire, Northamptonshire, Nottinghamshire, Rutland, Derbyshire and Cheshire. It was clear that Eleanor was sickening as the progress was characterised by very short journeys such as the stop at Pytchley only twelve miles after Northampton en route to Geddington, itself only eight miles further on. Edward was clearly very worried about Eleanor as he paid for three hundred poor men to be fed and given alms in penance for the king and queen not attending mass whilst at Silverstone on 6 August. The implication being that Eleanor was simply too sick to attend mass and Edward was seeking divine intervention for her cure. On 23 September, shortly after a brief stop at Clipstone, Edward sent for her doctor Peter of Portugal to tend to the ailing queen.[344]

Eleanor was so ill during the parliament that medicines were sent for from Lincoln and, perhaps most tellingly, the royal children Joan, Edward and Elizabeth were summoned. Edward and Elizabeth were so young that their grandmother Eleanor of Provence elicited a complaint that the long journey would be a danger to their health. It must have been tragically apparent that this might be the last few moments that they would be able to spend with their dying mother to take such a risk. Edward would have been painfully aware of the decline in his queen's health and was unable to return south to Westminster in time to hold a Michaelmas parliament. The king improvised by convening the assembly at his palace of Clipstone with overspill accommodation catered for at Rufford, Newstead, Warsop and several other great houses in the area.[345]

Eleanor's health continued to worsen after the parliament as the royal couple continued their painfully slow progress on to Laxton by 14 November and crossed the Trent at Marnham before staying at Harby near Lincoln on the 20th. Eleanor was clearly so very sick by this point that the household then halted until the 28th when she eventually passed away. Famously her embalmed body rested at twelve locations on the way back to Westminster and crosses were erected on the orders of Edward to mark those places, although only three now survive.

The Great Cause

Tragedy hit Edward in two ways during the autumn of 1290. The death of Eleanor led to a period of mourning spent at his manor at Ashridge in the Chilterns. Whilst he was there he was able to begin to contemplate the implications of the death of Margaret of Norway, the intended bride for his young son Edward, and key to the Plantagenet succession to the throne in Scotland. Her passing marked the end of the line for the Scottish royal dynasty which led directly to the feud between various rival houses – Balliol, Comyn, Bruce – for control of the beleaguered kingdom. Edward eventually declared the results of his ruminations on Scotland at Norham Castle during May 1291. As the feuding Scottish lords also owed him fealty for their lands held in England, he declared himself to be their overlord and therefore rightly the ruler of Scotland.[346] So began Edward's Great Cause, a tactically disastrous decision which led to decades of warfare between the two kingdoms. By 1300 the English had still not made any lasting progress in the war which had broken out in 1296 and the new season of campaigning opened with an invasion of south-west Scotland via Carlisle. The first action was a lengthy and costly siege at Caerlaverock Castle followed by a march on Dumfries, both of which led to largescale desertions from the army caused by a fundamental lack of pay and provisions. Edward's depleted forces attempted to bring about a battle near Wigtown but after a brief skirmish the Scots headed for the hills and left the English army isolated so that by August they were in retreat back to Sweetheart Abbey. Further disaster overtook Edward when he learned that Pope Boniface VIII had written a stern criticism of the pious king's campaigns in Scotland and, with the weather now against him, the king was left with little choice but to return south and consider his next move. Parliament was summoned to meet in January 1301 and, in the very depths of both winter and despair, Edward called in to the King's Houses at Clipstone for the very last time on his journey to the assembly convened at Lincoln.

A coin of the period – a hammered silver penny minted 1299–1300 in Bristol – has been excavated from the topsoil in Castlefield (Plate 6 B). The penny was minted as part of a recoinage by Edward which required an additional temporary mint to be set up at Bristol to help cope with the demand. The coin that was discovered is very worn and has evidence of a deliberate reduction in weight which makes it more comparable to coins in use after 1351 and may therefore have been in circulation for quite some time before it came to rest in Castlefield.[347] The value of a penny amounted to one third of the daily wage of a labourer in 1300,[348] a wage that remained stable from the period of Edward's castle-building in Wales during the 1280s until the later fourteenth century.[349] The coin bears a portrait of Edward I on the obverse and he can be seen wearing a very distinctive crown also visible in the portrait of the king in the sedilia at Westminster Abbey.

The Lincoln parliament once again brought up the subject of Forest Law. Edward was in sore need of funds to continue his campaign north of the border and was backed into a political corner by magnates determined to for the overdue perambulations which eventually found that roughly half of the royal forests were unlawful extensions. Edward was granted his war tax, but he had been humiliated over the forests by his chief opponents Roger Bigod, Earl of Norfolk, and Robert Winchelsea, the Archbishop of Canterbury. Even at this very low ebb, Edward played the part of the canny politician and ensured that it was on record that the decision was made not by himself but by the coalition led by Bigod and Winchelsea. His memory was very long and he harboured this grudge so that when Bigod ran into financial troubles the following year the king was named heir to his estates in return for a generous annuity which effectively put the earl in the king's pocket. Winchelsea eventually overextended himself in 1305 by supporting the inheritance claim of John de Ferrers, the son of a dispossessed supporter of Edward's old enemy Simon de Montfort. The king went after the archbishop and countersued him for £4000 in unpaid taxes. At the same time a new pope, Clement V, was elected after the death of Boniface and this incumbent was not inclined to take the side of the churchman in the face of vengeful Edward who dismissed Winchelsea from his see. The king may have lost his battle over the royal forests, but the forceful Edward eventually brought down both of his opponents during the Lincoln parliament. He never did extinguish the Scottish state and when he died on campaign in July 1307 his son Prince Edward was in London having declined to take part in that season's campaign. The new king eventually travelled to Scotland the following month[350] and it was his return journey south which led to the next extended visit to the King's Houses at Clipstone by the royal household.

Chapter Five

A Century of Turbulence:
1307–1399

'This period comes closest to the popular conception of what is 'medieval',
with its chivalry, jousts, etiquette, art and architecture... containing civil
wars, battles against the neighbouring kingdoms of Scotland and France,
sieges, outlaws... famine... and (above all else) the Black Death.'
~ Ian Mortimer, 2008, *The Time Traveller's Guide To Medieval England* ~

Edward II

The pattern of Edward II's use of his residences is distinct from any king that
we have so far encountered. Unlike the fast moving monarchs such as John,
Edward made short stops with the intention of reaching favoured residences
such as Winchester, Kings Langley, Windsor or Westminster where he would
then stay for an extended period of time. Prior to Edward's lengthy visits to
Clipstone, only his father's parliament in 1290 had led to more than two or
three days spent at the palace. Clipstone seems to have immediately become a
preferred manor as his first visit as king occurred in only the second month as
monarch (albeit prior to his actual coronation in February 1308).

Edward II is a much maligned king. His reputation was tarnished both in
his own lifetime and by later historians. The fact that he ended his reign
wandering around the south Welsh valleys with a mere handful of retainers,
prior to being forced to abdicate by his own queen and her supporters who then
kept him under house arrest at Kenilworth, and later Berkeley Castle, testifies
to the abject failure of his sovereignty. The end of his life is shrouded in great
mystery with large gaps in the record, perhaps created deliberately by Isabella
of France and Roger Mortimer as they sought to balance their power as regents
to the young Edward III. It is commonly held that Edward II ended his days in
September 1327 face down in a bed at Berkeley with a red hot iron burning

out his bowels via a horn thrust into his anus.[351] This is a much later story which did not become current until the 1350s[352] and contemporary accounts are a confusion, reporting his death as variously brought about by natural causes, grief, trickery, strangulation or suffocation.[353] If Edward died at all in 1327. Both Ian Mortimer[354] and Kathryn Warner[355] have asked some very awkward questions and presented very compelling arguments suggesting that the king was first moved to Corfe in Dorset before being allowed to live out his days in exile on the continent into the 1340s. Seymour Phillips has written a comprehensive critique,[356] but many questions remain and debate rages.[357]

The criticisms levelled against Edward II relate to a nineteen year period of conflict, civil war, failed military endeavours, over-reliance on unpopular favourites and an inability to maintain good relationships with his barons. He was accused of listening to evil councillors, losing lands in Scotland, France and Ireland, and of tyrannical behaviour towards his magnates and churchmen including imprisonment, disinheriting and executions. One of the most serious accusations against Edward was his deep curiosity regarding peasant activities – in short that he was simply not suited to kingship. Edward himself responded in tears '*I greatly lament that I have so utterly failed my people, but I could not be other than I am.*'[358] What may have endeared Edward to a twenty-first century populace only served to reinforce the notion that he was simply unfit to be monarch in the eyes of his contemporaries. His interest in the pursuits of ordinary folk such as thatching, blacksmithing, ditching, fishing, swimming, rowing and the fact that he was not above going out to buy his own bread or fish was entirely anathema to his barons.[359]

Above all Edward's greatest crime was that he was simply not either his father nor his son. Although both Edward I and Edward III had very great personal flaws in their characters and policies, these are often glossed over in a slavish appreciation of their martial capabilities and high-handed aristocratic bearings.[360] Edward II was an extraordinarily complicated character. He did not have nearly the same reputation as a huntsman as his predecessor or successor, yet there is compelling evidence that Edward enjoyed the pleasures of the chase in equal measure. He employed chief huntsman William Twiti, giving him a stipend of 9d a day until his retirement to Reading Abbey in 1327, the latter paid for by the king himself.[361] Twiti wrote a manual *The Art of Hunting* around 1320 which gave a very detailed account of practices in early fourteenth century England and it is likely that Edward had a hand in the patronage of this text. The king spent lengthy amounts of time hunting at his palace at Kings Langley, Hertfordshire[362] and a pattern emerges when the dates of Edward's visits to Clipstone are interrogated:

Period of Visit	Deer in season
16 – 27 September 1307	Red hind; Fallow doe (14 September – 2 February) Roe buck (Easter – 29 September)
29 October 1315 – 25 January 1316	Red hind; Fallow doe (14 September – 2 February) Roe doe (29 September – 2 February)
27 February – 14 March 1316	n/a
9 December 1316 – 17 January 1317	Red hind; Fallow doe (14 September – 2 February) Roe doe (29 September – 2 February)
18 August – 15 September 1318	Red stag (14 June – 14 September) Fallow buck (24 June – 14 September)
1 – 3 February 1320	Red hind; Fallow doe (14 September – 2 February) Roe doe (29 September – 2 February)

Figure 3: Table comparing the visits to Clipstone of Edward II with deer hunting seasons

All of the deer species cited in the table above have been found within the archaeological record at Clipstone[363] and can therefore be reasonably expected to have inhabited the deer park to the west of the palace. The timing of Edward's visits appear to be remarkable in the precision with which the hunting seasons were pinpointed. His 1307 stay at Clipstone began just two days after the red hind and fallow doe came into season and he departed the palace two days before the end of the roe buck season. These twelve days perfectly complemented and maximised the availability of three seasons. His later visits to the palace, with the exception of spring 1316, also fit this pattern with at least two types of deer always available. Political events can be cited to help explain the presence of Edward at Clipstone, but it is still noteworthy that he chose the King's Houses as opposed to other venues to conduct his business and the vast deer park must have acted as a draw for the king.

Politics was probably high in the mind of Edward in September 1307. The king had been attempting to pursue Robert the Bruce in Scotland during August, but the campaign was short-lived as Edward urgently needed to return south to formally take over governance and make arrangements for his father's funeral, his own coronation and his wedding to Isabella of France. Regardless, his progress was extremely leisurely as he delighted in the hospitality of his favourite, the recently ennobled Piers Gaveston at Knaresborough, before moving on to Clipstone which provided a convenient waypoint on the journey south via Nottingham, Northampton and Kings Langley to Westminster.[364]

Christmas at Clipstone

A great deal had changed for both Edward II and England during the eight years leading up to his next visit to Clipstone which began at the end of October 1315 and concluded at the back end of January 1316. Relations with his cousin Thomas, Earl of Lancaster had hit a nadir. Somewhere in the second half of 1308 Lancaster began to disappear from the lists of witnesses to royal charters. The origins of his disgruntlement are obscure, but may have begun trivially enough in a disagreement over the ownership of the manor of Wilton, Yorkshire between one of Thomas' knights and Edward's representative north of the Trent, Gerard Salveyn.[365] By 1311 Lancaster had emerged as the most powerful baron in England, holding a total of five earldoms with a total income of around £11,000 per year.[366] Anger at Edward's reliance on the hated Piers Gaveston had erupted and the king was forced, against his will, to sign the Ordinances of 1311, which regulated his power and led to the exile of Gaveston. The audacious royal favourite returned to England before the year was out, but in June 1312 he was abducted by the Earl of Warwick, given a show-trial and then taken by Lancaster himself to Blacklow Hill where he was summarily executed.[367] Matters got worse two years later when the English suffered the humiliating defeat at the hands of Robert the Bruce at Bannockburn in June 1314 and the Scots were more or less free to raid as far south as Castleford in

Yorkshire, which they reached in 1319.[368]

At exactly the same time the climate began to dramatically deteriorate, with the weather characterised by extremely wet summers and very harsh winters, lasting from 1314 until 1317 and then again between 1320–2. The entirety of Europe was hit hard by '*floods, crop failure, high mortality among animals from starvation and disease, food shortages, high prices, and sickness and famine among the human population*'.[369] Edward's own finances were hit very hard as the export of wool to the continent dropped from £12,200 in 1312–13 to just £7,100 in 1315–16.[370] Although never a great builder at Clipstone, Edward was mindful of the extreme weather when he ordered some of what money he did have in the coffers to be spent on 10 December 1315 on repairs to the chimneys at the King's Houses. The king also demanded that the royal official Robert Cliderhou, made good the fishponds as well as repairing St Edwin's Chapel, which was curiously listed as housing a hermit at this time.[371]

The population of England went into a sharp decline for the first time since the arrival of the Normans. There was essentially a perfect Malthusian storm of war, famine and pestilence created by a rising population competing for dwindling agricultural resources controlled by an aggressively greedy landowning class.[372] Crime statistics show that violence and murder increased exponentially in synchronicity with the astronomic rise in the price of foodstuffs. The inevitable breakdown in law and order was typified by the activities of the Folville and Coterel gangs – little more than highly-born bandits – who plagued the East Midlands in the latter years of Edward's reign. A Franciscan friar reported that '*men of this kind break into the treasure-houses of the great, carry off property, drive away herds, plunder churchmen, nor does this touch their consciences.*'[373] Analysis of English manorial court records show that the homicide rate for the country was actually in excess of late twentieth century urban America.[374] Breaches of the peace did not elude Clipstone. The Marshalsea Court held at the King's Houses on 13 November 1315 indicted a local man accused of homicide who was duly hanged.[375] We can see here something of the judicial role of the palace which was also seen in the presence of a gaol at Clarendon. The royal buildings in Sherwood offered a refuge to the population after the construction of a fortification on the edge of the park known as Clipstone Peel. Further disturbances occurred in 1317–18 when it was reported that '*local people…came several times to the peel when there was fighting in the country.'*[376]

The political situation towards the end of 1315 was therefore a complicated one. Lancaster and his adherents were notionally ascendant, however the influence of the king's cousin was on a knife-edge as his power was limited by a small number of allies after the death of the Earl of Warwick. An uneasy relationship developed with a constant flurry of messages exchanged between the cousins written from Edward's base at Clipstone and received by Thomas at his satellite castles in Leicestershire, Derbyshire and Lancashire.[377]

Edward's own response to the declining environmental conditions was typically confused. His interest in the common man led to the rather unusual decision to order that the number of courses served on his magnates tables should be limited due to the *'excessive and abundant portions of food'* that they consumed at the same time that the rest of the country was starving. However, he does not seem to have followed his own advice. The household at Clipstone during the winter of 1315–16 included men such as the earls of Hereford, Pembroke and Atholl as well as emissaries from the King of France.[378] Also present were the king's Welsh supporters the Bishop of Bangor, Sir Gruffydd Llwyd and Sir Morgam ap Meredudd – significantly there to advise Edward during a period of tension in Wales.[379] The high status nature of Edward's household at the time is pointed at through the discovery at Clipstone of a continental sterling from Florennes, Belgium minted in imitation of the English penny and issued by Gaucher of Chatillon between 1313–22.[380] It is coins such as this and the foreign imports also found at Clarendon and Kings Langley[381] that point to widespread links that the King's Houses maintained throughout the Mediaeval period.

So many people were with Edward that the household expenditure came to over £700 per month, peaking at £936 during December. It was remarked upon by a contemporary chronicler that the king was particularly generous in the distribution of gifts that Christmas,[382] perhaps a conscious effort to maintain good relations with his magnates in a time of strife? Edward himself was resplendent in a suit of scarlet at the Christmas feast[383] and his appearance was at the front of his mind when he ordered London goldsmith Roger Frowyk to make a new gold crown for him.[384] Over 100 pike and 1600 roach were taken from the Great Pond to the east of the palace and food stocks were depleted so much that foragers had to be sent into Lincolnshire via the ferry over the Trent at Marnham.[385] This of course was to be expected when such a large household was gathered in one place for such a long period of time, but the decision to remain at Clipstone for so lengthy a period cannot have been wise after the disastrous harvest of 1315.

Given the highly religious nature of the Christmas feast Edward also issued letters patent confirming the original foundation of the chantry at Clipstone.[386] Meanwhile sentimentality was part of the season as he gave 35 shillings to seventy Dominicans to say mass for his mother who had died shortly after her own lengthy stay at Clipstone in the autumn of 1290. Edward also commissioned a biography of his father from Nicholas Percy.[387] Family matters were furthered by Edward and Isabella who had been particularly close during 1315 (their households seem to have been joined together for much of the year and they made pilgrimage to Canterbury in June). This closeness seems to have led to the conception of their second son, John of Eltham, during the period spent at Clipstone. John was not recorded as being premature and nothing unusual was recorded regarding his birth on 15 August 1316, therefore his conception must have occurred whilst Edward and Isabella were at the King's Houses in early November 1315.[388] It is very rare to be able to pinpoint the location of Mediaeval conceptions due to the usually rapid itineraries of the royal household. The lengthy stay at one of Edward's most favoured residences therefore affords us an unusual glimpse of the sex life of the palace.

Chivalric adventure was in the air as Edward sent Sir William Montacute with three knights and thirty-six squires to Barnard Castle in County Durham on a mission to rescue a damsel in distress – Maud, the widow of a knight killed at Bannockburn, who had been abducted by John the Irishman. Romantically she was later married to one of her rescuers – Sir Robert Welle.[389] Closer to home, Edward began to develop an attachment to a new favourite, Roger Damory, a household knight who had fought at Bannockburn. The king began to make a series of grants in the knight's favour during December 1315 whilst at Clipstone. He also drew close to Hugh Audley and William Montacute, leader of the raid to Barnard Castle and the man who presided over the Marshalsea Court which led to the execution of the murderer at Clipstone. All three men began to exert an influence over the king far above their status so that one contemporary chronicler described their relationship as '*worse than Piers*'.[390] The seeds of continuing political and social discontent were sown at Clipstone by the king during Christmas 1315.

Clipstone Peel

Edward left Clipstone for a parliament assembled at Lincoln in February 1316 ostensibly to discuss the ongoing threat from Scotland, but in reality the proceedings were dominated by attempts to establish the place of Lancaster in the governance of the realm. Political embarrassment was caused by his deliberate late arrival and refusal to attend and it was only the intervention of the Bishop of Norwich that led to the appointment of Lancaster as head of the council, albeit isolated amongst a group of existing royal supporters.[391] After the parliament, Edward surprisingly returned to Clipstone again until mid-March with no apparent purpose other than further relaxation at a favourite residence. The king found himself unwillingly dependent on Lancaster who was often in the North and Midlands during the years 1314–18, and it may have been the powerfully fortified residences at Leicester, Castle Donington, Kenilworth and Tutbury, plus Thomas' new castle at Melbourne, which kept Edward in position at Clipstone for so much of this period.[392] Further insult was added by Lancaster in August when he was diplomatically named as sponsor for the king's new son John of Eltham, yet pointedly failed to attend the christening which was taken by Edward as a very great insult.[393] The king was so rattled that a chronicler commented that he was now armed against his cousin and in September he summoned Isabella to York in fear of her safety. The urgency of this demand can be seen through her rapid transit of 175 miles from Hertfordshire in just five days.[394] Edward appeared to be preparing for an imminent civil war as he attempted to gather a force about himself through the signing of indentures of military support with John de Mowbray, Bartholomew de Badlesmere, Hugh le Despenser, Humphrey de Bohun and John Giffard.[395]

Edward's second winter spent at Clipstone was every bit as tense as the previous year. The king arrived at his palace on 9 December 1316 before heading to Nottingham for Christmas on the 23rd. He was back in Sherwood again on New Year's Day and settled in until 17 January after which he made a rapid journey to Clarendon where he spent most of February, March and part of April. Despite his domestic problems, much of Edward's energies at Clipstone were given over to diplomacy with the new pope, John XXII, who had been elected eight days before the birth of the king's son back in August (and may have been the inspiration for the naming of the prince).[396] The king was hopeful that the new papal incumbent would look favourably upon his ongoing Scottish dispute with Robert the Bruce. Consequently many of the writs issued by Edward II during the winter of 1316–17 related to the papal nuncio Ammenenus de Pelagrua who brokered a two year peace with Scotland that was announced at Clipstone on New Year's Day. For his pains de Pelagrua was presented with a number of jewels plus a silver-gilt basin with a matching ewer by the king himself.[397] A very similar gift was bestowed upon Sir William de la Beche during the New Year's feast as he was fortunate enough to preside over the event after being named King of the Bean – a tradition conferred by discovering a bean hidden in the food by the royal cooks.[398]

Doubtless Edward was relieved at the peace settlement with Scotland, but his ongoing dispute at home with Lancaster was still not steadied and it may have been this quarrel which had led to a message sent on 20 December regretfully declining to attend the coronation of his brother-in-law Philip V of France, a ceremony which would also have necessitated paying homage for Edward's lands held on the continent.[399] Another piece of evidence for Edward's nervous disposition was an order given on 4 January banning a tournament at Thetford and the arrest of all those involved, which was followed twelve days later by a total ban on tournaments everywhere in England.[400] Steane has noted that strong martial kings such as Edward III encouraged tourneys whereas weak kings, who did not successfully engage in warfare, such as Henry III and Edward II issued prohibitions[401] on what they may have viewed as events loaded with the potential for incendiary armed gatherings of their enemies. This ban was possibly made with very good reason as the coronation tournaments of 1307 at Wallingford and Faversham took on an increasingly partisan nature between the supporters and enemies of Piers Gaveston that the royal favourite encouraged Edward to cancel a third event due to be held at Stepney. Subsequently the only licenced tournament that occurred during Edward II's reign was at Northampton in 1323.[402]

During the winter months spent at Clipstone in 1316–17 the king's fears for his safety in Sherwood Forest were being directly addressed through the construction of a fortified peel which has been definitively researched and published in two ground-breaking articles by David Crook. Deriving from the French word 'pel' (meaning stake) a peel was a type of timber fortification often added to an existing castle or tower such as the one built at Nottingham in 1312. They were a constant feature of border warfare in the Scottish Marches but were rare in England.[403] Exactly when Edward ordered the construction of Clipstone Peel is unclear, however the employment of plasterers between 29 November 1316 and 17 January 1317 indicates that the superstructure of the peel was completed and the accounts of the first keeper, Peter le Pavour, began immediately after the plasterers had completed their task.[404]

The site of the peel lies three miles away from the King's Houses, beyond the south-western edge of the deer park, at a place called Snake Hill (Plate 5 A). Lying at the bottom of a long and low rise, stretching out to the east, is a riverine escarpment formed by the Maun which flows below, and to the west of, the fortification. Little remains to be seen on the ground today except for some low magnesian limestone foundations which once stood much higher as late as the 1950s. Historic maps reveal that this building was called Beeston Lodge in the early nineteenth century and it is shown as a group of two buildings on the map of 1630. A Mediaeval map of Sherwood Forest made c 1400 shows the placename 'ye pele' in just this location.[405] Immediately to the south-west of the peel site is a flight of fishponds (Plate 5 B). They are similar to their near contemporaries at Lyddington in Rutland which were constructed on the orders of the Bishop of Lincoln during the 1320s.

Aerial photographs reveal a large oval enclosure marked by a faint soilmark at Clipstone Peel. It is possible that Edward II reused a pre-existing earthwork that may have been of some antiquity. Heat effected stones, used for cooking during the prehistoric, Roman and possibly Anglo-Saxon period have been noted on the site and may be indicative of a much older purpose. The shape and size of the enclosure is not too dissimilar to known Iron Age sites such as Gateford near Worksop or Oldox near Oxton. The reuse of a pre-existing earthwork would also help to explain why the peel was so far from the palace. Naturally, proving or disproving this theory would require archaeological intervention.

The keeper of the peel's accounts and inventories reveal a great deal of information about the buildings. There was a palisade and ditch, the gatehouse had two windlasses for raising a drawbridge, and inside there was a hall, royal chamber, long chamber, a chapel with glazed windows containing a cross with an image of Christ, a statue of the Virgin Mary and a bell. There was also a pentice house '*near the great wall*', a bakehouse, kitchen, grange and sheds for sheep, oxen and cattle (whose roof was plastered on the underside to reduce the risk of fire).[406] Details of repairs to the peel made in 1360–3 after a great storm reveal that the master mason John de Hoghton rebuilt the chimney in the King's Chamber using stone from Mansfield, Mansfield Woodhouse and Basford. These accounts also make reference to additional structures including the Park Keeper's Chamber, Steward's Chamber and granary.[407] Retainers employed at the peel in the early fourteenth century included carters, ploughmen, shepherds, a cowman, a dairyman, reapers, mowers and the groom, Peter de Driby. The river was diverted to make a pasture and additionally there were 198 acres of arable land attached.[408] During the last two months of 1316 animals were driven to the peel – 244 cattle and 271 sheep came from manors belonging to the vacant see of Durham, and 309 more sheep were brought from York.[409] Widespread disease amongst animals hit the peel's stock immediately, with 159 out of 193 goats succumbing, alongside 135 sheep of which 60 out of 90 lambs perished. After weather conditions improved slightly in the mid-1320s sheep stocks increased to 470 and by 1327 there were 704.[410]

The peel was a very developed operation and should be seen as something significantly more than a mere temporary palisaded fort. The gatehouse in particular was constructed in stone and had a drawbridge over the boundary ditch. The latter enclosed a very substantial area in the north-west corner of the arable field in which the remains of the peel now stand. An inventory made in 1328 found that there were ninety chainmail shirts, twenty-four crossbows, four barrels of bolts, twenty-four lances and a springald present at Clipstone Peel. The same inventory also includes reference to three '*kysarines*' one of which was recorded as being broken. These were probably cider presses[411] and point towards the multifunctional use of the peel as both a farm as well as a defensive fortification along with the list of agricultural buildings and references to retained farmworkers working on arable and pastoral land. This makes sense in the light of Edward II's concerns in 1316. His country was suffering a dreadful famine which hurt the rich as well as the poor, there was the ever-present threat of invasion from the Scots, and Edward was in conflict with Thomas of Lancaster. A fortified farm was just the thing to provide foodstuffs for the household whilst resident at Clipstone whilst also offering a secure bolthole in isolated Sherwood Forest for a king nervous of his personal security. The latter was compounded in May 1317 when Lancaster's own wife was abducted by the Earl of Warenne, an action which Thomas blamed specifically on the king himself.[412]

Almost immediately the presence of the peel caused complaint from the men of Mansfield Woodhouse who bravely approached the king on 6 January 1317 to bring forward their grievance about the enclosure of a region known as '*les Holms*'. A place known as '*ye holmes*' was shown on the c 1400 map near the point where the River Maun flowed into the western end of the deer park. A boundary enquiry of c 1334 also referred to this area as '*Holmedale*'.[413] The word 'holm' has varied meanings and can refer to an island in a lake or river, a flat patch of ground adjacent to a stream or a stand of holly. In the context of the location of '*ye holmes*' immediately next to the River Maun on the c 1400 map it is likely to be an area of pasture on the flood plain of the river. It is not discounted that it could also refer to a plantation of holly grown as winter fodder for deer such as the placename which is also rendered as '*Hollins*' on the 1630 map to the north of the park. The men of Mansfield Woodhouse complained that they had lost their common right to husbote (timber for building) and haybote (timber for hedging) as a result of the creation of the peel and the seizure of its attached land. Crook points out how dangerously real this must have been to the community after the disastrous fire of 1304 which destroyed their village. They also protested that their cattle, beasts and hay had been taken for the king's use without full payment. This was clearly an endemic problem as it was later specifically prohibited nationwide in February 1317. Rather surprisingly Edward conceded their point regarding husbote and haybote, and along with this concession the king also accepted that fines for trespass by animals into the newly enclosed land would not be levied.[414]

The ongoing situation with Thomas of Lancaster was untenable, and on 9 August 1318 a treaty was signed at Leake in south Nottinghamshire. The location, although obscure, was deliberately picked as a middle ground between Lancaster's castle at Leicester and that of the king at Nottingham. Central to the negotiations were the earls of Pembroke and Hereford who had been present with the king at Clipstone during Christmas 1315. Concessions were made by Edward, who agreed to stick to the restrictions laid down in the Ordinances of 1311 and to send Damory, Audley and Montacute away from court. Lancaster was threatened with sanctions if he continued to gather a private army around himself.[415] After a brief sojourn at Nottingham, Edward was back at Clipstone between 18 and 20 August and then again from 27 August until 15 September. The king is known to have specifically lodged at the peel during this time as complaints made about the Marshalsea Court at the York parliament in October 1318 referred to Clipstone Peel as '*where the king lodged*' during the previous August and September. The reason for this complaint was that local legal cases were being heard by the Marshalsea Court, as the court moved with the king, rather than locally by the mayor and bailiff of Nottingham in direct contravention of the Ordinances of 1311.[416] Edward's decision to stay at the peel is interesting. Although we do not know whether he shuttled between fortification and palace, his presence at the peel immediately after the treaty of Leake indicates that he was still feeling insecure. Lancaster actually visited the peel himself on 18 September, perhaps hoping to catch up with the king on his way to the York parliament. Thomas' precise motives for the visit are unclear and he was instead met by the king's retainers John le Ditton and Master Robert le Gynur.[417]

Relations again worsened due to the unsuccessful 1319 campaign in Scotland which led to further recriminations between the cousins. Lancaster refused to attend parliament, again held at York, in January 1320. The assembly was cut short as Edward had to prepare to move south in order to finally pay his homage to Philip V which had been delayed whilst at Clipstone in 1316. On their route through Pontefract the king and queen were jeered by Lancaster's retainers from the walls of the castle[418] and it must have been in a very sour mood that Edward stopped off at Clipstone during the first three days of February for the final time in his reign. Despite the fact that Edward II never stayed at Clipstone again, the palace remained on his mind as he ordered further repairs to be made in October 1320, June 1323 and December 1325.[419]

Meanwhile the peel provided some gifts of animal stock to Edward's new favourite Roger Damory,[420] who was soon to be involved in the campaign which brought about the final downfall of Lancaster. A private war on the Welsh Marches between the Despensers and the Earl of Hereford led Lancaster to overextend himself and he finally went into armed rebellion against Edward. For once the king acted with martial energy and his forces moved north to intercept Lancaster at Burton Bridge – where Damory was wounded in the skirmish and later died of his wounds at Tutbury. The royal forces now under the command of Sir Andrew Harclay pursued the Earl of Lancaster as far as Boroughbridge where Thomas, in a hopeless situation, finally surrendered. He was taken to Pontefract Castle, put on trial and executed on 22 March 1322.[421] The peel had its own small part to play in Lancaster's downfall as one of the earl's retainers John de Clif was imprisoned there under the control of the keeper Thomas de Merk, whilst animals seized from other supporters of the earl were driven from Derbyshire to the fortification.[422]

Edward II went on to place too much faith in the despotic Despensers and in 1326 his own queen, plus her adherent Roger Mortimer, landed in East Anglia and began the campaign that would end with Edward's imprisonment and abdication in favour of his fourteen year old son, Edward of Windsor.

The Minority of Edward III

Edward III's initial visit to the King's Houses bore a similarity of conditions related to the disappointing campaigns in the north that had plagued both the first and last stays by his father, and beforehand by his grandfather Edward I. Within hours of the new king's coronation at Westminster Abbey on 1 February 1327 the Scots had crossed the River Tweed and laid siege to Norham Castle, the site of Edward I's momentous decision to press the English claim to the Scottish crown back in 1291. The northern Marcher lords – the Percys and the Nevilles – were appointed to deal with the immediate matter and Edward began his own puzzlingly slow journey north with the intention of mustering an English army at Newcastle-upon-Tyne in mid-April. The royal household had only reached York, via Clipstone, towards the end of May and then attempted to pursue the various Scottish forces throughout the border regions. The hunted turned hunter when Sir James Douglas led an audacious raid on the English encampment at Stanhope Park, near Durham, with the Scot skirmishing his way right up to Edward's own tent which caused the young king to flee in fear of his life. The Scottish army then melted back into their own lands leaving the English once again overextended, frustrated and forced to retreat south with the intention of holding a parliament at Lincoln in mid-September.[423]

Small wonder then that, on their way to parliament, the dispirited royal household chose to halt at Clipstone again where a morale-boosting tournament was held on 28 August.[424] These early visits to the King's Houses by Edward III were made during the period of influence of his mother and Roger Mortimer, as the Marcher lord sought to fill the household of the young king with men loyal to himself rather than to the monarchy. The decisions to visit the residence related more to their needs than to the king's own autonomous preference and this may explain the unsatisfactorily slow progress made in reacting to the Scottish threat. The importance of the tournament at Clipstone is marked. Tournaments in the first year of the reign were still under close royal control, as they had been under his fretful father. In 1328 a tournament planned to occur at the same time as the spring parliament at Northampton was prohibited – ostensibly because it would have been a distraction from matters of state. In truth Isabella and Mortimer were concerned about outbreaks of violence during the early days of their regency.[425]

The Lincoln parliament was dissolved on 27 September 1327, the very day that the news of the death of Edward II at Berkeley Castle (which supposedly occurred on 21 September) reached the ears of the king. The remainder of the year was spent in the Midlands, including two halts at Clipstone during the second half of November lasting three and four days respectively. Presumably the time was spent hunting the red hind, roe and fallow doe as his father had done during his winter visits to the King's Houses.

The year 1328 saw the largest number of individual visits to Clipstone by the household during the reign of Edward III. This was partly related to an imperative to remain in the North and Midlands during the first half of the year due to continuing concerns over the Scottish situation. The first stay, in January, was of greatest significance as it involved another tournament held at the King's Houses. Whilst at Clipstone on 28 November 1327 Edward had ordered guides to be sent to escort his bride-to-be, Philippa of Hainault, and her father William, Count of Hainault, into the country from Dover.[426] The tournament held in January 1328 was part of a cycle of four such events held by Edward in the lead up to his marriage.

Philippa was intrinsically bound to the French throne as she was the granddaughter of Philip III. Her mother, Joan of Valois, was the sister to Philip VI, crowned on 1 April 1328 as the first French king from the house of Valois. In later years, Edward III pressed his own claim to the throne over Philip's through descent from his mother Isabella the sister of Charles IV who had died without a male heir in 1328 which led to the coronation of Philip VI. The ensuing conflict ,which lasted intermittently between 1337 and 1453, was later known as the Hundred Years War and was effectively a family struggle for power in which Philippa was married to the man at war with her own, and *his* own, first cousin. Despite this apparent tension, and repeated infidelities on the part of the king, the two had a strong affinity and Philippa of Hainault offered a strong cultural influence on Edward III similar to that of Eleanor of

Provence on Henry III.[427]

The tournament held at Clipstone to celebrate Edward and Philippa's impending union was a highly developed military, political and social event. The king often participated fully and took part in at least one a year, often fighting incognito as a simple knight. Tournaments were linked to almost any form of family celebration, religious festivity, diplomatic event or even actual warfare – the English and Scots fought in a ritualised combat at Roxburgh in 1341. Edward's attempts to create a great flowering of English chivalry during the mid-fourteenth century, through the re-founding of the Knights of the Round Table which was followed later by the establishment of the Knights of the Garter, had tournaments central to their rituals and the events acted as a form of social bonding for a martial culture in much the same way as hunting.[428]

The tournament at the King's Houses in 1328 was no ordinary affair. The jousting took place at night and was illuminated by torchlight. This was only one of two such recorded tournaments held at night, the other took place thirty years later on New Year's Day at Bristol. Edward's choice of garments must have been especially considered as the two suits of armour ordered for the tournament that cost £8 3s 4d were covered by purple velvet jupons into which 21,800 pieces of gold thread were stitched to form an image of crowns and oak leaves that must have caught the torchlight enchantingly.[429] The oak leaf had many symbolic connotations in Mediaeval England including endurance and eternity which would have been highly relevant within Sherwood Forest. However in this case the relationship of oak with crowns and a tournament would also have been understood as symbols of power and victory. Only one similar garment has survived in the archaeological record from the period, the blue and crimson velvet surcoat stitched with gold thread to show the heraldic arms of a prince of England which belonged to Edward of Woodstock (1330–76), popularly known as the Black Prince, eldest son of Edward III and father of Richard II. The surcoat is now hung over the Black Prince's effigy at Canterbury Cathedral along with other ceremonial pieces of tournament equipment – his shield, scabbard gauntlets and helm – although they are understandably much damaged and faded.

Quite where these tournaments were staged within the lordship of Clipstone is open to question. The palace enclosure must be considered a possible site, but it is not clear whether there would have been the space amongst the buildings, courtyards and gardens. The two surviving formal tiltyards at Tattershall, Lincolnshire and Kenilworth, Warwickshire are both immediately outside of their castle enclosures and although the palace demesne land and open fields are unlikely locations as the ridge and furrows would have created an uneven ground, it is possible to conceive of the areas of laund to be fit for purpose. The equivalent inner park pale at Clarendon was possibly used for temporary accommodation during largescale gatherings at the palace as well as locations for tournaments.[430] The laund to the north-west of the King's Houses may have been especially viable for jousting as it lay on high ground immediately between the palace and park and was of an ideal size for witnessing the lengthy mounted charges of jousting knights.

During the spring of 1327 the decision by Edward III's father to enclose the fortification and agricultural land at Clipstone Peel had come back to haunt the monarchy in the form of the men of Clipstone lodging a petition over their rights to common pasture similar to that made by the tenants from Mansfield Woodhouse ten years earlier. Not to be outdone, the men of Mansfield Woodhouse also renewed their complaint referring to two hundred acres of woodland and one hundred acres of waste which had been enclosed to their loss by Edward II. An enquiry was held at Warsop and the matter rumbled on into the following year.[431]

Edward himself mediated the reiterated complaints when they were brought before him at the King's Houses in January 1328 by the men of Clipstone, Warsop and Mansfield Woodhouse regarding the enclosure of Clipstone Peel and their loss of common rights. Concessions were finally made after this second petition which was led by Robert de Clipstone along with his confederates Alan Stuffyn, Walter le Wolfhunt, Robert Kirlyngton, John de Hathelsay, Alan son of Matthew and Richard Stuffyn. The name Stuffyn was an old and respected one in the area as an earlier Alan Stuffin was agister in the park between 1250–70, his son Alan was a forester in 1288 and Robert Stuffin was also a forester in 1289. Hugh Stuffin was a forest supervisor and regarder in 1301–22 and Alan Stuffin himself a forest official in 1334.[432] The gravity of his complaint was taken very seriously indeed, and the leader of the petitioners, Robert de Clipstone, was such a trusted individual that he was named keeper of the manor of Clipstone later in 1328[433]– a post which he held until his death in 1339.

The vulnerability of the monarchy in 1328 was apparent in the decision to capitulate and accede to the demands of the tenants, who appear to have acted in planned coalition, and who were given common rights to pasture in Birklands which had previously been off limits to beasts in the 1250s. Their right to gather ferns and leaves in the park was renewed and the removal of the new agricultural enclosures was agreed, albeit at the sacrifice of the newly enclosed woodland.[434] The agricultural land given back to Mansfield Woodhouse was probably outside of the deer park and in what became known as the Peelfield in several fifteenth century leases. This placename survives in the modern Forestry Commission Peafield Plantation and adjacent Peafield Lane which links Mansfield Woodhouse to Bradmer Hill and follows the course of the north-west part of the park boundary.[435] Additionally, the peel was dismantled and several timber buildings were taken to the King's Houses and re-erected[436] (a fact indicative of how much space was available within the palace enclosure). The site was not abandoned as '*the greater gate of the pele, and the house built over it.* '[437] afterwards became a hunting lodge which was often referred to in later documents, and repairs were ordered in 1360–3 to the King's Chamber, Chapel, Park Keeper's Chamber, Steward's Chamber and Granary.[438] William Senior's map shows two separate roofed structures standing which suggests that in 1630 more than just the stone gatehouse was standing at the site of Clipstone Peel.

On 28 August 1328, the Close Rolls (letters issued to the Chancery by the king) recorded that Master Henry de Clif and William de Herlaston delivered the Great Seal of England to the king at his chamber at Clipstone whilst Edward was with his trusted retainers Sir Edward de Bohun and Sir William de Clinton. De Bohun was the twin brother of the future Earl of Northampton who later fought at Crecy and Clinton would go on to arrest Roger Mortimer at Nottingham Castle in 1330.

The seal was then passed to Henry Burghersh, the Bishop of Lincoln, who had been a supporter of Isabella and Mortimer against the king's own father. Despite this, Burghesh and Edward seem to have been close – perhaps because Henry was a very capable treasurer. He briefly fell from grace at the time of Mortimer's arrest, but by 1334 was again in office. The temporary fall of Burghersh was not surprising given the astonishing speed of lavish spending by Isabella and Mortimer. When Edward II abdicated there was in excess of £62,000 in the royal coffers yet by 1330 there was just a pitiful £41.[440] The time that the Great Seal was delivered to Edward in the late summer of 1328 was marked by a period when the king had begun to chafe against the authority of Roger Mortimer. Immediately after he left Clipstone, Edward went on his first progress, without his mother or the Marcher lord in attendance, to religious sites in East Anglia. At just the same time Mortimer was flexing his own power during a sequence of tournaments intended to demonstrate his authority over the Crown.[441] It was to be over two years before Edward gained full control of his own kingdom. However the acquisition of the seal followed by his solo travels demonstrates that the king was beginning to consider exercising his own autonomy, and the beginning of the usurpers downfall started at Clipstone in the summer of 1328.

The fall of Isabella and Mortimer at Nottingham Castle seems to have taken the pair completely by surprise. The notion that the eighteen year old Edward had quietly and purposefully gathered a band of trusted supporters about himself despite their best efforts to infiltrate his companions with their own men seems to have passed them by. Mortimer's behaviour towards the king was simply not tenable. His alleged participation in the supposed death of Edward II, his insistence on always walking precisely in front of the king and the execution of Edward's own uncle, the Earl of Kent, during the Winchester parliament of 1330 must have made the young monarch certain that a move to take the throne away from him was imminent.[442] Edward spent the spring and early summer of 1330 in and around the palace of Woodstock where Philippa spent her confinement during the birth of their first son. Subsequently the king made his way through Northamptonshire and Lincolnshire to Clipstone where he stayed from 29 August until 4 September and then again on 22–23 September before a brief move into Yorkshire and then on to Nottingham for the fateful arrest of Mortimer on 19 October.[443] These two visits to Clipstone must therefore be seen against the lead up to Edward's assumption of control.

More prosaically, the king ordered repairs to the King's Houses, enclosure pale, pond sluices and the mill during January 1331.[444] He also heard an outlying petition, again relating to the controversial peel, brought by Sir John de Sutton who claimed that 40 acres of his own private woodland had been enclosed by Edward II. Although the outcome of this complaint was not recorded, Warsop Wood was not recorded as being within the park in 1630 possibly because it was removed by Edward III.[445] During the summer visits in late July and early August 1331 Philippa of Hainault heard an extemporized choral concert given at the King's Houses by women from the nearby village of Bilsthorpe which lies just a few miles to the southeast of Clipstone. Music played an important part of court life, and it is known that Edward III employed around twenty secular musicians including those who played trumpet, drum, harp, lute, viol, psaltery, guitar and fiddle.[446]

A Waypoint to Scotland

The pattern of visits to Clipstone by Edward between the later 1330s and mid 1340s reflected a growing militarism by the English crown in the conflict with Scotland. By this period Clipstone was the only unfortified residence north of the Chilterns[447] and it offered a uniquely isolated set of facilities not available elsewhere in either the Midlands or the North that was a recreationally attractive waypoint for the king when travelling to or from the battlefront. Taxes were granted in 1334 '*to eject the Scots from the limits of England*,' yet the following campaign, which also featured the king's younger brother John of Eltham, was rather inglorious. Edward's small force of 5,300 men stalled at Roxburgh and Melrose during the winter of 1334 whilst the Scots dispersed to the north. The English retreated south after agreeing a truce until midsummer 1335 and held a council of war at Nottingham in late March. Edward's longest stay at Clipstone took place after the council and lasted from 11 April until 2 May before the household moved off in late May to a parliament at York followed by the muster of troops for the resumption of the war at Newcastle in June.[448] The subsequent campaign, which lasted until the autumn of 1336, was far more successful, despite the threat of French intervention, with Edward's much larger army speedily laying waste to much of the country, taking fortresses, penetrating as far as Perth and then moving on to confront the Scots at Lochindorb.[449]

The stop at Clipstone in mid-May 1337 took place between another parliament at York, which gave its consent for the war which Edward was so keen to press in France, and a council of war at Stamford. The latter was brought about by the news that the Scots had laid siege to Stirling Castle. The king's rapid progress north was matched by the subsequent retreat south, content that the castle was well provisioned and defended.[450] The ability of the king to vary his focus in 1337 can be seen through the dichotomy of the arrival of urgent news regarding the siege at Stirling coupled with Edward's attendance at the wedding of his esquire Roger Beauchamp to the queen's damsel Sybil Patteshull in the palace chapel at the King's Houses.[451] Beauchamp was a member of the family of the earls of Warwick and as a knight of the royal household he later held important posts such as the keepership of Devizies Castle, Captain of Calais and was Lord Chamberlain in the last year of Edward's reign.[452] Beauchamp was present with the king in the French war which was declared at the end of April 1337. Edward was preoccupied with this war for many years to come, including a period spent at Clipstone in September 1343 when he was gearing up for an expected renewal of the hostilities the following year.[453]

The traditional alliance made between Scotland and Edward's new enemies in France gave him great cause for concern as he was now effectively fighting a war on two fronts. Consequently, when he found himself at Clipstone again in December 1345, his attention was fixed on the fighting taking place in Brittany at the same time that a very serious raid was staged by the Scots on Carlisle. This resulted in a dash north which was curtailed by an illness that stalled the itinerary in Nottinghamshire. The crisis apparently ended without his intervention, and the king headed south again to spend Christmas at Woodstock.[454]

The constant travelling necessary for a king at war required access to quality horses whose provision fell to the Master of the Horse. The copper alloy seal of Sir John, Master of the King's Horse under Edward III, was discovered at Clipstone in 2011 and therefore helps to directly pin down this important member of the household to the King's Houses (Plate 6 A).[455] Brocas was another veteran of the Hundred Years War having fought at the sea battle of Sluys in 1340. As an official of the Marshalsea Court he was responsible for stocking the royal stud farms which led him to Ireland in 1340 on a mission to buy horses for the king's use. The cost of horses were varied from £50–100 for a destrier, £10–50 for a courser or palfrey to £5–10 for a rouncy. Brocas' purchases of horses named Grissel de Borton (£24), Lyard de Burgh (20 marks), Ferrant Mackgibbyn (20 marks) and Ferrant Moyn (12 marks) fit into this economy.[456]

A thirteenth to fourteenth century horse pendant was found during a comprehensive metal detecting survey of Castlefield[457] which helps to demonstrate something of what John Steane refers to as the '*authentic glimpses of chivalric splendour*' of the mounted men who rode into the King's Houses with copper alloy decorations fixed to their horse's peytrel, breast band, crupper and head ornaments (Plate 6 C).[458] Excavation has revealed the presence of horse in the bone assemblage from the King's Houses which have evidence of butchery marks. The taboo on human consumption of horse was in existence during the Mediaeval period, so the marks on the bones are probably a result of food preparation for dogs to consume the meat.[459] Overall the presence of horse bones are rare in the archaeological record of palace sites as they tended to be buried where they fell or alternatively the carcasses were sent to a tannery for their skins, Those examples that have been found tend to be of relatively small size in comparison to modern examples,[460] and the horses would have been housed within the King's Long Stable constructed during the reign of Edward I.

The Black Death

A virulent plague arose in central Asia during the very late 1330s which spread along the Silk Road and then swept across Europe. By the autumn of 1347 it had reached Messina and Marseille[461] and it arrived in England during the summer of 1348 via the southern ports of the country. Known at the time simply as the 'pestilence', the outbreak of 1348–50 was later called the Great Plague and after its final eruption in 1665 was routinely called the Black Death. This name referred to a form called the bubonic plague which was especially rife in the summer and whose symptoms included the dark coloured swellings known as buboes that grew at the nodal points of the lymphatic system (groin, armpits and neck). Bubonic plague a bacterial infection carried by fleas infected by rats that can lead to death in just ten days following incubation. Far more dangerous was the sub-set variety – septicaemic plague – that could kill in mere hours as the bacilli rapidly increased in the bloodstream. A third type which flourished especially in the winter was pneumonic plague. This was passed via airbourne droplets transmitted through coughing, sneezing, kissing or even breathing.[462]

John Gynewell, Bishop of Lincoln, was at Newstead Priory in Sherwood Forest on 25 July 1348 when he became aware of the mounting death toll in France at just the same time that the plague arrived on English shores. He ordered penitential processions to '*assuage the anger of the Saviour, who brings vengeance upon sinners in divers ways… from pestilences, stormy weather, and the deaths of men in sundry parts of the earth.*'[463] William of

Edington, Bishop of Winchester, wrote of the mounting horror of the pestilence on 24 October: '*We report with anguish the serious news which has come to our ears: that this cruel plague has now begun a similarly savage attack on the coastal areas of England. We are struck by terror lest (may God avert it!) this brutal disease should rage in any part of our city or diocese.*'[464] Edington's fears were far exceeded as the plague spread across the entire country. The Bishop had held the post of Lord Treasurer since 1344 and therefore occupied the Treasurer's Chamber at Clipstone which was being repaired at just the time that the plague struck.[465] Plague arrived into Nottinghamshire initially through Newark, probably during February 1349. The town of Newark was vulnerable as it lay at the crossroads of two major highways – the Fosse Way running from Exeter to Lincoln and the Great North Road between London, York and Edinburgh; and also had wharves which received river traffic along the Trent from the Humber ports of Hull and Grimsby. These northern seaports were possibly the conduit of the plague into the county as they were in turn contaminated by shipping from the south coast during the autumn of 1348[466] around the time that Edington wrote his panicked missive.

By 15 May 1349 William Zouche, Archbishop of York, had been made aware of the deteriorating situation at Newark and responded to the citizens: '*the mortality of plague which has been afflicting various parts of the world began to attack the townspeople of Newark some time ago, and has carried off numerous residents and inhabitants of the town, and is daily gaining in strength there, with the result that the burial ground of the church, because it is small and has no room to expand, is not adequate for the burial of the dead. With all this in mind, you have purchased, at your own expense, a certain plot of land, which is walled and lies in the street called Appletongate...we should deign to grant a licence and give our authority for the burial of the bodies of the dead there.*'[467] John Vaux, Sheriff of Nottinghamshire and Derbyshire, wrote in June to the Exchequer to inform them that his accounts were delayed due to the fact that most of his officials were either sick or dead, and he died himself soon afterwards.[468] Although we cannot be absolutely precise in assigning a figure to the death toll in Nottinghamshire the number of clergy who are known for certain to have died as a result of the plague can offer an approximation. Of the 126 clerical benefices which existed in the county 65 of the incumbents died during the outbreak of 1348–50 which hints at a staggering 51.58% mortality.[469] The precise mortality at Clipstone will never be accurately known, but probably reduced the local population from around 130 back down to a figure close to the Domesday estimate of 60–70. The Black Death affected absolutely every sector of Mediaeval society, and even Edward III lost his own daughter Joan to the pestilence at Bordeaux on 1 July 1348. The experience led him to write mournfully: '*But see, with what intense bitterness of heart we have to tell you this, destructive Death (who seizes young and old alike, sparing no one and reducing rich and poor to the same level) has lamentably snatched from both of us our dearest daughter, whom we loved best of all, as her virtues demanded. No fellow human being could be surprised if we were inwardly desolated by the sting of this bitter grief, for we are humans too.* '[470]

It is surprising to learn that the plague does not seem to have affected the progress of a fairly substantial programme of repairs being carried out at the King's Houses. A document held by the National Archives, and recently translated by the New Forest historian and archaeologist Richard Reeves, reveals that work began on 11 August 1348 – the very time that the pestilence was appearing in the southern ports – and continued unabated until 22 December 1349. There is no hint at all in the accounts that the plague caused a cessation of the work or that the masons, plasterers, slaters, plumbers and carpenters were in any way affected. It is perhaps too much to believe that none of the workforce died during the outbreak, but the chaplain of the King's Houses, Robert Rotor, who managed the project, gave no hint that anything was awry when he filed an account for £57 spent on the work.[471] Although there is good evidence that the plague halted building work on the west front porch at Bishop Edington's cathedral at Winchester,[472] elsewhere the pestilence seems to have acted as a spur to architectural development as the depopulation made land very much cheaper and more easily available to purchase. This resulted in the expansion of Merton College and the creation of New College, Oxford and Winchester College, Hampshire as well as several other new colleges at Cambridge including Trinity, Gonville and Corpus Christi.[473] Closer to Kings Clipstone, the industry of producing high quality carved alabaster tomb effigies began to flourish after the Black Death in south Nottinghamshire, south-east Derbyshire and eastern Staffordshire.[474]

The Great Plague of 1348–50 was not an isolated occurrence. Further waves of pestilence arrived in England again in 1361, 1369 and 1374; with the second outbreak being particularly virulent amongst children and creating a time-bomb

for the labour market during the final decade of Edward III's reign.[475]   The
effect of the repeated pestilence served to reduce the English population from
a peak in the early 1300s of approximately 5 to 6 million to an estimated 2.5
million in the late fourteenth century.[476] The shortage of labour led to an
increase in wages which began to show during the 1370s and 1380s and
reached a peak in the 1420s.[477] Aware of the potential calamity to the ruling
classes, king and parliament tried to hold wages down to pre-plague levels
through the Ordinance of Labourers (1349) and Statute of Labourers (1351).
The problem was that the laws were effectively unenforceable. The Black
Death had created a seller's market and as time wore on the labour shortage
became critical. Even on royal building projects like Clipstone the daily wage
of craftsmen began to increase significantly above the levels established by
the Ordinance and Statute. This can be seen acutely by comparing the wages
as supposedly fixed in 1351 with what was paid out in daily wages to
stonemasons, carpenters, sawyers and plasterers at the King's Houses during
repair campaigns between 1348 and 1395 (Figure 4):[478]

	Stonemason	Carpenter	Sawyer	Plasterer
Ordinance of Labourers 1349 **Statute of Labourers 1351**	3d	2d	-	-
King's Houses 1348–9	4d	-	-	4d
King's Houses 1360–3	4d	4d	4d	4d
King's Houses 1367–75	4d	4d	6d	3d
King's Houses 1394–5	6d	6d	6d	6d

*Figure 4: Table showing the increase in tradesman wages during the second half of
the fourteenth century*

Although daily wages for construction work increased substantially after
the Black Death the price of piecework for some items remained surprisingly
constant until the very end of the century. The cost per hundred of the
manufacture of laths (20d) and a quarter of lime (8d) was maintained from
1348 to 1395. Thatch board (a roofing material for hanging shingles on)

remained constant at 12d per hundred until a sudden rise to 2s in 1394–5 which was matched by a steady rise in the price of one hundred shingles from 4d in 1348–9, 8d in 1360–3 and 1367–75 to 12d in 1394–5.[479] The accounts also reveal some details of the piecework of interior fixtures and fittings at the palace including the production of slivers of walrus ivory for window glazing, trestle tables, seven foot high doors and dressers.[480] The architectural historian Salzman has shown how the tables and benches at Clipstone in the 1350s were made of lime tree planks – a particularly rare building material.[481] In 1357 3s 8d was spent on 800 spikes for eight great doors so that the bracing of the door could be attached to the planking of the face.[482] The records of the fourteenth century are littered with references to different sizes and purposes of nails including 'spikyng' (large), 'broddes', (broad) 'chinkelrodd' (for shingles) and 'lednayle' (for lead).[483] An iron nail measuring 61mm in length was discovered in the topsoil at Castlefield which is very similar to examples excavated at Clarendon.[484] Such finds are evidence of the work of smiths on the site who also appear in the building accounts producing piecework such as a very substantial number of nails for £7 14s[485] and four pieces of iron for hooks and hinges for the louvres of the stables (5s).[486]

The craftsmen who benefitted most from the rise in daily wages were the plumbers (rising from 6d in 1348–9 to 8d in 1360–3) and the carters. It is hard to compare prices across the late fourteenth century as the carters considered each job separately according to the type of load versus the distance travelled. What is clear is that the hauliers were always paid the highest rate on any construction project at the King's Houses. Works to the Great Pond in the 1360–3 account rendered by the surveyor Richard de Clifford showed that whilst the carpenters making the piles for the dam were paid 4d a day the carters taking away rotten timber and bringing in fresh materials were paid 8d. Similarly the labourers digging out the gravel held in place by the piles were paid a standard wage of 3d and the carters again made double this amount for transporting the aggregate.[487] By 1367–75 this wage had been increased to 12d per day, three times the price of the masons or carpenters.[488]

Edward's Palace

The mid-fourteenth century building accounts are the most detailed to have survived from the Mediaeval heyday of the King's Houses. The documents were first published in summary by Howard Colvin as part of his majestic, six volume account of the *History of the King's Works*. The second volume includes a short three-page synopsis of the known principal building phases at Clipstone from the hunting lodge of 1164 to the survey of 1525 and the section on Edward III gives a straightforward list of the buildings referred to in the accounts.[489] Colvin had worked closely with Philip Rahtz on the article detailing the latter's excavations which was published by the Thoroton Society in 1960, and Colvin came to much the same conclusion as the archaeologist that the site was nothing more than a hunting lodge. This is puzzling as Colvin had access to documentary evidence for a palatial complex. When the second volume of the *History of the King's Works* was published three years later Colvin was, at 44, a very experienced academic employed at St John's College, Oxford. His work has been described as '*the definitive history of the castles, palaces and religious foundations of the medieval kings*' and Colvin himself as '*the greatest architectural historian of his own time, and perhaps ever.*'[490] Prior to Colvin other researchers had also come to the same conclusion about Clipstone. His colleague Rahtz had positively identified the site to be a hunting lodge,[491] as had the architectural historian Nikolaus Pevsner in 1951.[492] The first person to make this identification was the local historian Alfred Stapleton from Carlton Road in Nottingham when he stated that the site '*was merely a royal "hunting box" so far as my observations go, however, I think this term is more suitable than that of "palace"*.'[493]

Prior to Stapleton there does not seem to have been any dissension from the conclusion that Clipstone was anything less than a palace. Both White[494] and Throsby[495] were clear on the matter and prior to them Thoroton used the terminology '*king's old houses*' or '*manor*' in much the same way as many contemporary Mediaeval descriptions did. Stapleton was an amateur historian who pieced together an admirable amount of data from published sources held at the Nottingham Free Library and admitted himself that he had only ever visited Clipstone twice. He simply made an amateur's mistake in dismissing the conclusions of the antiquarians in an otherwise exemplary piece of research. However this was to be a very influential mistake. It is almost certain that Pevsner relied upon the local historian's text when he assessed King John's Palace in 1948. Pevsner made his breakneck survey of Nottinghamshire in a 1932 Wolsley Hornet as part of the research for *The Buildings of England* series without his customary driver, his wife Lola, and was therefore forced into the position of '*playing the parts of driver, leader and assistant.*'[496] Never one to pull his punches, Pevsner was not impressed with the county stating that '*Neither the architectural nor the picturesque traveller would place Nottinghamshire in the first dozen or so of English counties.*'[497] His time in Sherwood Forest during September 1948 does not seem to have been happy as he described Retford as '*unattractive*', Rufford Abbey as '*depressing*' and in a letter referred to his mood whilst visiting Worksop as '*the downest down at the moment.*'[498] His biographer Susie Harries pointed out that Pevsner rarely conducted any original research as he simply did not have the time and as a result was often inaccurate in his conclusions.[499] In his description of King John's Palace as '*a venerable wall*'[500] we can hear an echo of his reading of White's words published in 1832: '*some venerable ruins remain.*'[501] The likelihood then is that Pevsner also followed Stapleton's interpretation when he wrote that '*it was a royal hunting lodge for Sherwood Forest*'.[502]

We have already seen how Pevsner's contemporary Philip Rahtz made several errors in his conclusions relating to King John's Palace, and the archaeologist even admitted himself that '*the degree of destruction makes any interpretation of the site hypothetical, especially on the basis of such limited excavation.*'[503] Equally revealing is the point in his career that Rahtz worked at Clipstone. His towering reputation for later work at Glastonbury Tor, Bordesley Abbey and Cheddar, which led to his appointment as professor at the University of York in 1978, masks the fact that in 1956 he was aged just 35 and had only been a professional archaeologist for three years.[504] Prior to 1953 he worked as an accountant, enlisted with the RAF and then became school teacher.[505] Rahtz's relative inexperience may have led to misidentification of the site as his career was still in its very early stages when he excavated at Kings Clipstone and his interpretative skills were only beginning to develop.

Colvin, however, had both the professional experience and time to conduct his own original research and yet he still chose to see the King's Houses as a mere hunting lodge. This error simply cannot be explained beyond a suspicion that under the weight of data he had to deal with to outline the history of royal building projects in England he simply overlooked what was right under his nose. In the light of the work done by Richard Reeves as part of the research for this book, which went back to the original manuscripts of the building accounts from the fourteenth century, it is apparent just how much detail Colvin glossed over – and this detail points unequivocally towards a palatial complex at Clipstone (Figure 2).

The documents that Reeves translated are written in ink on vellum in clerical Latin intermingled with technical building terms added in Middle English. The texts are the accounts of those responsible for monitoring the financial accounts of building work at the King's Houses, and within is a welter of detail relating to the craftsmen and the structures on which they worked. The most illuminating passage comes from the 1348–9 account of the chaplain Robert Rotor who described the activities of two carpenters working at felling thirty oak trees in Clipstone Park between 1 January and 5 February 1349 which were then hauled to the King's Houses in sixty loads (2d per load). The timber was then trimmed to make posts for a palisade fixed into a groundsill and supported by two rails which was specified to be ten feet in height. The carpenters then constructed forty and a half rods of paling during the twenty weeks between 5 February and 29 June. A rod equated to sixteen and a half feet and therefore the total amount of palisade required stretched to 203.68 metres and cost a total of £6 15s 3d. The carpenters were paid an additional 9s to make five doors and gates for various palisades and buildings within the complex.[506] The importance of this passage is that it gives very specific details of exactly where the palisades and gates were in relation to the built environment of the palace and this allows a highly detailed ground plan to be constructed based on the pivotal location of the Great Gate already established as being on site of Maun Cottage and Brammer Farmhouse.[507]

A visitor to the King's Houses entering through the Great Gate in 1349 would see Robert de Mauley's Chamber. Robert de Mauley (otherwise spelled 'Morley', but consistently referred to as 'Mauley' in documents relating to Clipstone) was the keeper of the manor, and the chamber was located immediately to the south of the entrance. Next to his chamber was the King's Long Stable stretching alongside the village street. Running out into Castlefield between Robert de Mauley's Chamber and the King's Long Stable was a palisade which stopped at the porch of Henry III's Great Hall A visitor could then turn north, taking them past the shingle-roofed King's Kitchen and eventually to another gate which stood directly opposite the Great Gate. If that person turned in through that second gate they would enter the royal courtyard through the king's own private entrance. However if, instead of turning left at the Great Hall porch, the visitor turned south then they would enter the Screen's

Passage at the low end of the Great Hall. To the west would be the service area of the palace complete with kitchen, pantry, and buttery. Due south was a door allowing access beyond the Great Hall and into the area of King John's Palace as well as two chambers for retainers which stood directly off the Great Hall. Alternatively the visitor could turn east into the cavernous space of the Great Hall which was open to a roof covered with shingles. At the very far end of the Great Hall there stood the raised dais and three doors. Those doors would allow access to either the chapel (via a small covered passage), a garderobe or to the royal quarters. The royal quarters were reached from the dais and consisted of a range of buildings including the Great Chamber, King's Chamber and Queen's Chamber. The latter were two storeys in height with the high status rooms constructed for Edward I and Eleanor at first floor accessed by external steps. The king had a porch, private chapel, garderobe, chimneys and a great door which would give him a view down the slope of the hill out across the gardens to the lake and rabbit warren beyond.

There was a third courtyard to the west of the Great Hall. The palisade between the keeper's chamber and stable had a gate which allowed access to the south into a service court that had the stable on its west side hard up against the main village street. At the far south end of the service court and directly opposite the courtyard gate was the Queen's Hall and Kitchen. The location of these buildings in a fairly low status area of the palace means that they were probably not intended for use by the queen herself, who had her own apartments next to the king's, instead they were likely to be facilities used by the members of her own household. Beyond the Queens' Hall and Great Hall was King John's Palace which seems to have sat in a completely separate part of the complex suggesting a horizontal stratigraphy stretching from the earlier focus of Henry II to the south which was developed to the north under Henry III. Even further out, on the line of the boundary ditch, was Rosamund's Chamber, possibly an even earlier structure. Running back from Rosamund's Chamber to the south-western corner of the service courtyard and terminating between the King's Long Stable and Queen's Kitchen was another palisade, which may have divided off a paddock for horses. At the north end of this pale was a gate directly opposite the Queen's Kitchen.[508]

Spectacular as the detail of these passages are they still fail to pinpoint the locations of further buildings listed in the account of Robert Rotor including the Knight's Chamber, Treasurer's Chamber and Lionel's Chamber.[509] The latter was near or possibly attached to the Great Hall as the two had an interconnecting gutter. Later documents also reveal the presence of the Earl of March's Chamber.[510] It is worth noting that the nucleus of the palace was further to the north-east of King John's Palace and quite a lot of it appears to have been located within Castlefield's adjacent enclosure known as the Pheasantry. In 2014 an architectural fragment of a high status piece of window tracery was recovered by a local developer from this area of the site. Analysis of the chamfer cusps of the trefoil head indicates that the window was designed during the Curvilinear Gothic period c 1290–1350, and was stylistically similar to the contemporary windows of the Baron's Hall at Penshurst Place, Kent. By the period of the next programme of repairs to the King's Houses, in the early 1360s, Perpendicular Gothic had become the dominant style of architecture and it is deemed unlikely that the tracery could date from this phase of work.[511] The only known substantial masonry work carried out during the Curvilinear period were the seven weeks in 1348–9 that two masons spent working on the gable, cornice and chimney of the Great Chamber. It is plausible that the architectural fragment originated in this part of the palace which otherwise had a garderobe and a lead roof 35 foot long (10.67 metres) which was later re-clad with tiles.[512]

Across the royal courtyard from the Great Chamber was the king's kitchen and Salzman pointed out that it was fitted with a chimney flue made of stone and chalk in 1368. There were also references to timber framed chimneys rendered in plaster[513] similar to both of the chimneys blown down by the wind at Windsor in 1236[514] and the '*uncountable chimneys the colour of chalk*'[515] depicted in *Sir Gawain and the Green Knight*. A large number of the buildings at the King's Houses were plastered both internally and externally so that the render, pargetting, and whitewash would make the structures very visible to the traveller and focusing attention on them in the landscape.

The repairs of 1360–3 were specifically carried out because many of the buildings at the King's Houses had suffered from '*the tempest they were blown down and broken to pieces*' and one man was employed for eight days to cut down fallen trees and thorn bushes whilst also making intrusive inspections into the state of the foundations.[516] This helps to explain why so much of the work carried out was to roof structures which must have been largely stripped of their coverings. The Great Hall alone required 7,500 new shingles. Clipstone was probably a near constant building site with scaffolding erected on ranges throughout much of the second half of the fourteenth century. It is revealing to see mention of the builders tools and materials in the accounts such as the birches taken from Birklands to make scaffolding, wattle hurdles for scaffold walkways, a fifty foot long ash ladder, hemp ropes for binding the ladders to the scaffold and hauling up materials such as the lime brought from Warsop which was mixed with a sieve and a bowl especially bought for the work on the chapel at Birklands.[517] During the reign of Richard II barrels were bought for 20d from John Pawe whilst John Lole supplied shovels, spades, mattocks, pickaxes for 3s and John Boxworth was given 16d for large and small ropes.[518]

The Royal Household at Clipstone

Most of the buildings referred to in the mid-fourteenth century building accounts were already in existence by the period of the Black Death and it appears that the documents contain information on repairs to structures commissioned by Henry III (Great Gate, Great Hall, Chapel, Great Chamber, Queens Hall and Kitchen) and Edward I (King's Long Stable and King's Chambers). The only one '*of new making*' was the Knight's Chamber on which work began when masons built a groundwall 60 foot long by 2 foot wide (18.29 by 0.6 metres). However there are hints that even this was more akin to a wholesale rebuilding of a structure which was still partially standing as carpenters were paid for 120 feet of walling – twice that of the masons – suggesting that only one length of groundwall required rebuilding. Later a more explicit reference was made to the reuse of an existing garderobe. A similar project took place in 1539 when Thomas Cromwell ordered the rebuilding of the Lieutenant's House at the Tower of London on exactly the same location as the previous Mediaeval structure.[519] The new Knight's Chamber contained four individual spaces internally, each with its own garderobe and the specified sixteen windows point towards each room being lit by four windows, perhaps two on each long elevation. Only three new doors with iron braces were paid for, again hinting at the reuse of a fourth. The timber framed walls were daubed in clay and lime and the structure was roofed with Mansfield stone slabs capped off with decorative glazed tiles from Nottingham which may have been similar to the coxcomb ridge tile excavated by Philip Rahtz.[520]

Along with the Knight's Chamber, all of the other buildings that were referred to for the first time in 1348–9 and 1360–3 were for household members. Lionel, son of Edward III, had a chamber with a lead guttering; the keeper Robert de Mauley's Chamber had a stone chimney and Mansfield stone roof measuring 40 by 15 feet (12.19 by 4.57 metres); the Treasurer's Chamber used by Bishop Edington was timber framed and also had a clay and straw daub wall which was in turn plastered.[521] The Earl of March's Chamber was part of a larger range of buildings measuring 80 by 18 feet (24.38 by 5.48 metres) and was again timber framed with plastered walls made of clay and lime. Something of the carpentry was also revealed through the payment for posts, beams, a gable truss and notched rafters.[522]

Purpose built retainer ranges were generally a feature of the late Middle Ages such as those surrounding the Green Court and Stone Court at Archbishop Bourchier's late fifteenth century great house at Knole, Kent. The regular courtyards which are characteristic of complexes such as Knole, Hampton Court, Eltham or South Wingfield were beginning to make an appearance during the late fourteenth century and the analysis of the documentary accounts hints at a possibility that such ranges may have existed at Clipstone. Clarendon had its own similar retainer apartments such as the de Nevill Chamber.[523] It is useful to look at exactly who occupied these spaces at the particular time that they were identified as a means to populate the palace with individual members of the household.

Roger Mortimer (1328–60), Earl of March, whose chamber was repaired in 1360–3 was the grandson of the more famous traitor executed by Edward III for usurping the power of his father. Like many of the king's household knights he fought at Crecy in 1346 and was later named as one of the founders of the Knights of the Garter. As such he would have known the Lord Treasurer William Edington (died 1366), who was also chaplain to the Garter Knights. Edington's rise to prominence began when he was recommended as a cleric to Edward III by his employer Adam Orleton, the Bishop of Winchester. By 1341 the highly capable Edington was named the Keeper of the Wardrobe, eventually rising to hold the position of Treasurer and later Chancellor. His skill at carefully budgeting all revenues and expenses brought about an end to the crippling debts that Edward suffered in the earlier part of his reign, thus leaving Edward free to pursue his wars in France. Edington also progressed through a steady rise in the church and held several rectorates and benefices until he was elected Bishop of Winchester in 1346 which entitled him to be buried in the chantry chapel that he bestowed in the nave at Winchester Cathedral.

A contemporary of both Mortimer and Edington was Robert de Mauley (often rendered as de Morley), 2nd Baron Rodyn (died 1360), who can be accurately described as a fourteenth century swashbuckler. He fought at the battle of Boroughbridge for Edward II against Lancaster, yet in 1327 he joined Isabella and Mortimer's rebellion. Robert fought the Scots at Halidon Hill and the French at Sluys where, as Admiral of the East Coast, he was one of the principal commanders of the English fleet. Following the death of Robert de Clipstone, de Mauley was named as keeper of the manor of Clipstone in 1339. Following further action at Crecy and Calais, de Mauley pressed his claim to be able to wear the coat of arms of the Burnell family. He seems to have had a stubborn streak as when Edward III queried the claim Robert threatened never to fight in the king's name again if he was refused. Wisely Edward acquiesced to his veteran commander whom he later named as Constable of the Tower of London in 1355. Both de Mauley and Mortimer died of disease during the 1360 campaign in Burgundy.[524]

The chamber of Lionel of Antwerp, Duke of Clarence (1338–1368) and second surviving son of Edward III, was located close by to the Great Hall Despite this proximity to the high status part of the King's Houses, when he died Lionel was buried in a very remote location. His grave lies at Clare Priory in Suffolk, far away from the royal mausoleum at Westminster or the tomb of his brother the Black Prince at Canterbury Cathedral. Clare was founded in 1248 by Richard de Clare (1222–1262) and is also the location of the grave of Lionel's wife Elizabeth de Burgh, Countess of Ulster (1332–1363). Richard de Clare's first wife, Margaret, was also a de Burgh and it seems that the family connection to the priory was maintained across more than a century. Elizabeth was a direct descendant of Margaret de Burgh's brother – John. Consequently she was eventually buried at a priory with a close family relationship to her. The de Burgh family have a curiously recurring relationship with Kings Clipstone as Robert de Mauley's first wife Hawise was the granddaughter of Devorguille de Burgh and Lionel's wife Elizabeth was the great-granddaughter of Devorguille's sister, Margaret. Family networks were vividly alive in the Mediaeval period and as such Lionel, Elizabeth, Robert and Hawise would have considered themselves to have been kin and probably used the familiar term "cousin" to describe those relationships. These relationships are apparent in all of the people who held chambers at Clipstone, as Lionel's daughter, Philippa (named after his mother who also brought up the orphaned Elizabeth) was married in 1368 to Edmund Mortimer, the son of Roger, 2nd Earl of March.[525]

The household expense books of Elizabeth de Burgh contain the earliest known documentary reference to the existence of the poet Geoffrey Chaucer, listed between 4 and 9 April 1357 when he was probably in his mid-teens. Chaucer was a page in the countess' household and the account referred to clothing provided for him to wear at the Easter feast held in London.[526] Chaucer can then be traced from time to time in Elizabeth's household accounts as she travelled to Reading, London, Windsor, Woodstock, Doncaster, Hatfield, Anglesey, Bristol and London.[527] In the autumn of 1359 Lionel came of age and his household merged with that of Elizabeth, and at this stage Chaucer went on campaign in France until May 1360 during which period he was briefly held to ransom.[528] After this there are seven lost years in Chaucer's biography during which it is assumed, but cannot be proven, that he served in some capacity within the royal household as when he reappeared in the records in June 1367 it is because he was granted a life annuity of 20 marks given for good service to Edward III as a yeoman of the chamber.[529] As a member of these royal households it is therefore entirely plausible that Geoffrey Chaucer, who went on to become known as the father of English literature, spent time at the King's Houses either as a member of Elizabeth, Lionel or Edward III's households during the period 1357 to 1363 (the date of Edward's last visit to the palace). Later in life Chaucer was Clerk of the King's Works from 12 July 1389 to 17 June 1391 and was responsible for building projects at royal properties including the Tower of London, Westminster, Berkhampstead, Kennington, Eltham, Clarendon, Sheen, Byfleet, Kings Langley, Feckenham and the New Forest Lodge of Hatheburgh.[530] The routines and construction of royal palaces was imbued into the character of Chaucer and he would have understood the rhythms of the King's Houses so completely that the text of his first major poem *The Book of the Duchess*, written in 1368, is full of the allegory of courtly love and hunting which could only have been penned by a man familiar with that world.

Donald Howard's research into the life of a mid-fourteenth century page, published as part of his background portrayal of the life of Chaucer, allows us a glimpse of what the lower status activities of the King's Houses may have been like. The day began at dawn with mass followed by a breakfast of breaded porridge made with wine or ale. Pages would then attend their academic lessons with a cleric or martial training with a knight. Meanwhile the rest of the household servants would be busied with cleaning, cooking and laundry. The main meal of the day was served during the late morning and would be preceded by prayers and then accompanied by both music and entertainments. Chaucer would then have been allowed a period of recreation which often involved reading publicly from bound illuminated books. The painted frontispiece of an early edition of Chaucer's *Troilus and Criseyde* shows a courtier standing at a lectern placed within a garden reading to an assembly.[531] On seeing such an illustration it is hard not to think of the gardens lying on the lower slopes of the hill at the King's Houses or of the Mediaeval book clasps found in Castlefield in 2012 (Plate 6 D).[532] It is also possible to consider the Mediaeval winged belt fitting punctured by three rivet holes that was excavated in 2011 and must have once adorned a courtier's clothing.[533] In the early evening there were more prayers and a light meal after which, Howard is of the opinion that, a large amount of heavy drinking of ale, wine or cider took place into the night before the household retired.[534]

Dining was a highly ritualised activity in which members of the household were seated in order of prestige from the most high-ranking at the centre of the dais to the lowest at the far end of the hall. The trestle tables were spread with white linen tablecloths set with metalware goblets and dishes from which the household ate with fingers, spoon and knife. Food was served in many courses, each shared between two people – the higher status partner serving the lower. Fish courses were eaten often as meat was regulated against on holy days. Between every course hands were washed in a ewer and people ate 'subtleties' made of sugar or marzipan. Food was usually as much a spectacle as the surroundings in which it was served and often consisted of vibrantly coloured and sculpted dishes made to look like structures such as castles or fountains spouting wine. A theme that would have been highly popular in the hunting environment of Clipstone was a cooked pheasant served with its feathers covering it as if it was still alive.[535]

From the later 1360s Edward III's travels were contained within the south and south-east of England and often did not include the entire household but instead involved a very select number limited to perhaps fifty people. One reason for this was the king's advancing age, which can be seen through the regular appearance in the household accounts of his physicians John Glaston and John Paladyn, alongside increasing numbers of potions purchased for the ailing queen.[536] The king's last visit to the Midlands in 1363 was in the presence of Philippa of Hainault and a number of French hostages captured during the wars and concentrated primarily on hunting parks in Northamptonshire, Leicestershire and Nottinghamshire.[537] Prior to a lengthy stay at Clipstone between 25 July and 10 August – coinciding with the hunting season of the red stag and fallow buck – eight women cleaned '*the hall and chamber and diverse houses of office in the manor against the coming of the Lord King, during the course of two days*'. It is noteworthy that they were each paid 3d per day – a wage equivalent to the male labourers who also worked at the King's Houses.[538]

Richard II

During the period 1384–6 Richard II excelled himself in causing outrage to his first cousin Henry of Lancaster, Earl of Derby, the eldest son of John of Gaunt (himself the younger son of Edward III). The two had been rivals since childhood but, starting with a move by the king to hand out the inheritance of Henry's second cousins the Mortimers, the king had consistently antagonised Lancaster. Richard sacked his chancellor, favoured the incompetent Robert de Vere, Earl of Oxford and slandered Henry's cousin Thomas Arundel. More dangerously Richard had been involved in the attempted murder of the Archbishop of Canterbury, allowed his half-brother John Holland to get away with the murder of Sir Ralph Stafford and had been angling for the death of John of Gaunt through either execution or assassination.[539] What became known as the 'Wonderful Parliament', during the autumn of 1386, sought to settle the issue of Richard's abuses once and for all. Henry of Lancaster's personal grievances with Richard aligned with the national mood that the king had placed his trust in the wrong men. Michael de la Pole, Earl of Suffolk, was particularly blamed for mishandling the ongoing war in France.[540] The criticism is highly reminiscent of Edward II's reliance on his favourites Gaveston, Damory and the Despensers; and this similarity was specifically cited during the parliament alongside other dark mutterings that there was, after all, now a precedent for how to deal with an unsatisfactory king.[541] Parliament eventually took a very strong line and elected a council of fourteen lords headed by

Henry's uncle, Thomas of Woodstock, Earl of Gloucester, to restrict the king's powers. The council met regularly for the course of one year at Westminster.

Richard's reaction was initially to confirm the succession to the throne on the twelve year old Roger Mortimer, Earl of March (grandson of the earl who had a chamber at Clipstone), essentially a malleable puppet descended from Lionel of Antwerp's daughter Philippa. The decision was expected, but was provocative as it bypassed Edward III's brothers Thomas of Woodstock and John of Gaunt in favour of a boy descended from a female lineage.[542] The king's second tactic was to go on an extended progress through the farther reaches of his kingdom so that quite simply he would never be in reach of the restrictive council at Westminster.[543] The 'gyration', as it became known, started in February 1387 and took in places such as Beaumanoir, Nottingham, Royston, Beverley, Windsor, Coventry, Drayton Bassett, Lichfield, Stafford, Stone, Chester, Shrewsbury, Acton Burnell, Worcester and then back to Nottingham in late August. Richard's wanderings were not completely aimless as he maintained the work of kingship, as he saw it on his own terms, by settling a dispute between the canons of Beverley and attending the installation of the Bishop of Lichfield.[544]

Aware that his delaying tactics could only work for a finite period of time, Richard summoned a panel of handpicked judges to Shrewsbury and demanded that they consider the legality of the restraints imposed upon him by parliament. The judges were then summoned to appear before the king again at Nottingham to answer the question posed to them on whether the council of lords was '*derogatory to the regality and prerogative of the lord king*' and, if so, how those who had enforced it should be punished.[545] The judges decided in Richard's favour and declared that the king had the power to choose and dismiss his advisors at will. This legal solution to the problem opened up the way for Richard to declare Thomas of Woodstock and his fellow councillors as traitors.[546]

The judges had little choice in their deliberations. Robert Bealknap refused to fix his seal to the judgement several times until Michael de la Pole threatened to kill him.[547] William Skipwith claimed to be too ill to attend the meeting at Nottingham, perhaps a convenient excuse to avoid Richard's wrath due to his Lancastrian sympathies.[548] The decision provided a blueprint for a potentially new model of royal authority in which parliament became less of a political institution voicing the concerns of the people and more of an extension of the monarch's court.[549] Richard was effectively trying to outlaw any criticism of his governance of England.[550] This behaviour is entirely in keeping with his character which can be accurately described as narcissistic with a strong streak of crippling self-doubt brought about by a very sheltered childhood surrounded by those who acquiesced to his every demand. It was this background which led to him insisting that for the first time ever the monarch be addressed as '*your highness*' or '*your high royal majesty*', rather than the more simple '*my lord.*' In particular he delighted in sitting ostentatiously on his throne after dinner where he demanded that anyone he looked at had to prostrate themselves before the king.[551]

As soon as the matter was settled with the judges at Nottingham, Richard headed off to Clipstone where he remained between 2 and 8 September 1387. This was the most overtly obviously example of the use of the King's Houses as a location for royal rest and relaxation. Richard had suffered many setbacks to his personal authority in the previous year and after securing what he considered to be such a neat solution to his problems he went to enjoy the pleasures offered by Sherwood Forest. Richard was noted to be a keen hunter[552] who paid a goldsmith £25 in 1386 for a hunting knife and a golden horn '*embellished with green silk tassels*'[553] and would certainly have taken advantage of the red stag, fallow buck and roe buck hunting seasons during his visit to Clipstone.

Hunting was of such paramount importance to the king that in 1390 he imposed the Game Laws which restricted the right to hunt to only those who possessed land worth 40s or more a year in rent. The law specifically prevented '*butchers, shoemakers, tailors, and other low persons,* [to] *keep greyhounds and other dogs, and at times when good Christians on holy days are at church, hearing divine services, go hunting in parks, rabbit-runs, and warrens of lords and others.*'[554] Perhaps Richard was reminded, with some revulsion, of the demand Wat Tyler had made during the Peasant's Revolt of 1381 that '*all warrens, as well as fisheries as in parks and woods, should be common to all; so that throughout the realm, in waters, ponds, fisheries, woods and forests, poor as well as rich might take the venison and hunt the hare in the fields.*'[555] The Game Laws restricted the right to hunt throughout the land to the gentry and above and must be seen as a painful extension of the Forest Law. This was imposed due to the fear that the common man was getting above his station and either hunting or poaching. The right to hunt was now confirmed by the law as an exclusively upper class activity only.[556]

Richard's French contemporary Gaston Phoebus wrote his manual the *Book of the Hunt* between 1387–8 and described a scene which indicates the kind of relaxation that the king may have indulged in after a day's hunting at Clipstone: '*Back in his hall, while a supper of suet, venison, and wine is being made ready for him, he strips off his clothes and shoes, washes his legs and sometimes his whole body. Once he has eaten and drunk, he is thoroughly warmed and contented, and can lie down in his bed between fine, fresh linen, and sleep wholesomely through the night, without any thoughts of committing sin.*'[557] This is a passage very reminiscent of the arrival of Sir Gawain to his chamber at Sir Bertilak's castle in the poem also written during Richard's reign:

> '*In a while he washed and went to his meal.*
> *Staff came quickly and served him in style*
> *With several soups all seasoned to taste,*
> *Double helpings as was fitting, and a feast of fish,*
> *Some baked in bread, some browned over flames,*
> *Some boiled or steamed, some stewed in spices*
> *And subtle sauces to tantalize his tongue.*[558]
> *... Then, blissful, bound for bed,*
> *Sir Gawain waved goodnight.*'[559]

Phoebus' use of the words '*without any thoughts of committing sin*' and the *Gawain* poet's use of the word '*blissful*' are ironic as, of course, later in the story Gawain accepts three kisses from Sir Bertilak's wife as she tries to seduce him whilst her husband is off out hunting. We must also recall the words of the Monk of Evesham who recorded that Richard II had a reputation for '*staying up half the night, and at other times right through until the morning drinking and indulging himself in other unmentionable ways.*'[560]

When Richard finally met the lords at Westminster in November 1387 they arrived armed and demanded that all of Richard's favourite courtiers be tried for treason. Robert de Vere absconded to the king's stronghold of Cheshire where de Vere's support was greatest and raised an army. Gloucester and the lords headed north and shadowed de Vere's progress until there was a confrontation at Radcot Bridge near Oxford. Henry of Lancaster was present at this skirmish and played a key role in trapping de Vere north of the Thames so that he only narrowly escaped from the fight and was subsequently exiled to the continent. Eventually Richard was forced into a private meeting at the Tower of London on 27 December and agreed to the curtailment of his powers alongside accepting the council of the lords. Gloucester and Arundel argued for deposing Richard, but they were persuaded to maintain the status quo by Henry of Lancaster.[561] An irony, as it was Lancaster who eventually forced Richard's abdication in 1399 so that he could himself become Henry IV.

Richard II's next connection to Clipstone was apparently more benign, as on 4 July 1391 he confirmed that the local people should '*be quit of payment of toll, pontage, picage, pavage, carriage, murage, stall-age and passage upon their goods and merchandise…as by custom hitherto kept and approved in England men and tenants of the ancient demesne have been thereof quit throughout the realm time out of mind*.'[562] This order is somewhat anomalous as it was a reaction to an enquiry as to whether or not Clipstone was part of the ancient royal demesne land, the prerequisite for which was that it was in the hands of the Crown at Domesday. Clipstone was not in royal ownership in 1066, so the decision that the manor was ancient royal demesne was not strictly legal[563] and may have been related to the presence of the substantial palace. The next link between Richard and Clipstone is also similarly anomalous as David Crook placed the monarch at the King's Houses in 1393 based on the '*survival of a signet letter attested there*'[564] which has traditionally been viewed as the final royal visit to the palace. Nigel Saul has reconstructed the itineraries of Richard and his complete list of locations and dates for 1393 reveals that the king's whereabouts can be traced for every single day in the year. Richard's time was spent in the south and he never went further north that Kings Langley in Hertfordshire,[565] over 130 miles away from Clipstone.

Repair work to the sum of £30 took place at the King's Houses during the regnal year 1394–5 which was accounted for as the final year that the keeper of the manor and park William Danyell was alive.[566] The programme of documented works was only loosely specific in terms of the actual buildings that were repaired with brief mentions of '*diverse ruinous houses*', the stables, paling, chapel, King and Queen's Chambers. The accounting is distinctly inaccurate and there are several occasions when payments were not added up correctly or where entire lines were crossed out in error. Danyell's death may have left a hole in the records or they may have been compiled by a less able man. Another difference from the earlier accounts, especially that of 1348–9, is that rather than listing a specific building separately and then accounting for all of the tradesmen working on it, the 1394–5 account lists each type of craftsman in the first instance. For the first time we start to see individual names of those people that worked at the King's Houses. The carpenters who felled and hauled trees from Clipstone Park were called William Togby and John Pawe, whereas those working from Birklands and Bilhaugh were called John de Ednestaw and John Eton. Togby and Pawe were paid more than Ednestaw and Eton as they had further to transport the timber, although the former pair were later able to earn an extra 27s for roofing work at the palace. They were joined in roofing by the carpenter William S. and the slaters John Karre and Henry Sclatter who purchased 18 quarters of lime from Adam Lymer of Crich. Another team of carpenters including Hugh Lekke and Thomas Gerneld manufactured and built groundsills and stairs whilst Henry Chamberleyne and three others laboured at daubing the walls for a total of six days. The carpenters were supplied with finished materials by the sawyers John and Richard Sagher. Ironwork for the gates of the park and doors and windows of the palace was supplied by William Renerege, whereas specialist material in the form of twenty pieces of timber from sapling oaks for the same was provided by John Bulkote. As ever, it was in the leadwork and transportation of materials that the serious money was to be made. A total of 47s 8d was paid out to John Fletcher and John Carter for haulage and 62s 10d went to Robert Plumbar for repairing the lead roofs of the chapel, King and Queen's Chambers.[567]

It was entirely normal for surnames to reflect the occupation of the individual during the late fourteenth century so that the Poll Tax returns of 1379 for Derby list the name and occupation of '*William Plummer, plummer.*'[568] Many of the names in the 1394–5 accounts for the King's Houses relate to the trades in which the men were employed: Sclatter (slater), Lymer (lime burner), Sagher (sawyer), Plumbar (plumber), whereas John Carter's colleague John Fletcher may have either had multiple occupations as a haulier and arrow maker or had transferred to a new trade. Other names may relate to the point of origin of the man such as Eton, Bulkote (Bulcote, Nottinghamshire) or Ednestaw (Edwinstowe, Nottinghamshire). Adam Lymer is listed as being from Crich in Derbyshire which may also have been the location for his lime kiln.

The year after Danyell's account of repairs at the King's Houses was a pivotal one for Richard II. On 9 March 1396 a twenty-eight year long truce was signed by proxy with the French, bringing a temporary end to the hostilities opened by Edward III in 1337. During the negotiations of this truce one of the requests made by Richard was for French military assistance, should he require it, against his own people. The king was still in a very difficult relationship with his magnates and was trying to ensure he had a fall-back plan.[569] The central symbol of the treaty was the agreement of marriage between the twenty-nine year old Richard and the six year old Isabella of Valois. Richard was at Clipstone on 16 March at a time when he must have been considering the implications of the peace with France and his planned second marriage to the infant Isabella which took place near Calais in October.[570] There was nothing special about this stay at the King's Houses. It was simply part of a perfectly routine journey through the Midlands which began at Woodstock in November 1395 and took in places such as Oxford, Abingdon, Kings Langley, Gloucester, Tewkesbury, Worcester, Warwick, Coventry, Leicester and Nottingham. Afterwards the king headed into Yorkshire before returning south through Nottingham, Leicestershire, Northamptonshire and Bedfordshire.[571] The only reason why this visit to Clipstone is in any way noteworthy is that, with hindsight, we are able to identify it as the very last time that an English monarch visited the King's Houses.

In a very influential article on the connection between the chivalry of Richard II's court and *Sir Gawain and the Green Knight* Sylvia Federico has demonstrated that the poem can be read as a satirical allegory of the failings of the king's reign. The mythical court of King Arthur was established after the heroic exploits of his youth and the foundation of the Knights of the Round Table. After this Arthur rather slips into the background and the collection of tales revolve around the adventures of his knights until right at the very end of the legend when the court is destroyed from within by Mordred. Federico points out that the contemporary chroniclers were all in agreement that, aged just fourteen, Richard II's heroic confrontation of the rebels at Smithfield during the Peasant's Revolt was the high point in his reign. The documentary evidence from the rest of his reign is then a catalogue of criticisms of a passive king that valued a kind of chivalry that was not martial in tone but relied on '*games, feasts and musical and literary entertainments*' whilst Richard himself was '*noted for his taste in fine clothes and a fondness for self-display*'. Henry Knighton referred to Richard's favourites as '*seducers of the king*'; Adam of

Usk stated that it was partly the king's '*sodomies*' which led to his deposition, and Thomas Walsingham described the court as being '*knights of venus…more powerful in the bedchamber than on the field, more vigorous with words than with weapons, quick in speaking but slow to perform the acts of war.*'[572] The court of Richard was seen by contemporaries as a decadent and un-martial place full of effeminate knights, and such descriptions are highly redolent of the words that the *Gawain* poet puts into the mouth of the Green Knight when he enters Camelot:

> '*So here is the House of Arthur,' he scoffed,*
> '*Whose virtues reverberate across vast realms.*
> *Where's the fortitude and fearlessness you're so famed for?*
> *And the breathtaking bravery and big-mouth bragging?*
> *The towering reputation of the Round Table,*
> *Skittled and scuppered by a stranger – what a scandal!*
> *You flap and flinch and I've not raised a finger!*'[573]

Federico's point that the poem is '*invested in its historical moment*' is a valid one. It was written in a north Staffordshire and Cheshire dialect during the last quarter of the fourteenth century and may have been inspired by one of Richard's repeated visits to his stronghold at Chester.[574] The world that Gawain inhabits is an allegory on the royal court of the period of Richard II and the observations made by the poet are steeped in the reality of sites such as the King's Houses. This world, so familiar from the research at Clipstone, is contained in descriptions of tournaments: '*time after time, in tournaments of joust, they had lunged at each other with levelled lances*'; horse harness decoration: '*a saddle which flickered with fine gold fringes*'; the comfortable and warm chambers: '*beautifully furnished with fine silken fabrics finished in gold*' with '*his host's own chamber and the heat of its chimney*'; the dining facilities in the hall: '*a table set on sturdy trestles covered entirely with a clean white cloth*'; multiple places of religious devotion: '*chaplains went off to the castle's chapels to sound the bells hard*'; Christmas festivities: '*a diary of delights: banquets and buffets were beautifully cooked and dutifully served to diners at the dais*'; the carousing: '*they lounged by the lord's fire, and were served unstintingly with subtle wines…and drank on the deal and went on drinking till late*' and the gorgeous surcoats worn at a palace: '*he clothes himself in the costliest costume: his coat with the brightly emblazoned badge mounted on velvet.*'[575] The world of *Gawain* is precisely the same world as that of Mediaeval Clipstone, and in the next chapter we shall see how the poet's descriptions of the landscape and hunting are also directly applicable to the park and palace.

Chapter Six

Beyond the Palace

'The most commanding castle a knight ever kept, positioned on a site of sweeping parkland… in the midst of tall trees'
~ Anonymous, c 1400, *Sir Gawain and the Green Knight* ~

Clipstone Park

To the west of the King's Houses lay Clipstone Park. By the time that William Senior drew his estate map in 1630 the park comprised 1457 acres of enclosed woodland either side of the valley of the River Maun. The park pale measured almost seven miles in circumference, an identical dimension to the royal park at Woodstock.[576] The earliest representation of Clipstone Park was made on a map of Sherwood Forest drawn in the early fifteenth century and now housed at Belvoir Castle, Leicestershire. The map may have been created for Ralph Cromwell when he became Warden of the Forest and Constable of Nottingham Castle in 1437;[577] significantly Cromwell also became keeper of Clipstone Park in 1445.[578] The park is shown as a circular enclosure bounded by a pale fence with a groundsill, rail and sharpened posts similar to the palisade described at the palace in 1348–9 and reminiscent of other Mediaeval depictions of deer parks such as the Flemish tapestry, dating to c 1500, held in the Burrell Collection by Glasgow Museums and Art Galleries. Documentary analysis at Madeley Great Park, Staffordshire, has shown that in 1467–8 the pale fence consisted of repetitions of four vertical pales placed between two posts which were supported by two horizontal rails and 'stipers' which may have been diagonal braces.[579] The park pale was a construction that was in need of constant maintenance if the deer inhabiting the park were to be prevented from escape, and there are references to sawyers, carters and carpenters working on its repair at Clipstone throughout the later fourteenth century.[580] The circuits of parks were bordered by an area of cleared land known as freeboard which allowed access to the pale for maintenance. At Clarendon the freeboard was eighteen feet wide back from the park's three metre high earthwork banks.[581] Although very little remains to indicate it archaeologically, documents confirm that at least part of the circumference of Clipstone Park was ditched;[582] slight earthworks in Peafield Plantation may be the vestige of a corresponding bank. The pale fence was the defining feature of the park, a fact shown dramatically by the exaggerated size of the paling on the Belvoir map, which inevitably led to the need for access gates of which four were specifically named in 1630 – Taberner, White, Warsop and Woodhouse. Other gates may have existed, including one near the village of Clipstone referred to in the mid-fourteenth century when money was spent on locks and keys.[583] Clipstone gate was possibly depicted on the 1630 map slightly to the west of the end of what is now Squires Lane.

There was an imperative to keep the deer from escaping from the park, but there was an equal need to ensure that stray animals from the wider forest were able to naturally add to the stocks. Consequently a number of deer leaps were incorporated into the boundary enclosure which were lowered sections of fence with reduced earthworks internally to ensure that a deer could jump into, but not out of, the park. The 1630 map appears to show such a feature at the end of 'Deer Leap Dale' near Bradmer Hill and the physical remains of a possible leap from an earlier, and slightly larger, boundary of the park may survive in nearby King's Wood.[584] These earthworks take the form of a curving ditch with an internal bank and an entrance placed near the centre; it is possible to imagine that a reduced height pale stood on the outer lip of the ditch enabling a deer to leap down and then exit through the break in the bank with the steepness of the face of the ditch acting as a barrier to animals attempting to leap the fence. Crook claimed that no changes were made to the park enclosure between 1327 and 1630[585] so if the King's Wood earthworks are the remains of a deer leap then, under this interpretation, they could be from a twelfth or thirteenth century enclosure.

Crook's assertion may be open to question. The boundary of the park as described in a document of c 1334 indicates that the enclosure was to the north of the road between Kings Clipstone and Edwinstowe. The text refers to a deer leap immediately adjacent to St Edwin's Chapel on the very edge of Birklands pointing towards the possibility that Clipstone Park, Birklands and Bilhaugh were all directly interconnected. The boundary description had its

Plate 1 A: King John's Palace, looking north-east, viewed from a similar direction to several antiquarian illustrations made of the building in the eighteenth century

Plate 1 B: The former interior of King John's Palace, looking north-west, the openings in the centre and to the left are relict doorways whereas the masonry blocking to the right was inserted during 1991

Plate 2: A mid-thirteenth century illustration by Matthew Paris of Henry II, Richard, John and Henry III (British Library Board Royal 14 C. VII, f.9)

Plate 3 A: Romanesque carved stone beast head discovered at King John's Palace during Philip Rahtz's excavations in 1956

Plate 3 B: Stone voussoir with a recessed roundel from Clipstone similar in character to those from the twelfth century, moulded, central door at St Mary's Guildhall in Lincoln

Plate 4 A: Maun Cottage to the south of Mansfield Road is a post-Mediaeval building that was formly a public house known as the Gate Inn

Plate 4 B: Arundel Cottage (left) and Brammer Farmhouse (right) contain in situ remains of the Mediaeval boundary wall and great gate of the King's Houses

Plate 5 A: The site of Clipstone Peel, looking north-west, lies three miles to the south-west of the King's Houses and was constructed in the early fourteenth century for Edward II

Plate 5 B: The Spa Ponds were probably created in the early fourteenth century as part of the agricultural enterprise at Clipstone Peel (Tim King)

Plate 6 A: Fourteenth century seal matrix of Sir John Brocas (Portable Antiquities Scheme)

Plate 6 B: Silver penny of Edward I excavated in 2012 (David & Anthony James)

Plate 6 C: Mediaeval horse pendant from Clipstone (David & Anthony James)

Plate 6 D: A Mediaeval book clasp from the King's Houses (David & Anthony James)

Plate 7 A: Parliament Oak, looking south, has apocryphal legends associated with it involving assemblies under its branches called by King John and Edward I (Mark Fretwell)

Plate 7 B: The Old Churn Oak is one of the ancient pollarded oaks marking the north-western boundary of Clipstone Park (Mark Fretwell)

Plate 8 and Plate 9: William Senior's estate map of 1630 shows the lordship of Clipstone at a pivotal moment caught between the semi-fossilised landscape of the

Mediaeval period and the later changes brought about by enclosure. North is orientated to the right hand side of the map. (A private collection)

Plate 10: The estate map of 1766 contains many field-names relating to the historic topography as well as evidence from the encroachment of enclosure onto the former Mediaeval landscape (A private collection)

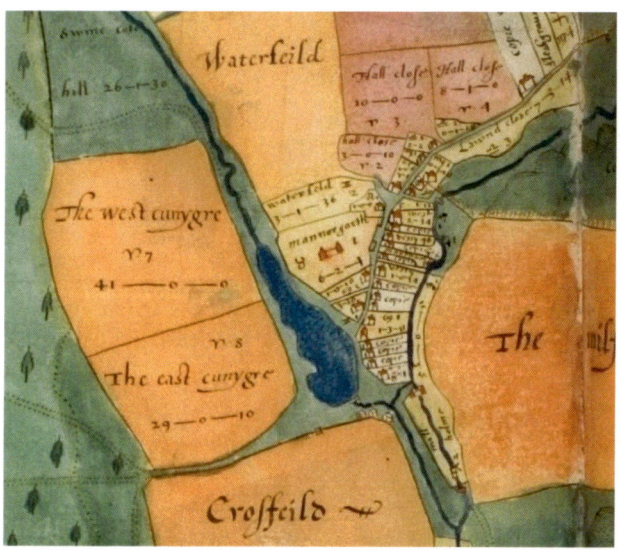

Plate 11 A: A detail of Clipstone village from the 1630 map. North is orientated to the right hand side of the map (A private collection)

Plate 11 B: A detail of Clipstone village from the 1766 map (A private collection)

Plate 12 A: Ritual protection mark scribed into a beam in Arundel Cottage

Plate 12 B: Lead token containing a ritual protection mark discovered at Clipstone (Portable Antiquities Scheme)

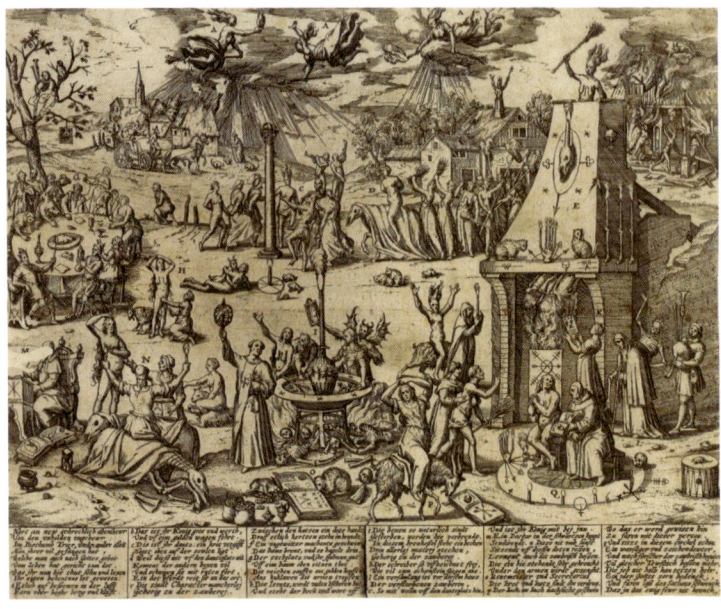

Plate 12 C: German scene of a witches sabbat dating c 1600 and showing ritual protection marks on the fireplace lintel of the foreground chimney (Trustees of the British Museum 1880,0710.1582)

Plate 13 A: Hayman Rooke's illustration of King John's Palace published by Francis Grose in 1772 (Nottinghamshire County Council)

Plate 13 B: John Throsby's 1790 illustration of King John's Palace was probably copied directly from Hayman Rooke's earlier version (Nottinghamshire County Council):

Plate 14 A: Samuel Hieronymous Grimm's view of Clipstone, looking east, was made in 1775 and is therefore closely contemporaneous with the 1766 estate map (British Library Board Add.15543, f164, online gallery)

Plate 14 B: Hayman Rooke's prospect of Clipstone, looking east, dating to c 1790 shows King John's Palace and the village in the background and the bank and pale fence of the deer park in the foreground

Plate 15 A: Mansfield Road, looking north-east, photographed c 1915 with the Gill family stood outside of the village shop that they ran from Maun Cottage (Michelle Bradley)

Plate 15 B: Emma Bradley and her family photographed stood outside Brammer Farmhouse c 1915 (Michelle Bradley)

Plate 16 A: An early twentieth century photograph of King John's Palace, looking north-west, and showing the great state of disrepair that the building stood in (Michelle Bradley)

Plate 16 B: King John's Palace photographed in 2009 during a programme of comprehensive conservation carried out by Paul Mendham Stonemasons

first marker fixed as being near the village: '*beginning from the pounde at Clipstone* [this is not the Great Pond and was probably a secondary pond somewhere in the vicinity of Cavendish Lodge, *and extending to the Toyst Cross* [unknown location], *and from the Toist Cross to the holm dale* ['ye holmes' marked on the Belvoir map close to Clipstone Peel] *unto the bancke of Mane* [River Maun], *and from the water bancke of Mane going to well dale* ['heldale' on the Belvoir map], *and from the well dale going to the herthe pitt, and from the hearth pitte to bradmeer* [Bradmer Hill] *and from the bradmeer to the leaping place* [deer leap] *beside the chappell of St Edwynnes* [St Edwin's Chapel] *and so going by the way unto another leaping place* [deer leap], *and so from thence unto said ponde at Clipston where it began.*'[586] A map made in 1606 showing the conjunction of Clipstone, Warsop and Birklands made after the sale of the estate by Lord Mountjoy to the Earl of Shrewsbury confirms that the park pale was in the same place as found in 1630. However, the 1606 map also depicts '*The Olde Leape, by St Edwins Chappell, a boundary marke of Clipstone parke*' which was actually outside of the seventeenth century boundary.[587] The logical conclusion is that the park boundary altered between c 1334 and 1606 and this is backed up by the Belvoir map which notes an area called 'ye holynes' to be within the park whereas in 1630 Senior drew it as just outside the northern boundary indicating that a possible contraction of the park had occurred.[588] This helps to potentially narrow the chronology of the park boundary changes to somewhere between the early fifteenth century and 1606.[589] Archaeologically these earlier northern boundary features may have left very faint earthworks in the form of linear trenches on the parish boundary north of Bradmer Hill and as a low woodbank near to St Edwin's Chapel.[590] Alterations to park boundaries were by no means unusual as Clarendon Park initially consisted of only the northern lawns which were added to c 1319 by the addition of forest assarts to the south-east.[591]

Parks provided an amenity in which their owners could enjoy the thrill of the hunt, which in turn provided entertainment for themselves and their guests. The deer often acted as diplomatic gifts for the services of retainers, family members or peers alongside the provision of a living larder supplying meat to be consumed at feasts.[592] Forests, parks and residences usually developed together as the monarchs required a base from which to hunt and enclosing reserves within the forests was an entirely logical progression. Some parks, such as that at Clarendon, which had reached 4292 acres in size by 1350,[593] or Bestwood, Nottinghamshire, which had a nine mile circumference, were so big that they could be considered a forest in their own right.[594] Comparable parks to Clarendon and Clipstone were owned by the bishops of Winchester in Hampshire at Bishop's Waltham (1000 acres) and Bramshill (3000 acres)[595] and during the twelfth and thirteenth centuries it was only the high ranking churchmen, magnates and royals who owned parks. By the fourteenth and fifteenth centuries this had been extended to lesser men[596] and there were approximately 3,200 parks in England, most averaging just 90–180 acres in size. All shapes and sizes of parks can be seen in the record, although most were circular or elliptical, and modern field boundaries very frequently still respect the pre-existence of the now now-vanished enclosures.[597] This is certainly the case at Clipstone as both Peafield Lane to the north-west, and the road between Kings Clipstone and Edwinstowe to the north-east, respect the historic boundary of the park as shown in 1630.

The interior of Clipstone Park was dominated by the woodland marked on the 1630 map and by the River Maun which flowed from south-west to north-east through its centre. This provided a source of water for the deer and other animals and allowed the opportunity for wildfowling. The southern bank of the river is characterised by bluffs and cliffs, such as Snake Hill and High Rocks, and the land rises to a central plateau within the park. Hoult Hill Wood, also marked in 1630, was probably a fenced and protected coppice within Clipstone Park similar to those marked on a map of Clarendon Park in 1650.[598] Interestingly, the word 'hoult' or 'holt' is a word of Saxon origin denoting a wood or wooded hill. Potentially this enclosure was also marked within the park on the Belvoir map as a shaded oval. Perhaps the location of Hoult Hill Wood near the northern boundary indicates that it was used for growing timber with which to repair the pale fence as described in 1394–5: '*To John Fletcher for 46 carriages of palys, bordes and rewles from diverse places within the same Park as far as diverse places of the pallisade of the same Park during the course of diverse times, namely 4d a carriage, 15s 4d.*'[599] The park also regularly provided oaks for construction work at the King's Houses.[600] The eighteenth century antiquarian Major Hayman Rooke referred to a tree near the north end of Clipstone Park called the Broad Oak which measured 27 foot 6 inches (8.38 metres) in circumference and may survive in the modern placename Bradmer meaning 'broad boundary mark.'[601] The north-western boundary is still marked by two ancient pollarded trees known as the Old Churn Oak and Parliament Oak (Plate 7 A and 7 B).

Clipstone Park was part of an area of forest administration known as the Rumwood which also consisted of the hays of Bilhaugh and Birklands to the north. The latter were administered by two foresters on horseback and two on foot whereas Clipstone had two verderers and two agisters. Verderers were usually unpaid knights appointed by the sheriff of Nottingham whose responsibility was to present cases of infringements to the forest court. Foresters were lower status men who received their appointment from the forest wardens and received a salary to ensure that forest laws were enforced. The agisters collected fees, mainly from forest residents for common rights such as grazing within the park.[602] In 1251 the men of Clipstone had rights to common within the park, although not in Birklands or Bilhaugh, all of which were administered at the time by the Chief Forest Justice Beyond the Trent.[603]

Documents from the later thirteenth and fourteenth centuries imply that the upkeep of the park pale was not maintained as it was referred to as a 'hay' enclosed by a hedge rather than a pale or '*the king's wood of Clipstone called le parke*' and there is a hole in the lists of park keepers throughout much of the thirteenth century. The complaints about the extension to the park and peel in 1327–8 by the men of Clipstone made reference to the new enclosure of the park implying that it was a recent landscape feature not present before in living memory. New keepers Roger Dobman and Roger de Warsop were then subsequently employed to maintain the pale indicating a re-founding of the deer park which may not have been fully functional during the thirteenth century.[604] We have already seen how Edward II's re-imposition of the park pale caused outrage to the local communities and although Edward III diplomatically settled those issues by confirming common rights and removing some of the enclosures it seems probable that the park was still slightly larger during his reign than the dimensions recorded in the early seventeenth century by William Senior.

Hunting

Prior to the arrival of the Normans, hunting in the Anglo-Saxon period seems to have been relatively sophisticated and required land and stock management to ensure that the beasts thrived. Hunting infrastructure ensured that the deer were being driven by beaters into hedgelines which funnelled the highly prized animals into a killing zone where they would be dispatched by hunters armed with bows.[605] The drive hunt (often called the bow and stable method) was a uniquely English phenomenon that the Normans readily adopted[606] and was a common activity within parks that relied on large amounts of men and dogs to provide substantial yields of meat. It was also a method which enabled women to take part in the hunt as well as men.[607] Deer parks in England were essentially a Norman import, created as a habitat for the less hardy fallow deer which they brought with them, and venison was the food of social prestige for the new regime.[608] Orderic Vitalis' description of William II's death in the New Forest depicts a drive hunt '*as they stood on the alert waiting for their prey with their weapons ready*'[609] but it was the *Gawain* poet who left us a fully developed impression of the pace, excitement and techniques of this type of hunting:

> '*But the hinds were halted with hollars and whoops*
> *And the din drove the does to sprint for the dells.*
> *Then the eye can see that the air is full of arrows:*
> *All across the forest they flashed and flickered,*
> *Biting through hides with their broad heads.*
> *What! They bleat as they bleed and they die on the banks,*
> *And always the hounds are hard on their heels,*
> *And the hunters on horseback come hammering behind*
> *With stone-splitting cries as if cliffs had collapsed.*
> *And those animals which escaped the aim of the archers*
> *Were steered from the slopes down to rivers and streams*
> *And set upon and seized at the stations below.*
> *So perfect and practised were the men at their posts*
> *And so great were the greyhounds which grappled with the deer*
> *That prey was pounced on and dispatched with speed.*'[610]

Although the action of the hunt described in the poem was of its moment and has left no trace beyond the butchered bones of the deer excavated archaeologically, the landscape of Clipstone Park fits the scene depicted by the poet as he writes about the deer being chased across the high ground and then down into the river valley. The plateau at the centre of Clipstone Park and the steep descent into the valley of the Maun must have witnessed such scenes many times during hunting by the monarchy in the Mediaeval period.

The bow and stable method of hunting was usually reserved for hunting fallow deer within parks and although it was relatively efficient and provided a type of meat which was considered to be the tastiest venison, it was the *par force des chiens* hunt (first mentioned in the fourteenth century although probably much older) which was thought of by contemporaries to be the higher status form of hunting. This involved the selection of a male deer over the age of five – often a red stag – who was then chased on horseback with a pack of dogs across the countryside for many miles until the animal was tired and eventually dispatched at the point of a sword.[611] Geoffrey Chaucer wrote about the method in a very easy and leisured manner[612] and was not afraid to leave us with an observation of a failed hunt in which the stag evaded the hunters:

> '*There every man was doing just*
> *As he by laws of hunting must.*
> *Three long notes blew the master then*
> *Upon his great horn, telling men*
> *To unleash and urge on every hound.*
> *And quickly then the hart was found,*
> *Hallooed and keenly hunted fast*
> *Long time with shouts; until at last*
> *The hart zigzagged and stole away*
> *From all the hounds a secret way.*
> *The pack entire thus overshot*
> *And lost the scent they'd had so hot.*
> *At once the master-huntsman knew,*
> *And on his horn the recall blew.*'[613]

Very few parks were large enough to have been hunted in on horseback, but the size of Clipstone and certainly Clarendon and Bestwood must have allowed for this technique.[614] The *Gawain* poet also described a boar and a fox hunt[615] and other animals that were pursued included hare, otter, marten, badger, rabbit and (until the beginning of the thirteenth century when the species became extinct in England) wolf.[616] However it was the deer that was prized above all which is why their numbers were protected during rut, fawning and cold seasons when food would need to be artificially provided for the animals.[617] A survey of 1532 showed that there were 1,340 red deer in Sherwood Forest of which 310 – almost one quarter of the total – were at Clipstone. Surveys in later years show varied numbers: 1,000 in 1538, 1,263 in 1616 and 1,361 in 1635[618] and regular programmes of breeding and culling must have been maintained. Approximately 10% of the deer herd were taken per year. At Clarendon this amounted to between two and four hundred deer per year from a park which was approximately three times the size of Clipstone, where perhaps sixty to one hundred and thirty were culled.[619] Oliver Rackham calculated that in 1260 Henry III took 607 fallow, 159 red and 45 roe deer, and of the fallow deer he took 81 from parks.[620] Disease could also reduce numbers significantly such as the disease which killed 350 roe and fallow deer in Sherwood Forest during 1286.[621]

During the month of May in 1212 King John's hunting pack which travelled on itinerary with him were recorded as being 167 greyhounds, 38 'dogs of the pack', 32 bercelets with 52 handlers. By September this group had increased to 300 greyhounds, 16 boarhounds, 9 bercelets with 64 handlers.[622] Although John does not seem to have visited Clipstone during these periods he was certainly in Nottinghamshire during the autumn. In the fourteenth century, Edward II's huntsman, William Twiti, indicated that fallow and roe deer were hunted with a type of bloodhound known as a lymer which would seek out the quarry, whereas the hart, hare, boar and wolf were hunted with running hounds who would pick up the scent. A single arrow was unlikely to kill outright a fallow deer, therefore the hounds would be employed to kill the wounded animals.[623] Twelfth century accounts indicate that the administrative organisation of the hunt was complex with officers including '*knight huntsmen, keepers of the kennels and hounds, huntsmen of the wolf hunt, horn blowers, hunt servants and archers*'.[624] It is somewhat depressing to read that the dogs were often fed better than the communities local to royal residences – in May 1265, during a period of eight days, half a quarter of grain was distributed to the poor at Odiham, Hampshire, whereas the royal hounds received three quarters of grain in ten days.[625]

Both dog and deer bones have been archaeologically excavated at Clipstone,[626] as they have at other high status sites such as Portchester Castle where hunting was conducted in the Forest of Bere.[627] Bone does not survive well in the acidic sandy soils of Sherwood, but the presence of a high quantity of lime mortar from the demolition of the palace site has helped to preserve the 179 animal bones that were excavated in 2011. The domestic animals in the assemblage included sheep, goat, cattle, fowl, pig, horse and dog; the wild animals included rabbit, red, roe and fallow deer. The proportions of animals were found to be very similar to those found at Nottingham Castle[628] and Strelley Hall[629] which also had attached deer parks. At Clarendon, fallow deer was found in a high proportion, and although red and roe deer bones were present they were probably those of animals hunted within the wider forest instead of within the park by the king himself. The presence of metapodials and phalanges showed that whole carcasses were butchered on site, but the relative scarcity of forelimbs and scapulae points towards the redistribution of meat that was prepared and then sent on to other sites.[630] The majority of deer bones at Clipstone were either skull fragments or limbs with a preponderance for the right hand side of the carcass. This is a preference commonly found at high status sites as the butchery of deer was a highly ritualised process, related to the status of the hunt participants, with the most important members being offered the meat from the right side.[631] This highly ritualised butchery is described in graphic and visceral detail by the *Gawain* poet, a man who must have been eyewitness to such carnage, given the precise and truly gory specifics:

> *'Through the sliced-open throat they seized the stomach*
> *And the butchered innards were bound in a bundle.*
> *Next they lopped off the legs and peeled back the pelt*
> *And hooked out the bowels through the broken belly,*
> *But carefully, being cautious not to cleave the knot.*
> *Then they clasped the throat, and clinically they cut*
> *The gullet from the windpipe, then garbaged the guts.*'[632]

Remarkably this minutely observed and bloody depiction continues for another twenty-five lines. The butchery was always carried out at the place of the kill, which may explain why evidence of only the highest quality cuts of meat are found in palace bone assemblages.[633] Although the very practical details of the butchery are described by the poet, showing a very controlled and ordered process, there are also hints towards certain rituals: '*a fee for the crows was cast into the copse*' and '*using pelts for plates the dogs pogged out.*'[634] The poet then goes on to provide an idea of the soundtrack of the hunt:

> '*The kill-horn was blown and the bloodhounds bayed.*
> *Then hauling their meat they headed home,*
> *Sounding howling wails on their hunting horns*'[635]

The learned cleric, John of Salisbury, alive in the mid-twelfth century, also wrote that a successful hunt was announced by blowing pipes and trumpets to signify the kill. He then went on to describe the deer's head being paraded in triumph at the front of the hunting party as they returned home[636] and that may go some way to explaining the presence of the skull fragments excavated at the King's Houses.[637]

Although the choice cuts of meat would be offered to the most high status members of the hunt during the equally ritualised dining procedures, there is an irony that the *par force des chiens* type of hunt was less about food provision and more about demonstrating status and power. The forests were reserved for kingly hunting, and parks were so expensive to maintain that only the richest men could afford them. Additionally, the late fourteenth century Game Laws made hunting a strictly aristocratic activity, taking the right away from the common man altogether. In a discussion about the twelfth century depictions of hunting in the poems *Tristan* and the *Romance of the Horn*, the bloodsports historian, Emma Griffin, is emphatic that hunting was '*not a means of obtaining food; it is an art to be studied and mastered by those with time on their hands*'. Consequently, hunting was a mechanism for a leisured practice of martial behaviour and horsemanship within a peer group who demonstrated their courage as a method of social bonding. Magnates hunted for high status recreation whereas the provision of food for the larder was enacted quietly and stealthily by professional huntsmen.[638]

Gardens

Archaeological evidence for gardens at palaces during the Mediaeval period is generally lacking, yet where they have been investigated there seems to be a specific spatial link between gardens and immediately adjacent royal quarters.[639] This relationship has been recorded at Marlborough, Woodstock, Westminster and Windsor; with the gardens at Clarendon lying on a terrace to the north of the royal chambers so that they were directly visible from the windows.[649] The enclosed nature of such gardens, surrounded as they were by the apartments and boundary walls, increased royal privacy[641] enabling a quiet enjoyment of architectural features such as pools or fountains often found within.[642] The late twelfth and thirteenth century climate was very warm leading to the introduction of exotic garden plants[643] which complimented more common fruit trees and orchards alongside grass lawns which could be scythed for haymaking.[644]

Views out across the gardens from royal chambers were very important, hence the construction of a balcony at Woodstock in 1354[645] and the gallery built in 1244 at Clarendon for Eleanor of Provence, who was known to be especially fond of gardens.[646] There was overall a very strong link between the Plantagenet queens and their gardens, although they also appear to have been precious to both Edward I and Edward II.[647] The connection between palace, gardens and the aquatic landscape of moats, ponds, rivers and lakes was particularly important in the Mediaeval mind[648] so that the wider management and framing of the landscape meant that gardens acted as the controlled intermediary between the built environment of the palace and the wilder areas of woodland on the fringes of the panorama.

It is certain that gardens existed at the King's Houses as an exchequer document from the reign of Henry IV refers to the profits of the verdure and herbage of the garden in Hall Garth (as the King's Houses were referred to in the fifteenth century) at Clipstone.[649] The excavation of a trench located thirty-five metres to the south-east of King John's Palace proved to be archaeologically barren[650] which helps to give some credence to the notion that the gardens at Clipstone were located between the concentration of palace buildings towards the top of the hill, close to Mansfield Road, and the lake further to the east.[651]

Fishponds

There were three different groupings of ponds related to the infrastructure of the park and palace at Clipstone. The location of the twelfth century Great Pond to the east of the King's Houses is well understood through the study of historic maps and existing landscape features. Immediately adjacent, to the west, is the earthwork of a smaller stew pond, now known as Cellar Hole, which was used for breeding fish which were then released into the main lake. Surviving in a modified form after alterations in the mid-twentieth century is the early fourteenth century flight of fishponds stretching down a tributary valley of the River Maun adjacent to Clipstone Peel. The c 1334 boundary description of the park refers to another pond that can no longer be traced, but which was probably in the vicinity of Cavendish Lodge and could possibly have been the second pond close to the palace referred to during the 1180s. The latter was described as the 'old pond' by the fifteenth century and must have been unmanaged and silted up by this point.[652]

Royal fishponds became an increasingly common and desirable landscape feature throughout the Mediaeval period with just ten known from the twelfth century such as those at Feckenham, Eye and Newcastle under Lyme, rising to thirty-three by the end of the thirteenth century.[653] Most commonly, fishponds involved the creation of an earthen dam, possibly with a stone revetment, which blocked up a river valley to create an artificial lake. This basic arrangement can be seen in the Great Pond at Clipstone with a dam holding back the Vicar Water in its valley to the north east of the palace. Construction work involved a significant force of labourers such as those employed at Woodstock in 1249.[654] The digging of the fishponds usually yielded river cobbles which could then be used as foundation materials like those excavated from the rectangular structure to the north of King John's Palace.[655] The prevalence of sand and gravel in the natural geology would have also provided a ready source of aggregate used for mortar and levelling, although extra quarry pits would have been required alongside what materials could be retrieved during the cutting of foundation trenches.[656]

The impressive effect of the lake would have been diminished once silting and leaf litter began to dull the appearance of the feature and it is therefore no surprise that regular orders to carry out maintenance work on the Great Pond appear in documentary sources. In 1194 repairs totalling £12were ordered immediately after Richard I's visit[657]; in 1208–9 John spent £42 on house and pond[658] and further work occurred in 1219–20.[659] In 1290 repairs to the house, dam and weir amounting to £160[660] took place after the tremendous wear and tear caused by Edward I's parliament. The sluice gates were in danger of breaking by 1327[661] and in 1348–9 masons rebuilt the head, fish trap and bridge between 29 September and 24 June under the direction of Thomas de Breton.[662] In 1360–3 the revetment timber piles and dam were renewed by a team of six labourers, two carters and two carpenters whilst a further twelve men dug the gravel used in the embankment.[663] The lake was still extant in 1630 but by 1766 the lake had begun to silt up and in the early nineteenth century it was remodelled as part of the Duke of Portland's flood meadows irrigation scheme.

Thirteenth century royal fishponds produced large quantities of fish such as the seventeen hundred taken from the Great Pond to feed the household during Christmas 1315. Common species farmed were pike, eels, tench, bream, perch and roach. Fish constituted an important part of the Mediaeval diet, being eaten at least two or three days a week, as well as throughout Lent and on certain holy days.[664] Research in Warwickshire has demonstrated that the local village population were also allowed access to royal ponds, indicating that the importance of fish as a source of protein for the entire population during periods of fasting was taken very seriously indeed.[665]

The Great Pond fulfilled a dual practical and ornamental role. Alongside the provision of a fishery, it was a habitat for wildfowl and stored up water to power the mills located further to the north. Aesthetically, it acted as a landscape mirror to reflect the gardens and buildings on the hill when viewed from the road and the laund to the north-east. It also provided a venue for boating and aquatic entertainments, whilst also making a statement as a symbolic and defensive boundary on the east of the palace enclosure.[666] Such vast ponds were common to the Mediaeval lordly landscape and can be seen at Kenilworth, Leeds Castle, Somersham and Bishop's Waltham.[667]

Coneygarth

The 1630 map depicts two very large enclosures to the east of the lake which amounted to slightly over seventy acres called the East and West Cunygre. The word 'cunygre' derives from 'coneygarth' indicating an artificial rabbit warren often known as a pillow mound. Rabbits were probably introduced by the Normans, however the first reference to them does not come until Henry III gifted ten rabbits from his park at Guildford. Vast numbers were kept – two thousand rabbit skins were brought from Lundy Island in 1274 – and enclosures were required to keep rabbits penned in and predators out. These enclosures could be of great size sometimes even exceeding a square mile. The rabbits within were taken using hawks, dogs and ferrets[668] and hunting them was an activity which was often undertaken by women as depicted in the fourteenth century Queen Mary Psalter where two women are using a ferret and nets to snare their prey.[669]

The 1348–9 building accounts specifically referred to the King's Chamber being directly opposite the coneygarth[670] which points towards the status of the feature and may also have been intended to ensure that it was highly visible from the palace to deter poachers.[671] A timber paling around the warren was specifically mentioned during the 1360–3 repairs at Clipstone[672] and the coneygarth was still recognised as a landscape feature as late as 1839–40, when a paper in Journal of Royal Agricultural Society referred to its survival right up until the flood meadows irrigation scheme.[673]

Small amounts of rabbit bone have been excavated from the King's Houses[674] indicating that the coneygarth provided a source of food for the palace and as rabbit is not a meat that can be cured it was consumed fresh on site. The Archbishop of Canterbury supplied two hundred rabbits for the feast of St Edward at Westminster in 1305[675] and *'the chief Master Cooks to King Richard II'* who wrote the fourteenth century collection of recipes known as *The Forme of Cury* gave a method for cooking rabbits in syrup.[676] The Clarendon assemblage showed only a modest representation of rabbit bones and their consumption at the feast was more popular before the Black Death than after. The plague led to many rabbits turning feral due to a lack of management so that they became more commonly eaten by all sectors of society and therefore less highly prized.[677] The real worth of coneygarths lay in the economic value of rabbit skins which were worn by the servants of lords, grooms and artisans according to Mediaeval sumptuary laws.[678] A lease of the rabbit warren at Aldbourne, Wiltshire shows the high value of a coneygarth worth at £30 a year which produced 5,000 rabbits. Those at Clarendon produced an annual total of 15,000 rabbits per year.[679]

Woodland

The outer reaches of the lordship of Clipstone was largely given over to woodland in the Mediaeval period, a time when timber was still to be found in plentiful supply especially in the north and west of England.[680] Woodlands were maintained adjacent to royal residences as the land was set aside as part of the hunting reserves. This picture at Clipstone is reflected at other estates, such as Feckenham in Worcestershire which also survived into the seventeenth century.[681] The 1630 map depicts Clipston Hollins and The Asserte to the north, Fless-greave Wood and Ann at bows Wood to the south and The Shroges to the east. The woods of Clipstone Park lay to the west. Referred to as Clipston Wode on the Belvoir map, the 'Shroges' is a word denoting bushes and underwood and perhaps the presence of managed coppice woodland as opposed to the pollarded oaks of the park which enabled hunters to ride freely beneath the branches. Clipston Hollins was probably an enclosure for growing holly trees as winter feed for the deer.[682] The tree species present in the Mediaeval woods framing Clipstone were the commonly found oak, birch, beech, chestnut and sycamore, along with the slightly rarer larch, yew and silver pine.[683] In common with most manors in the Midlands the woodland at Clipstone could be found furthest from the centre of the village and on what may have been less fertile soils.[684] Much of this woodland is still under tree cover as a result of plantation by the Forestry Commission which enables the modern eye to be able to appreciate the character of the Mediaeval landscape, albeit with the largescale replacement of deciduous species with coniferous plantations.

The common woodland management technique of coppicing was employed to supply timber for broom handles, skewers, spindles, hurdle-fences, charcoal and firewood.[685] As such coppices were vital to the rural economy and woods were often enclosed with banks, ditches and hedges as a deterrent to deer that would otherwise eat the young saplings.[686] The woodlands of Clipstone Park, Birklands and Bilhaugh provided the raw materials for the timber framed buildings at the palace, the roofing of thatch board and shingles and the scaffolding used in the construction projects during the later fourteenth century. The woods also provided building materials for external projects such as the six oaks taken from Clipstone in 1292 to ensure that the facilities at Pleasley Park were fit to entertain the king.[687] Grants of timber for non-royal building projects ceased after 1257 as there was increasing concern over the growing shortage of woodlands[688] during the later Mediaeval period which led to the resource being reserved.

The local village community at Clipstone had the right to husbote and haybote as well as the right to pasture their animals within the woodlands. However the control over the woods which were under Forest Law was jealously guarded as the chaplain of the King's Houses found out in 1318 when he was fined for collecting a load of branches which was an action considered to be harmful damage to the habitat of the king's deer.[689] Letters Patent were issued forbidding the men of Clipstone to take firewood from the adjoining woodland owned by Rufford Abbey,[690] presumably after a number of transgressions had already been made. In the early part of Edward III's reign the village community were allowed to pasture agisted foals, heifers and calves within the woods of Clipstone Park. This was later restricted along with herbage in 1334 due to drought and from 1342 no profits were recorded, presumably because there was barely enough growth to sustain the deer herd. In 1341 and then again in 1366–6 the right to gather ferns and leaves in the park was shared with the men of Warsop. By 1363 the men of Clipstone were granted a charter relieving them of all payment for the privilege, and this must have been a great relief in such trying economic times.[691] By the late Mediaeval or early modern period, areas of woodland such as the two enclosures called Wood Close and another adjacent called the Fleassegreave Close may have been pastoral fields carved out of former woodland as the need for cleared land outweighed the requirement for wood pasture.

An Idealised Romantic Landscape

Every square foot of the lordship of Clipstone was stage managed to project the wealth, power and status of the monarchy. The palace stood at the heart of this landscape and the gardens, fishponds, coneygarth and woodland all revolved around this epicentre in a manner intended to overawe visitors. The designed landscape of Clipstone was unique within Sherwood Forest and was linked entirely to the management of the crown comparable to other estates such as Clarendon, Woodstock and Kenilworth. Fundamental to this stage management were the three launds marked on the 1630 map. Unusually two of these launds were entirely separate to the deer park – it was more common for such cleared grasslands to have been created internally such as the Gallops at Knole, Kent or the northern laund at Bestwood.[692] The reason for keeping the launds external at Clipstone was to enhance the views to and from the palace.[693] The laund to the north-west of the palace was on a locally elevated position, standing above the village, which occupies a shelf on the slopes of the Maun valley. It probably acted as an extension to the park which formed and entrance from the palace. The laund to the north-east of the palace created a very dramatic view of the King's Houses which could be seen from the branch approach off the main road north to York with the wooded parkland directly behind the palace and in the foreground a reflection of the buildings created by the Great Pond. South of the palace a very large laund would have been framed on all sides by the peripheral woodlands of the lordship when viewed from Castlefield.[694] The semi-fossilised nature of this Mediaeval landscape in 1630 is proven by the existence of a document dated 1463 which specifically refers to one of the two external launds to the park.[695]

This design of the landscape was deliberate. Amanda Richardson has shown a direct inter-relationship between park and palace and the romance literature of the day.[696] The ideal was for a park surrounded by woodlands with launds stretching out from the residence so that the wild wood was contrasted perfectly with the tamed landscape of the park in a conscious combination. Clipstone fits this ideal and in fact exceeded it by altering the appearance of the entire lordship, not just of the enclosed parkland. In every sense the *Gawain* poet once again portrayed an accurate representation of how the castle of Sir Bertilak standing on its hilltop was framed by the managed woodlands, park and water-filled moat around it:

> '*He became aware, in those woods, of high walls*
> *In a moat, on a mound, bordered by the boughs*
> *Of thick-trunked timber which trimmed the water.*
> *The most commanding castle a knight ever kept,*
> *Positioned on a site of sweeping parkland*
> *With a palisade of pikes pitched in the earth*
> *In the midst of tall trees for two miles or more.*
> *From the corner of his eye this castle became clearer*
> *As it sparkled and shone with shimmering oaks ...*'[697]
> '*Out of water of wondrous depth, the walls*
> *Then loomed overhead to heavenly height*'[698]

The similarities to Clipstone in this description of a fictional lordship are apparent. Gawain sees the castle standing on a mound just as the King's Houses stood on the summit of the hill. Bertilak's residence is surrounded by a moat analogous to the presence of the multiple lakes and ponds in the valleys of the Vicar Water and River Maun. The fictional castle has a direct inter-relationship with its wooded deer park surrounded by a pale fence in much the same way that the palace of Clipstone stood immediately adjacent to the park and was depicted in the early fifteenth century as having a pale constructed with sharpened stakes. he entire scene is bordered by a frame of wild woodlands out of which Gawain emerges into the civilised and managed landscape of Bertilak's lordship as a visitor to Clipstone must have viewed the countryside after riding through the surrounding woods to catch sight of the launds, park and palace reflected in the Great Pond.

The *Gawain* poet's impression of woodland is one of the dangerous and 'other'; the woods outside of the castle are alien, barbarian and uncivilised. This impression is first made through the terrifying appearance of the Green Knight as the personification of the wildness of the woods, then confirmed through Gawain's perilous journey through the wilderness and made absolutely explicit on his arrival at the Green Chapel: '*Green church? Chunters the knight. More like the devil's lair.*'[699] In the Mediaeval mind, the woods were quite sinister places. Leaves were depicted in Christian writings as metaphors for sin and lust, whilst the woods were places where the devil sought to ensnare the sinful; a latter day place of temptation analogous to the desert of the Bible. The popularity in Mediaeval ecclesiastical carving of wild men or 'woodwoses' and the green man hiding within or spewing forth foliage was brought about not as a result of a latent paganism and reflection of the concept of rebirth and renewal, but rather such figures represented visual warnings against the chaos, evil and temptation of the wild places. Indeed this link is made explicit in many early representations of the green man as he was depicted with devil's horns, such as the example on the chancel arch at Garway, Herefordshire.[700] Consequently, we must see the artfully designed landscape of Clipstone as a complex juxtaposition which balances the perceived threat of the wild wood against the harmonious management of the park and palace and in this way it becomes a metaphor for the good management of the kingdom.

Despite this idealised and romanticised symbolic stage management, the landscape that framed the aesthetic views at Clipstone still provided a pragmatic purpose. We have already studied the very practical realities of the use of the fishponds and woodlands, and the launds may have been used for grazing, a habitat for edible birds, orchards, exercising horses and hunting;[701] they were also probably the location for Edward III's tournaments of 1327 and 1328.

Although there was no apparent pattern in the relationship of palaces to parks – Clarendon in the centre, Woodstock to the east, Gillingham to the west[702] – the location of the King's Houses to the south of the village and with the deer park to the north-east is reminiscent of Somersham in Cambridgeshire which stood in a very similar managed landscape. Owned by the Bishops of Ely from 1109, Somersham Palace lay to the south of the east-west orientated linear village and was approached from a causeway between two fishponds, one of which measured approximately 100 by 150 metres. The palace enclosure was enormous – by the sixteenth century it covered some 8.6 acres and was surrounded by a very large moat which was up to 22 metres in width. The very developed aquatic landscape at Somersham can be perhaps partially explained by its location in the fenlands, with a spot height of just 10 metres above sea level. However, it cannot be denied that the use of combined ponds and moats provided a very eye-catching seigneurial landscape. The palace itself sat in the north-east corner of a 621 acre deer park which lay upon higher ground that would have afforded majestic views back over the designed landscape below.[703] Meanwhile, in Wiltshire, visitors to Clarendon Park were required to pass through an enormous managed landscape lying underneath the palace buildings and the specific access routes, which may have been prescribed relating to elite status, was designed to intimidate.[704]

Somersham, Clarendon and Clipstone were not special in realising a concept of landscape vistas in the Mediaeval period; rather, they were typical in being designed with their wider landscapes specifically in mind. What is distinctive here is the sheer *scale* of the private, managed landscape around the palace. The precise chronology of this stage management is not fully understood and it is worth considering that the landscape may have been developed in a piecemeal fashion and that there may not have been a single architect.[705] Despite this, the King's Houses and Clipstone Park were created to take advantage of their wider landscape setting – ultimately the end product as interpreted through the semi-fossilised landscape represented by the 1630 map is one of a harmonious process of creation that possibly took place over several centuries.

Chapter Seven

The People of the Palace

'*The lower orders, peasants, artisans, even wage earners, had their own interests, which often diverged from those of the ruling elite, and while they laboured under many disadvantages, they were able to check and restrain, sometimes even reverse the actions of the aristocracy.*'
~ Christopher Dyer, 2000, *Everyday Life in Medieval England* ~

The Village of Clipstone

The word 'peasant' is problematic. It can be interpreted in a pejorative sense and it can often be imbued with condescension to describe a little people with little power leading a little life. We should be extremely cautious in taking this view as the picture was one of much greater complexity. The word derives from the Anglo-Norman 'pais' meaning country, which ultimately comes from the Latin 'pagus' which referred to a country district. It was first recorded towards the end of the Mediaeval period, during the fifteenth century,[706] and peasants have been defined by Christopher Dyer as '*small-scale rural cultivators, occupying a relatively subordinate social position, and having relatively low incomes*'. Over 80 per cent of the Mediaeval population fell into the category of peasants,[707] although as we have seen the fourteenth century altered the terms of both economy and society so the picture was not one of inertia, and social mobility began to be more common during the later Mediaeval era. However, at Clipstone the life of the ordinary people was relatively static throughout the period that the Plantagenents occupied the palace, and even between the fifteenth and seventeenth centuries the peasant existence remained one that would be recognisable to someone in the thirteenth century. Essentially they were not a free people – they could not own land, were not free to move between estates, paid rent on their homes, were committed to unpaid labour on the demesne land of the king, ground their cereal crops for a payment at the estate mill and even at the end of their lives had to pay a death duty, known as the 'heriot', of their most prized possession or animal.[708]

The presence of the King's Houses had a widespread impact on the ordinary lives of the village inhabitants as such rural residences also functioned as manorial centres with a small permanent staff of occupants to administer the estate.[709] Many locals would have found gainful employment as a result of the palace such as the king's foot messengers (known as 'cursers') William Warsop in 1306, Nicholas de Clipstone in 1313–14 and Robert de Warsop who was paid £18 8s in 1328–9 and again in 1339 for shoe money after several years of wear. In 1208 a messenger took 16 days to travel from Clipstone to York to collect saddles and cloths for the king's use.[710] For the majority though, life was intimately connected to the land owned by the king. Indeed, Thoroton mentioned several of these individuals who lived at Clipstone during the turbulent fourteenth century. In 1336 Peter Witheberd held two messuages and two and a half bovates of land for the cash rent of 2s 6d per annum, whereas his son William was fined in 1384 for handing over a bovate to his younger brother John without a licence from the king.[711] In the following century, John Bever of Clipstone rented a similar parcel of a toft and one bovate for 12d a year during 1409–10.[712]

George Sanderson's map of 1835 *Twenty miles around Mansfield* indicates that the villages within the area of Sherwood Forest were nucleated and distributed along the river valleys.[713] In an area of relatively poor quality free-draining soils which did not retain enormous amounts of water in its rivers this was a very practical reaction by communities who clustered together, maximised their shared plough teams, and communally utilised the limited water sources. It is debateable exactly when the present village conjoined the earlier centres, on Squires Lane and around the mill, by occupying the land directly to the north of Mansfield Road with the properties stretching back down to the banks of the River Maun. It is possible that the establishment of either the mid-twelfth century hunting lodge or slightly later palace helped to focus a planned settlement which may have been laid out on either the instructions of the monarchy or equally plausibly by common consent of the community. A second period that is also possible for the regular design of the settlement to have been reorganised was after the disastrous village fire recorded in 1221 when the keeper Brian de Insula was ordered to view the damage and allow the men of Clipstone an allowance of building wood to make repairs.[714]

Senior's map of 1630 is the first to give us a clear picture of what the late Mediaeval landscape of Clipstone looked like (Plate 11A). We have to be extremely cautious in assuming that it represents an accurately fossilised depiction of what the estate looked like throughout the entire Mediaeval period, but the presence of the royal estate does appear to have mitigated against dramatic change and left a partially preserved earlier landscape well into the mid-seventeenth century. The road systems can be read against those of today as what became Squires Lane existed and ran as far as the deer park and edge of the north-western laund. Gorsethorpe Lane was merely a route down to the river and across a bridge to the Millfield. There does not appear to have been a direct short track that led around the deer park to Warsop in this direction, as there was from the eighteenth century, the latter being reached via a track running across the Broomhill and connecting with a way along the northern boundary of the lordship via St Edwin's Chapel. Both Squires Lane and Gorsethorpe Lane branched off from a small triangular space which interconnected with the Rathole leading off to the south-west and the main street through the village to the east. This central junction was a sub-triangular space which may have functioned as a simple, informal local marketplace operating without a charter where the residents could sell their surplus stock. The Rathole sits in a deep Holloway and skirted around the north-western edge of the palace enclosure and then headed across the Waterfield before running off to the White Gate entrance to the park. In the opposite direction the village street, now known as Mansfield Road, led between the peasant community houses to the north and the palace to the south before running over Clipstone Dam and off between the coneygarth and Crossfield. Within the village itself tracks went down to the water sources. One led, between the main palace enclosure and a triangular portion of land reached, down to the shore of the Great Pond; whilst another lane headed north, between two properties down to the Maun. The only regular street that would have received maintenance according to the presence of potholes, weathered surfaces and erosion of sections of the way[715] was the main road through the village. Other routes were simply informal routes between plots or a mass of tracks and green lanes acting as access between watersources, fields, pasture, meadow, waste and woodland.

The areas of settlement, defined by narrow linear hurdles or hedges, were known as either tofts or messuages and stretched back from the road edges with the peasant dwellings lining the front of the street. There were a number of principal areas of occupation. To the extreme west were three long and wide divisions out beyond Hall Close that may have originated as enclosed strips in the Waterfield of which just one had a building located within it. A further three dwellings in irregular plots of land were drawn by Senior immediately to the west of the possible market place. To the south of the main road was the palace compound. A rectangular enclosure that projected out into the village street was probably the village pinfold used for penning stray animals, although this may have been a post-Mediaeval creation. The main distribution of village residences lay in a neat row of fifteen tofts along the north side of Mansfield Road which stretched right down to the resources offered by the river to the rear. Two of the properties had two buildings shown within, all of the others had just a single dwelling depicted. There were two empty tofts one of which had an area of land that wrapped around the back of its neighbour and may have represented a former enlargement that had subsequently become disused. Three outlying buildings were located on the opposite side of the Vicar Water dam to the village. A further three buildings spanned the course of the River Maun to the east of the village and these probably related to the presence of the watermill. Additional water channels known as mill leets required extensive surveying and sophisticated engineering and were intended to concentrate the small volumes of water produced by the Maun and Vicar Water so that they ran along the contours. The manorial court demanded that all peasants ground their cereal crops at the mill which provided the opportunity to exact a toll that brought an income to the crown. A secondary opportunity for money-making came from rents charged to the miller.[716]

There were twenty-six occupied plots of land in the village of Clipstone in 1630 which probably equated to a population of around 100–130 – an equivalent to the number of people in the village prior to the depletions of the fourteenth century. Although recovery had occurred by the seventeenth century, the population was still limited to just 134 in the early eighteenth century and only began to substantially rise in the nineteenth century, in line with a national increase. Census data reveals an 1871 population of 220 increasing to 256 ten years later. This Mediaeval agrarian system allowed a moment of fairly static planforms within the village that only began to see substantial alteration as the system itself changed[717] from largely arable to largely pastoral, from open fields to enclosure, from labour intensive to fewer workers required, from a subsistence feudal economy to a cash economy based on surplus and rents. The latter had certainly come into being by the mid-fourteenth century at Clipstone, however some of the other changes took until the late seventeenth and eighteenth centuries. Nucleated village plans survived longest in regions where the open field system survived the longest[718] as it did at Clipstone well into the seventeenth century. The introduction of new property boundaries in the settlement indicated a subdivision to smaller spaces whereas conversely the removal of such boundaries might indicate the need or opportunity for larger spaces so that the village plan was inherently dynamic. A hypothetical situation for such a story is the case of the Witheberds where Peter left his eldest son a parcel of land which William then appears to have subdivided to cater to the needs of his younger brother John. This was perhaps related to a rising population and their need for land. Later in time the population depletions created by repeated outbreaks of pestilence led to the opportunity for more wealthy tenants to combine plots of ground into single larger entities.

The boundary hedges around the village properties were probably limited in height so as to allow the free passage of deer unhindered by obstacle,[719] and of course under Forest Law the animals were strictly off limits for the peasants to hunt even when the deer were consuming produce in their fields and gardens. The food grown within the tofts included '*onions, garlic, leeks, cabbage, peas, spinach, beans, parsley and borage*' alongside fruits and nuts like hazel, walnut, plums, cherries, pears and apples. Pens would be provided for horses, cattle, pigs, geese and chickens whilst other areas would be devoted to pits for rubbish. Those tofts which were empty would probably have been utilised in their entirety for livestock and gardens although may have been returned to occupation as dwellings at later times.[720]

It used to be thought that the majority of Mediaeval rural peasant houses were poor quality structures erected by the occupants themselves out of locally sourced and inexpensive building materials which have left little trace in the architectural and archaeological record. Trevor Rowley made much of buildings at Old Wittam, Lincolnshire described as '*old hovels, decayed beams and half-destroyed walls*' by contemporaries.[721] This characterisation compares favourably to William White's early nineteenth century summary that Clipstone was the most decayed village in Bassetlaw. Archaeologically, fingers were pointed to houses excavated at Wharram Percy, Yorkshire that were found to be just ten by twenty feet or an example at Seacourt in Berkshire which was even smaller at ten by twelve feet in dimension. An interpretation held for many years in which it was believed that peasants lived a very impoverished and architecturally meagre existence until the reorganisation of agriculture in the late Mediaeval period began to lead to the creation of more substantial buildings. Most commonly these were the cruck frame structures seen across the Midlands which could be as small as a single bay, heated and lit by an open hearth and open to the roof structure.[722]

A reason for thinking that the peasants lived in what were effectively hovels was the interpretation that the commoners were all at a single, dire socio-economic level and were responsible for paying for their own construction and maintenance regime that was enforced (in the courts when necessary) by the landowning elite. The argument ran that the substantial housing stock which survives from the fifteenth and sixteenth centuries was constructed by a peasantry made wealthy after the Black Death before which they lived in ephemeral structures which left little trace. This picture has been challenged by Dyer who pointed out that within peasant society there were varying levels of wealth, building materials were often granted by landowners from their woodland estates in order to ensure that their workers were suitably provided for, and skilled carpenters were usually contracted by the peasants themselves as they were simply too busy with their own agricultural activities to spend time on advanced methods of construction.[723] Documentary analysis of building descriptions in the Midlands has shown that up to eighty per cent of peasant buildings were really quite substantial buildings of two or three bays in length equating to 13.8 by 4.6 metres in dimension and consisting of a hall, chamber and service with external animal byres, barns, granaries and perhaps additional combinations of bakehouse, brewhouse, stable, pig sty, workshop, dovecote, cart and wood stores.[724] A three bay structure required around twenty trees that might cost somewhere in the region of 10s, equating to forty days of wages for a labourer; and a similar cost of 9s 10d was paid to a carpenter to build such a house at Pattingham, Staffordshire in 1444. It has been estimated that a complete new build house in the mid-fifteenth century would cost at least £2 and up to £4 – a very significant investment in a substantial dwelling by a peasant and equivalent to the annual wages for a carpenter or the price of six oxen or thirty sheep.[725] Although the vast majority of surviving peasant buildings date from the late Mediaeval era, they were not necessarily preserved because of a great rebuilding using more durable materials and styles. Evidence suggests that the cruck houses of the earlier period were every bit as substantial, however the design of the cruck frames did not allow for an upper floor to be inserted as easily as the later box frame style of vernacular architecture and were therefore often demolished and replaced. Documentary and archaeological research has shown that thirteenth century properties were of similar dimensions to those of the fourteenth and fifteenth centuries and a range of costs were incurred during construction from as little as 10s stretching right up to as much as £2. Equally, the paucity of timber buildings within Nottinghamshire in particular could also relate to the surprising longevity of earth-fast structures which went out of fashion elsewhere due to the practical problem of rotting posts around the year 1200, yet seem to have remained in popularity throughout the East Midlands.[726]

Based on studies of surviving buildings from the thirteenth to sixteenth centuries in Nottinghamshire, the presumed architecture of much of Mediaeval Clipstone would have been single storey timber-framed buildings. Timber was expensive to transport and must have been obtained locally and under licence from royal officials. The nurture of a mature oak tree on the Sherwood sandstones was a significant investment taking around two hundred years to reach full maturity, at which point it could be expected to be perhaps twenty metres in height.[727]

It is not possible to comment on the vernacular architectural style of the twelfth century in Nottinghamshire. However, the surviving examples of buildings from the thirteenth and fourteenth centuries point towards the rarity of upper floors until they began to be inserted into older buildings during the fifteenth and sixteenth centuries[728] and were then built as a matter of course from the later sixteenth century. The ground floor open hall was the norm for those that could afford them, such as the simple two bay structure at the Old White Hart, Newark. Floors were constructed from a variety of materials – flagstones, tiles or beaten earth mixed with ox blood, lime or gypsum plaster. Open hearths provided warmth and rudimentary lighting, the smoke was allowed to drift up through the thatch or in higher status properties through a louvre. A slightly elaborated planform constructed in 1266 at The Gables, Little Carlton incorporated a single aisle and cross-passage which then had a service wing and solar added c 1540[729] and marked the beginnings of the separation of rooms for specific purposes in vernacular architecture. In Nottinghamshire crown-post roofs were the most popular form of roof structure until the sixteenth century when the clasped-purlin roof took over. The earliest crown-post roof is the Old White Hart, Newark, dated to 1313; the very latest is from the 1460s at the Saracen's Head, Southwell, whereas the earliest known clasped-purlin roof is the Woolpack, Newark (now the Prince Rupert) which originated as a Wealden-style townhouse dated c 1452.[730]

Lower down the social scale, Mediaeval cruck frame buildings were prevalent and these were found throughout the county from the Wolds, in the south, all the way up to Yorkshire. Sadly, many have been demolished including those at Glapton, Sutton Bonington and Kirkby-in-Ashfield. However, surviving examples can be seen at The Hollies, Bathley (dated 1295–6), TIL House, Clifton (dated 1319)[731] and the sixteenth century Cruck Cottage, Skegby. The survival of the infill of wall structures is rare in the county because wattle and daub does not commonly survive, and alternatives were often used such as lath and plaster at the Woolpack, Newark or even stone slabs at the Saracen's Head, Southwell and roof tiles at South Muskham Prebend.[732] Given that the north-west of the county, and in particular Mansfield, is characterised by stone vernacular architecture it is possible that some of the village buildings at Clipstone could have been masonry structures, and at the very least stone groundwalls would have been a common sight from the end of the twelfth century. This was especially true during the post-Mediaeval period when the disused palace acted as a quarry.

One of the Mediaeval peasant houses at Clipstone may have survived, at least in outline, and is now known as Rauceby which stands on the north side of Mansfield Road, a little to the east of the former palace gatehouse complex. A standing building survey of the property would be beneficial to confirm or deny this likelihood, as the orientation of Rauceby matches that of a property standing directly opposite the north end of Dam Close in 1766 and a building was also marked in this precise location on the 1630 map (Plate 11 B). It seems probable that the footprint of Rauceby survived the aggressive re-planning of the village in the early nineteenth century and was standing at least as early as the mid-eighteenth century. Although Rauceby is now a characteristically post-Mediaeval brick and pantile cottage, it has a low groundwall of stone that may have originated as the sill for a timber framed house which was later either rebuilt or clad with brick. The groundwall is also noticeably lower than the surrounding ground level, again suggesting a degree of antiquity.

Furnishings within buildings were sparse – simply constructed tables, stools, perhaps a chair and a chest containing linen characterised a lifestyle that was dominated by perishable objects made of wood and basketry[733] which do not survive in the archaeological record of the acidic soils of the Sherwood region. Households generally relied on just a single functional cooking pot, bought at local market places such as the one in the village or perhaps Warsop or Mansfield, for holding liquid-based meals such as soups and pottage. The markets also provided villagers like the Witheberds with places to sell their own surplus produce including honey, wax, eggs, apples, poultry and vegetables to help with cash rents due to the Crown.[734]

Agriculture

Arable farming underpinned both the subsistence of the majority of the population and the landed wealth of a very small minority of clergy, aristocrats, and gentry during most of the Mediaeval period in the Midlands. This configuration only began to alter during the second half of the fourteenth century as demesne land farming decreased and pastoral farming began to grow.[735] The farming year revolved around ploughing in winter, harrowing and sowing in early spring, followed by weeding in the fields and haymaking in the pastures before harvest in the summer. During the twelfth and thirteenth century obligations were paid to the Crown in the form of agricultural service which was replaced by cash rents from the beginning of the fourteenth century.[736]

The fields were large and unenclosed, quite unlike those that we are used to seeing in the modern landscape, as they consisted of irregular strips grouped together to form very large expanses of ploughed land bounded by hedges bordering the outer limit of each of the open fields. The strips were tenanted by neighbours and an individual's landholding would be scattered throughout the open fields, which were in turn farmed on a rotational system that could pivot around both the strips and fields. Managing annual cycles of fallow land helped to increase the fertility of the soils. Stock would be raised on both pasture and waste as well as on the fallow fields where their manure would help to promote soil fertility. The strips were ploughed towards their centre leaving characteristic S-shaped curves related to the progress of the oxen team which left a ridge and furrow pattern often left fossilised in their final incarnation as arable fields prior to alternative uses, usually as pastoral land. The ridges were favoured as they increased the land surface available, acted as property boundaries and eased the drainage of the fields. The earthwork furrows are not necessarily contiguous with the individual landholder's strips, but there was usually an element of relationship and all of this was administered and kept in check by the manorial court.[737]

The Mediaeval arable system was rotational, based on multiple fields which could number between two and five, although two or three were the most usual. Analysis of the three fields located at Cuxham, Oxfordshire has shown that each field was sown with a winter crop one year, a spring crop in the second year and was left fallow during the third.[738] Winter sown wheat was the most valuable crop as it was the staple for making bread, but spring sown oats were also grown for animal fodder and barley was primarily used for making ale.[739] The size of the fields could vary enormously – Anglo-Saxon fields were probably smaller units than those of the Mediaeval period due to a lower population. The general rise in numbers of people, coupled with the nucleation of villages, led to an overworking of the land closest to settlements and a need for the extension of the size of the open fields to compensate.[740]

By 1630 there were four principal fields at Clipstone, which probably reflects only a semi-fossilised landscape from the Mediaeval period. To the south of the village was the Waterfield which had been partially enclosed to the west and south. Limited archaeological test-pitting of the sports field to the south of Squires Lane, which was part of the western enclosure, confirmed that this area was originally part of the open fields,[741] with indicative Mediaeval pottery ending up in the soils as a result of manure carted out from deposits within the tofts that often incorporated waste ceramics thrown out with the nightsoil. The northern end of the Waterfield was a separate enclosure which was probably originally part of the demesne land of the palace cultivated specifically to provide food for the royal household. Test-pitting of this land showed a stratigraphy of modern soils overlying earlier ploughsoils which lay directly on top of natural sands and gravels. Within the historic ploughsoils the only finds consisted of heavily abraded Mediaeval pottery, suggesting that this area was under arable use and was never under occupation.[742] To the north-east and north-west of the village were the Crossfield and Millfield which were largely untouched areas of arable land. It stands to reason then that Mediaeval Clipstone was probably farmed on a three-field system – the Waterfield (named after the Vicar Water), Crossfield (named after a nearby crossroad of trackways) and Millfield (named for its proximity to the village mill). The majority of Midlands estates operated on the two-field system but three fields were sometimes favoured to link in more closely with the three-course crop rotation or to increase the amount of land under cultivation.[743]

In the High Forest area of Sherwood the open fields accounted for approximately twenty per cent of the total area of the manors and the poor quality soils coupled with low population led to the adoption of the infield-outfield system.[744] This arrangement relied on permanent cultivation of the infield which was closest to the village settlement and the temporary ploughing of the outer fields cultivated alternately with one area being left fallow for several years to recover through manuring during the pasture of animals. Such a system has been identified from historic mapping at nearby Carburton. Carburton, located seven miles to the north of Clipstone, had three small enclosures close to the village centre under permanent arable use with the rest of the parish as temporary outfields to the south known as 'brecks' – common land used mainly for pasture but which occasionally came under the plough when required.[745] Such a system was certainly in existence at Clipstone by the early seventeenth century, as a plot of cultivated ground immediately to the north of the Millfield was called 'The Breake' indicating the adoption of infield-outfield farming which plausibly began during the Mediaeval period.

Within the estate, peasant farmers were highly mobile and were reliant on walking between their homes and the varied strips out in the arable fields, to the open pastures and woodlands alongside trips to the mill, markets, manor court and church. The land of Clipstone was therefore more accessible during the Mediaeval period than at any subsequent time because the privatised enclosure of both fields and woodlands put much of the land off limits.[746]

The food and drink produced by the peasant community in the fields and tofts were based on cereals grown for use in ale, bread and pottage alongside vegetables such as peas, beans, onions and brassica. This was perhaps complemented by cheese, milk and honey. Meat was a rare commodity and the presence of animal bone may be equally indicative of their use in soups, stock and pottage as much as actual flesh consumption. Fowl were primarily kept for eggs although birds such as rooks may have been consumed in pies. The staple diet relied upon fish, bacon, sausages and eggs, with grain, pulses and legumes made into pottage together with a very gritty bread baked from wheat with either rye or barley. Ultimately the peasant diet was low in saturated fats and high in fibre, and was subject to seasonal variation but was low in both vitamins and calories[747] – the latter ably added to by the drinking of ale. Significantly the origins of the names given to foods derive from Norman French as opposed to the words used to describe animals which all came from Old English. The Norman-speaking, aristocratic viewpoint was one of high levels of meat consumption whereas the English peasant experience was more aligned to the rearing of the live animal. Consequently we have *beef, pork* and *mutton* which originate in the Norman language whilst *cow, pig* and *sheep* come from the English language.

To the south of the coneygarth the 1630 map shows an enclosure of approximately twenty-six acres named Swine Cote Hill which formerly operated as a Mediaeval pig farm supplying the palace. Pig bones were discovered at the King's Houses during the 2011 excavations and are redolent of a payment of 10s 10d to William Brewer, Sheriff of Nottingham, made in 1201 for the transport of bacon from Clipstone to Northampton.[748] Only five bones were confidently identified as being from pigs and it is notable that this animal was also the least abundant in the domestic bone assemblage at Clarendon, although evidence of three suckling pigs from the north kitchen there was suggestive that they were indeed consumed.[749] Beyond the Swinecote, the pasturing of pigs, known as pannage, was allowed within the park and woodlands during good mast seasons[750] as it still is within the New Forest in Hampshire.

Subsistence, or near-subsistence, farming was the pattern of existence across England until the thirteenth century and the ideal pattern of tenant farming was the even distribution of land across varied types of soils in the lordship. Peasant farmers could have access to very diverse sizes of landholding, from a mere one or two acres up to quite substantial estates of forty to fifty acres, with an average of between five and thirty acres.[751] However over time the pattern of landholding altered as the amalgamation and swapping of strips began to occur. From the fourteenth century, there was a desire to create consolidated packages of land through sale and exchanges by private agreement[752] and although the open field system stubbornly remained at Clipstone, as enclosure required the compliance of everyone working in the system, it did gradually begin to become of a feature of the agrarian economy.[753]

It is not possible to be precise about exactly when enclosure of the open fields began to occur, however by 1630 the process was underway as exemplified through the existence of closes to the south and west of the Waterfield. The enclosures had significantly impacted upon the size of arable land available, perhaps resulting in bringing the former coneygarth into the ploughland. Enclosure came about as a result of many factors during the late Mediaeval period such as rising wages, exhaustion of the soils, and a booming textile industry that was reliant on less labour to manage flocks of sheep reared for their wool. This was not necessarily a direct result of the Black Death (although the reduced population did seem to hasten the process) as the amount of common arable land and demesne land was already beginning to shrink across the country during the earlier fourteenth century. The process tended to make initial inroads across England in areas of poor quality soils, such as Devon, than it did in the fertile Midlands which saw slower diversification and the continuation of open field systems for a lot longer.[754] The free-draining soils of the Sherwood area were not of exceptional quality, and inevitably Clipstone began to succumb to the process.

Archaeologically this type of early private enclosure can be identified by examining early maps which show new field patterns conforming to the pre-existing open field strips which had a characteristic S-shape curve. Later, Parliamentary enclosure of the eighteenth and nineteenth centuries tended to be far more formal in the creation of regularised square or rectangular plots of ground which bore no resemblance to the earlier open field systems.[755] Consequently it is possible to interpret the three long and narrow closes to the west of Hall Close drawn in 1630 as having potentially derived from enclosure of the strips of the open field system. The more detailed 1766 estate map also reveals closes which fossilised the earlier land boundaries, in particular to the south-west of the former Waterfield, the middle section of what had been the Crossfield and possibly the north-east of the old Millfield and the coneygarth.

Alongside the preponderance for the enclosure of open fields, the woods were also under threat during the late Mediaeval era as areas of trees were cleared to increase the amount of land available for both arable and pasture. This process, known as assarting, became increasingly common across Sherwood Forest. Assarts were added to the older core of open fields so that historic maps often show an outer ring of hedged fields surrounding an inner block of earlier open fields.[756] This phenomenon was possibly present in 1630 in the two enclosures known as Wood Close to the south of the Waterfield which were probably carved out of Fless-Greave Wood. It had certainly occurred in the north of the estate where an area specifically titled 'The Asserte' lay to the north-east of the Broomhill waste and must have been added to the Millfield and its breck during a time of agricultural necessity. It is worth noting that the assart was cut out from the wood of Clipstone Hollins but had subsequently been allowed to be re-wooded as the need for extra land diminished.

Common Rights

We know something of the common rights enjoyed by the local peasant communities largely from the pleas and court cases in which they sought to preserve them. During his 1200 visit to Clipstone King John was petitioned by the men of Mansfield over their loss of common pasture rights within the lands enclosed by Henry II in the park. John demanded a fine of 15 marks for the renewal of the rights but no record of its payment is ever made.[757] A more specific indication of what exactly these rights entailed comes from the enquiries surrounding the foundation of the peel. The men of Mansfield Woodhouse complained at the loss of timber for hedging and building, alongside losing areas of wood and waste pasture for their animals. In 1327–8 a degree of collusion between the men of Mansfield Woodhouse, Warsop and Clipstone must be assumed as they all took advantage of Edward III's visit to Clipstone very early on in his reign to present their grievances against his father. Their complaints had some variation – Clipstone had lost common rights of pasture in the park, Mansfield Woodhouse and Warsop had lost lands due to extensions to the park. The men of Clipstone were given alternative pasture rights in Birklands and their historic rights to gather ferns and leaves in the park were renewed.[758] What is apparent is that the presence of the deer park and especially the Forest Law had a controlling influence on many aspects of daily life in Clipstone. Although some concessions were granted to the peasantry by the monarchy these were of a practical nature to ensure that the estate remained well managed and concerned the provision of building materials for the construction of living quarters and agricultural buildings, coppiced timber for making property boundaries and permissions to gather brushwood for fuel as well as leaves and ferns for bedding. Animals were allowed to pasture in the royal enclosures so long as there was no inherent danger to the grazing resources of the deer herd and in times of poor growth the deer were given priority.

Forest Law specifically forbade anyone without full royal authority to hunt in Sherwood. Prior to the establishment of this law peasants had been free to hunt animals that strayed onto their land and the prohibition became a problem for both survival, through supplementing meat intake, and utility for farmers whose crops were regularly grazed by wild animals that they were helpless to deter. The maximum penalty for killing a deer was the sentence of blinding and castration brought in during 1198, although there is no evidence that it was ever used as punishment for poaching and fines or imprisonment were far more usual.[759] Nevertheless both transgressive poaching of deer parks and opportunistic scavenging of dead deer was just too much of a temptation for many peasants living a near-subsistence existence[760] and it comes as little surprise to read that Henry Curson of Breadsall was charged with killing a hind in Clipstone Wood in 1334.[761] Reports of poaching in Sherwood Forest included a description of two brothers who set snares '*placed in such a way to strangle the animal*' and court documents referring to poaching made it clear that peasants hunted on foot, often with dogs, and made extensive use of snares that were placed either high enough to entangle the antlers or neck and others placed ground ropes and cords to trap the animals hooves. The late Mediaeval poem *The Parlement of the Thre Ages* is emphatic that the poachers, by nature, had to operate stealthily and wore camouflaged clothing festooned with foliage.[762]

Low status participants could legitimately join the hunt as paid, skilful retainers of their lords and it was those men who provided the majority of the meat eaten at feasts and ensured that the vermin population of the woods was controlled. In the twelfth century *Tristan* poem there is a clear division of purpose in hunting between the king and his retinue who hunt very ostentatiously for recreation whilst the professional huntsman, Orri, hunts much more stealthily to stock the royal larders. Anglo-Saxon descriptions of hunting show that the populace relied on dismounted hunters using nets and dogs in a drive hunt as depicted in the Bayeux Tapestry. This type of quietly efficient hunting was no doubt the mainstay of peasant techniques which has not been registered in the contemporary aristocratic manuals and tracts that were far more concerned with recreation and the status of hunting. The business of a professional huntsman was a potentially lucrative one as they were paid up to 8d a day – twice the mid-fourteenth daily rate of a mason or carpenter and equivalent to the wages of a knight.[763]

Ultimately the Forest Law was a constant source of tension in Mediaeval society. Despite the imposition of the Charter of the Forest in 1217, and its eventual full adoption during the fourteenth century, the peasant communities did not benefit as the laws were upheld by the barons for themselves. As Griffin puts it: '*for the small hunter, depressingly little changed. Thousands of acres were removed from the royal forests and returned to the commonalty in the thirteenth century, yet it hardly heralded the dawn of a new era of hunting for all*'.[764] For those living outside of the forest, the Game Laws of 1390 forever installed the hunt as the prerogative of the upper classes, and for those within Sherwood the forest remained legally intact until 1818.

Small wonder then that the fourteenth century – characterised by climatic change, famine, pestilence, rising prices, the Poll Tax, warfare and rebellion – was the period which saw the literary debut of the Robin Hood myth. The very first reference to the heroic outlaw comes from William Langland's *The Vision of Piers Plowman* written circa 1377 in which an indolent priest confesses that he cannot recite the Lord's Prayer but does know '*rhymes of Robin Hood*'.[765] The impression is that by this point in time the stories were already widely in oral circulation. Clipstone itself was linked to the legend much later when Spencer T. Hall's 1841 book, *Forester's Offering*, connected the royal visits to the palace to the story about the meeting between Robin Hood and the king, and the action was located at the King's Houses. The chapter entitled *The Outlaws' Excursion to Clipstone* related that it was based on stories current in the nineteenth century forest villages, which notably placed the narrative during the reign of Edward I rather than those of Richard or John.[766] Many of the earliest accounts of the legend, such as Walter Bower's *Scotchichronicon*, written in the 1440s, put the stories during the reigns of Henry III or Edward I. Bower described Robin as a very pious outlaw alive in 1266; a significant year that fell just after the defeat of Simon de Montfort at the battle of Evesham during his attempt to replace the monarchy with a parliament assembly. Robin and his band of outlaws can be seen in the light of de Montfort's disinherited followers, such as the very real Roger Godberd, who terrorised much of the East Midlands from his base in Sherwood until his capture in 1272.[767]

The first fully-fledged and detailed accounts of the legend *A Gest of Robyn*

Hode and *Robin Hood and the Potter* date to the later fifteenth century. The character of these stories is slightly at odds with the popular modern renditions; again the setting was the reign of Edward I and the action takes place between South Yorkshire and Nottinghamshire through the forests of Barnsdale and Sherwood. Robin was not a dispossessed Saxon nobleman leading a resistance movement against an oppressive Norman regime charging exorbitant taxes. The outlaw was described as a former yeoman who lived in the woods with his band of men and there was no outright altruistic motive of robbing the rich to give to the poor.[768] The notion of the Saxon freedom fighter was blended in during the sixteenth century from tales of the real eleventh century fenland rebel Hereward the Wake, alongside the idea of Robin as a former aristocrat who slipped into redistributing wealth after he lost his own lands.[769] Despite this late development, the early tales made it clear that Robin's arch nemesis was usually the grasping Sheriff of Nottingham, and the outlaw was often presented as a man sympathetic to the downtrodden, such as the poor knight Sir Richard at the Lee. Pointedly, Robin was always steadfastly loyal to the rightful king whose authority was never challenged by the outlaws; rather it was the evil servants of the Crown who the band laboured against. Obviously this motif was bound by the social constrictions of the day and Robin was usually taken into the service of the king once the righteousness of his cause was established.

There is here a kernel of truthful Mediaeval experience in which landlords enlisted trusted members of the peasantry into their service as '*court officials, the jurors, chief pledges, ale-tasters and affeerers*' and this mechanism of power-sharing actually made the exploitation of the common workforce for the profit of a landowner a viable socio-economic system.[770] Perhaps here we can see something of the struggle of Robert de Clipstone who fought against what he saw as the social injustice of the establishment of the peel and extension of the royal enclosures at the expense of the common rights of the local people in the early fourteenth century. Whilst it is going too far to suggest that Robert was a model for Robin Hood, his story does show certain similarities. Robert was an ordinary man from Sherwood Forest who stood up to the power of the monarchy to promote the well-being of the peasants against an unfair reduction of their rights. So determined was de Clipstone that he appeared in front of Edward III to plead his case and was not only successful, but was later promoted to the post of keeper of the manor and park of

Clipstone. Robert's struggle illustrates the everyday conflict between classes in a region dominated by draconian laws that dictated so much of which resources were, and crucially were not, available to the common people. One of the defining features of all myths is that they speak loudly of the time in which they were created, yet do so from a point of view set in the past. The early tales of Robin Hood, set in the thirteenth century, fit this characteristic as the stories began to circulate as a result of the very real turbulent experiences of fourteenth century Sherwood.

Chapter Eight

The Decline of the Palace:
1399–1568

'ther is in great dekay & ruyne in stonework tymber lede and plaster'
~ Survey of the manor of Clipstone, 1525 ~

William Senior's map of 1630 shows that the Mannorgarth was largely devoid of buildings by the early seventeenth century and that the great list of structures known from the late fourteenth century accounts had been largely demolished. Three cottages lined the south side of the road, the central one almost certainly on the site of the palace gatehouse, and King John's Palace was shown in isolation as a roofless building with two steeply pitched gable ends. Henry II's hall, built in the mid-twelfth century French style, was well on the way to becoming the three-walled, rubble core fragment that we can see today. The reasons for this decline stretched back to the heyday of the King's Houses in the fourteenth century, as Edward II began to focus on south-eastern residences by acquiring and developing sites such as Kings Langley (Hertfordshire), Eltham (Kent), Byfleet, and Sheen (Surrey). This pattern was continued under Edward III who added to the royal residences by procuring Foliejohn, Hampstead Marshall and Wychmere in Berkshire, East Worldham in Hampshire, and Rotherhithe in Surrey. Meanwhile he spent increasing amounts on existing properties at Sheen, Havering, Hadleigh, Queenborough, Easthampstead and Windsor. Richard II maintained strong affiliations with his childhood home at Kennington and his summer house on the Thames at Sheen.[771] Within Sherwood Forest the establishment of Bestwood Park in 1349, with its lodge that was so much closer to Nottingham, may have led to the decline in popularity of Clipstone which is clear from the dwindling visitations by the monarchy from the mid-1340s.

The toppling of Richard II in 1399 led to a pivotal swing in interest away from the former Plantagenet residences under Henry IV. Sites such as Leicester were of greater importance to this new royal house which had acquired the castle after the marriage of John of Gaunt to Henry of Grosmont's heiress daughter. This began the favouritism shown towards an alternative residence within the East Midlands at the expense of Clipstone alongside the rebuilding of Kenilworth in the West Midlands. Meanwhile, the favoured south-eastern palaces continued in popularity as Henry chose Eltham as the location for his marriage by proxy to Joan of Navarre in 1402 and held a total of five Christmas feasts there.[772] The Lancastrian kings spent very little time in the midlands or the north preferring to concentrate their time and political energies in the south or in France. Even their own manors in Derbyshire, such as Belper and Ravensdale, saw minimal expenditure in the fifteenth century.[773] Clipstone itself was granted to George Dunbar in 1401, within the first two years of Henry IV's reign, along with Somerton Castle.[774] Dunbar had recently absconded from Scotland after a perceived slight to his family when Archibald Douglas had objected to a marriage between Dunbar's daughter and the heir to the Scottish throne, David Stewart. Dunbar soon made good on his allegiance to the English as he fought resolutely alongside the Earl of Northumberland, against his former countrymen, at Homildon Hill during September 1402. It is unlikely that Dunbar ever visited Clipstone and on his death in 1420 the manor reverted to the monarchy. To consign away such an important and lavish residence to a new ally indicates the fragile position that Henry IV found himself to be in on assuming the throne and also points towards a clear disinterest in the palace by the newly emergent Lancastrian monarchy.

Henry V continued to focus on the use of Kenilworth by building the Pleasaunce-in-the-Marshes across the lake from the great fortified palace but it seems that, despite being frequently abroad, he intended Sheen to become his favoured residence in England.[775] The early part of his infant son's reign was dominated by projects led by the royal uncles Gloucester and Bedford especially at Greenwich and Baynard's Castle. Later on, Henry VI was himself devoted to the point of distraction by the construction at institutions such as Eton and Cambridge.[776]

The final phase of building at the King's Houses for which we have evidence comes from the middle years of Henry VI's troubled reign. The continued use of the manor during this period can be attested to by the presence of a half-groat of Henry VI[777] and a French jetton[778] which points towards the continuing political and military connections in France by England in the fifteenth century. More specifically there was an issue of £200 on 5 November 1435 by William Stanlowe to William Clerk, deputy to John Arden, Clerk of the Works for construction at Clipstone. The money was given to Clerk so that he could pay the wages of the lath-makers, carpenters, sawyers, masons, smiths, ditchers, daubers, tilers, slaters, plumbers, hedgers, glaziers and plasterers employed to make repairs to the King's Houses, park lodge and in the '*making of a certain new tower*' at Clipstone. Clerk himself was to be paid 6d a day and the tradesmen's wages paid according to the Statute of Workers and Labourers made at Cambridge. There was reference made to materials that were carried to the site by both land and water, but which were specifically not to be sourced from church lands, and included timber, shingles, tiles, boards, laths, lead, iron and glass. The work was funded through the felling and sale of timber authorised on 22 March 1442 and the account was audited as complete during the Hilary Term of 1443 by R. Frampton and his clerk W. Haddon.[779]

Sadly, the document does not go into a similar explicit level of detail regarding which buildings and precisely what materials were used by the named craftsman that the late fourteenth century accounts left us with, but the reference to the construction of a new tower at Clipstone is most definitely intriguing. Whilst it is not clear exactly where the tower was located or what its function was, by this period a tower could serve as a residence, defence, gatehouse, belfry, a location to view a hunt or a tournament, and indeed could serve as a multifunctional combination of many of these. The presence of a massive feature partially excavated by Philip Rahtz,[780] and clearly located by ground penetrating radar in 2011,[781] immediately to the north of and abutting the north-west corner of King John's Palace, may be the archaeological remains of this tower. The square feature has foundations approximately two metres in width which descend to at least two metres in depth and the entire structure is approximately 5.4 by 5.7 metres in dimension. Most notably the corners of the building were supported by massive angle buttresses which may even have been big enough to contain newel stairs such as those of turreted gate towers constructed in the mid fifteenth century at Knole or Christ's College and Trinity College, Cambridge.

Two years before open hostilities began at St Albans between the houses of York and Lancaster, Henry VI granted the manor of Clipstone for life jointly to his brother-in-law Edmund, Earl of Richmond and Edmund's own brother Jasper, Earl of Pembroke. They were deprived of the estate when Edward IV granted it to his younger brother George, Duke of Clarence, but after the latter's death in 1478 it probably reverted back to the Crown again. Edward IV, ever the practical economist, concentrated on his south-eastern residences and began to maintain fewer palaces.[782] Lip service was still paid towards the upkeep of the King's Houses through the appointment of Gervase Clifton as surveyor of the works at Clipstone between 1471–8 and Henry VII selected Simon Digby as the Lieutenant of Clipstone and Keeper of the Park in 1485 after Digby's show of loyalty in fighting for the Lancastrians at Bosworth.[783] Henry's favourite palaces included Richmond, Greenwich and Baynard's Castle, and like Edward IV the Tudors rarely left the Thames Valley and had few palaces left elsewhere. Henry once again chose Sheen as his favourite palace which was rebuilt as a monument to Lancastrian military triumphs prior to its destruction by fire in 1499 and replacement by the ten acre Richmond Palace. The size of palaces during the Tudor age began to increase exponentially. Whitehall was the largest in Europe at twenty-three acres, dwarfing even Clipstone and Clarendon. Remote sites such as these were simply left to decay, and Clarendon was finally abandoned by the Tudors after over four hundred years of occupation.[784]

The decline in feudalism, rise of towns, less need to consume excess manorial produce through itinerary and wars with France led to a south-eastern focus by the monarchy especially during the reigns of Edward IV and the Tudors. Of the twenty houses inherited by Edward I, only Clarendon, Clipstone, Havering, Windsor, Woodstock and Westminster were still owned by the Crown in 1485[785] and the fifteenth century kings tended to stay at either castles or religious houses when they travelled north.[786] Government itself was changing and the late Mediaeval administration became centralised at Westminster so that palaces tended to survive only if they stood in a convenient location or if their use as a centre of government was maintained. Northern properties were frequently gifted to retainers.[787] This was preferable as royal income in the fifteenth century tended to be reliant on taxation as opposed to exploitation of the Crown Estates. The Lancastrians in particular were financially poorer than their predecessors which, coupled with a desire for a very high quality accommodation, led to the decline in many older, less fashionable palaces that needed major and expensive upgrades to bring them up to the standard required.[788] The change in architectural needs and fashions strayed away from organic and rambling sites which were either left to decline or were remodelled in favour of symmetrically arranged courtyards often constructed in brick, which had begun to edge in front of stone as the new high status building material of choice. Consequently the appearance of sites such as Clipstone and Clarendon were considered to be old fashioned by the late fifteenth century[789] whereas the ascendancy of residences such as Hampton Court Palace was just beginning.

The manor of Clipstone was granted to Thomas Howard, Earl of Surrey in 1514 as a mark of gratitude for his service against the Scots at the battle of Flodden Field, but was back in royal hands again by 1520 (despite Howard living until 1554) as William West, Groom of the Privy Chamber was granted its keepership.[790] A commission was given to the abbots of Welbeck and Rufford, the Prior of Newstead, Sir Brian Stapleton, Sir Richard Basset, Sir John Vyllers and John Hercy to survey the park, deer and manor of Clipstone in 1524. The rather sad and forlorn findings of that enquiry were reported the following year and are iterated here with modern spelling:

> '*First the south-east end of the high chamber there is in great decay and ruin in stonework, timber, lead and plaster; and the gable end of the same is fallen outward so that a part of the roof and floor of the same chamber is fallen down. Also there was sometime begun a stone stair and it is not finished which has been the cause of the ruin of the said chamber. Also the chapel there is in decay and has no covering upon it. Also the kitchen there was new plastered and the roof thereof wants pointing and amending of the slate, also on the said kitchen were two chimneys begun and not finished.*'[791]

The commissioners also went on to describe the pitiful state of affairs at St Edwin's Chapel: '*it has no mansion but a parlour under the chapel of no value*'.[792]

It is clear that, despite the programme of repairs and even new build at the King's Houses during the late 1430s and early 1440s, by 1525 a wholesale process of demolition had occurred at Clipstone so that only three structures are recorded as still standing at the palace, and all of those were in a catastrophic state of disrepair despite an attempt to plaster the kitchen. It seems that by the early sixteenth century the facilities had been downgraded to just those required of a hunting lodge – a residential chamber, a kitchen and a chapel. Rahtz noted that post-fifteenth century pottery was found exclusively in the disturbed demolition layers[793] and this was confirmed in four evaluation trenches dug during 2011 to be between 0.3 and 1.17m in depth which contained both redeposited Mediaeval and post-Mediaeval pottery fabrics indicating that the destruction had occurred during the latter.[794] The stratified pottery assemblage showed a relatively small amount of material dating from the twelfth through to the mid-fifteenth century, but crucially no Cistercian ware was recovered from sealed Mediaeval contexts relating to the palace infrastructure, which is a fabric abundant on sites occupied between the very late fifteenth century and early seventeenth centuries. Instead the demolition layers contained pottery forms dating to the period 1450 to 1550 and were primarily vessels such as jugs or cisterns which would have provided liquid refreshment for work-gangs involved in the heavy labour of demolition and stone-robbing.[795] The end of the palace was therefore one of a fairly sudden decline in use following the last visit by Richard II in 1396 and final programme of repairs which ended in 1443. The subsequent eighty-two years in the second half of the fifteenth and early sixteenth centuries witnessed unrecorded, but probably sanctioned, programmes of demolition which resulted in a greatly reduced facility that in itself was apparently in a grave state of disorder by 1525. An alternative point of view of the demolition was revealed by an archaeological test-pit within the properties lining the south of Mansfield Road which contained deliberately deposited plain and painted window glass in a post-Mediaeval pit. This has been interpreted as opportunistic robbing of assets deriving from the palace by stripping lead from the windows. The lead proved useful to the local occupants of the village, but the ancient glass served no purpose within the economy and was therefore buried as rubbish.[796]

The estate was next granted to the Duke of Norfolk by Henry VIII and then to Edward Fynes, Lord Clinton and Saye, in 1551. It was then briefly owned by John, Earl of Warwick and Henry Sydney under Edward VI before reverting to the Crown. A document dated 19 March 1568 which granted the keepership of the manor of Clipstone to Thomas Markham of Ollerton simply referred to the '*site of the late castle.*'[797] The King's Houses were no more.

Chapter Nine

Dukes, Antiquarians, Farmers and Community:
1568–2016

'There is every reason to suppose that Clipstone will soon emerge – under the fostering care of his Grace – from being the most decayed village in the county, and become the neatest.'
~ William White, 1832, *History, Gazetteer and Directory of Nottinghamshire* ~

Cultural Anxieties

Clipstone passed out of royal ownership for the very last time in the first year of the reign of James I The king granted the manor and park to Charles Blount, Lord Mountjoy, who then sold the estate to Gilbert Talbot, Earl of Shrewsbury. Talbot also held the nearby residence of Welbeck Abbey from which the Clipstone estate was now run. Shrewsbury was married to Mary Cavendish, the daughter of his own step-mother Elizabeth Talbot (more famous to history as Bess of Hardwick) and in 1606 he became embroiled in the scandal surrounding the marriage of his niece, Arbella Stuart, to William Seymour – a match that was seen to be politically dangerous by the new monarchy. Gilbert was confined to the Tower of London and Welbeck, complete with Clipstone, passed to his nephew Sir Charles Cavendish. The estate remained in the ownership of descendants of Cavendish until it was sold piecemeal in 1945. Welbeck itself began life as a Mediaeval Premonstratensian abbey and witnessed many additions and alterations at the behest of its post-Mediaeval owners who employed architects such as Robert Smythson (late sixteenth century) John Smythson (early seventeenth century), John James (1741–52), John Carr (1764–5), Humphrey Repton (1790) and Sir Earnest George (early twentieth century). The house at Welbeck was leased to the Ministry of Defence between 1945 and 2005, and has been in the ownership of William Parente, grandchild of the 7th Duke of Portland since 2008.[798]

Although several maps made during the post-Mediaeval period, including those drawn in 1576, 1606 and Speed and Saxton's map of 1610, show the broad outline of Clipstone Park, the earliest detailed information given for the estate was Richard Banks' 1609 survey for James I. This gave a relatively similar picture of the estate as William Senior's 1630 map although there was a slight discrepancy in the size of the park from 1,583 acres in 1609 to 1,457 acres in 1630. Banks also provided a glimpse of the names of some of the estate tenants such as Thomas Woodward, who leased woodland adjacent to the northern assarts. However it is clear that many occupants, including Woodward, were also landowners in their own right as Thomas had the freehold of over eight acres of pasture next to Hall Close. His neighbours William Lawe, Ralph Heath, Rowland Dand and Thomas Tomlinson also owned enclosed land at this time.[799]

The William Senior map was drawn in a very characteristic early seventeenth century hand. The boundaries of fields, closes and properties were shown in birds-eye view however buildings are shown isometric with two elevations and the gables of roofs visible. The buildings all appear to be depicted as archetypal symbols rather than true architectural representations, although it is significant that King John's Palace standing alone in the 'mannorgarth' was shown as being roofless, which it almost certainly had been for at least one hundred years by 1630. Senior himself tells us in the top right hand corner of the map that he was a '*professor of arithmetique, geometric, astronomie, navigation and dialing.*' He created nineteen estate surveys depicting manors such as Bolsover and Chatsworth for William, the son of Charles Cavendish, probably as a method of cataloguing the properties of a man on the rise. Cavendish was made Viscount Mansfield in 1620, Earl of Newcastle in 1628 and Lord Ogle in 1629.[800]

The character of the village architecture was beginning to change during this period and new features would have become noticeable such as the incorporation of fireplaces, upper floors, staircases and brick infill. The presence of chimneys, shown in nearly every property by Senior, led to a preference for the lobby-entrance planform whereby the stack was placed in the centre of a building so that on entering the door, usually placed in the middle of a property, a visitor would be faced with the side elevation of the chimney. Later building design favoured placing chimneys against the gables. The very end of the Nottinghamshire timber-frame tradition took place during the era of the mid-seventeenth century with surviving examples at Yews Farmhouse, Styrrup and Raven's Farm, Misterton. Such buildings represent construction in a tradition that was soon to be entirely superseded[801] as brick became the common building material. This changing tradition can be seen from a Welbeck estate survey of the village dated 1838 which lists ten village properties, all of which were noted as having been constructed from brick or stone with tile roofs.[802] Higher up the social scale was Clipstone Hall, built (possibly with stone robbed from the palace) to the south of Squires Lane in the early seventeenth century and listed as having ten chimneys in the Hearth Tax accounts of 1664–74. By the early eighteenth century it was inhabited by a tenant named Widow Ingall and was probably in a state of disrepair as John Cavendish gave permission to use it as a stone quarry for other building projects.[803]

As well as enclosure and architecture bringing an altered physical environment to Clipstone, the spiritual life of the village was also subject to radical change and tension. During the sixteenth century England's official religion had swung from Catholicism to Protestantism during the mid-1530s, back to Rome during Mary's short six year reign and then returned to the Church of England under Elizabeth. As the son of a staunch Catholic, Mary Queen of Scots, James I's allegiances were open to question prior to his emphatic adoption of Protestantism after his coronation and many English Catholics had held out a great hope that he would return the country to the faith. During the mid-seventeenth century James' son Charles I was married to a Catholic, Henrietta Maria, and, together with his ally William Laud, the unpopular Archbishop of Canterbury, made many anti-Calvinist overtures. Charles' younger son, the future James II, was an overt Catholic from the late 1660s. Added to this were dissenting groups such as the Anabaptists, Grindletonians, Presbyterians and hard-line Puritans so that the religious climate was one of great complexity. Although official lines were drawn through the Act of Uniformity, the relationship of the people to the church was often not as straightforward as orthodox Protestant or recusant Catholic, old traditions died hard and many continued to be quietly practiced by the ordinary folk.

Others in the village were more vociferous about their beliefs and conspicuously clung to their non-conformist faiths. Lists of those brought to court for non-attendance of Anglican church services show that a total of forty-eight individuals were fined for recusancy between 1605 and the outbreak of the English Civil War in 1642, with definite peaks in the trend of twelve individuals in 1619 and eleven in 1635–36 (Figure 5). The figures demonstrate that almost as many women were accused as men with twenty female recusants listed, some individually such as Ann Gowridge in 1638, as widows such as Margaret Hynd in 1620–4, in family groupings such as Elizabeth and Ursula Freeman in 1619 and, most commonly, along with their husbands such as the unnamed wives of Francis Bilby in 1613, Richard Anthony in 1623 and William Featherstone in 1630–2. Amongst the men a wide-ranging number of professions and social positions were represented from agricultural labourers and yeomen through to the stonemason Francis Hare and those who styled themselves as gentlemen such as John Johnson in 1640–1.[804]

Figure 5: Graph showing the reported figures of recusants in Clipstone between 1605 and 1642

Family names recur in the lists such as Freeman, Thorold, Bilby, Hynd, and the father and son both named Thomas Beeston. The Beeston family may have had a link to the former peel that became a hunting lodge and which was referred to as Beeston Lodge as late as the nineteenth century.[805] The yeoman farmer Thomas Beeston Senior began his lengthy spell as a recusant in 1620 and was still holding out against the Church of England at the time of the outbreak of the war. His son also made a determined stand between 1633–7 alongside other lengthy spells of recusancy, such as the five years by husbandman Thomas Smyth or fourteen years by spinster Ann Lawrence. Questions must be asked as to how punishment was administered,[806] as recusancy was considered to be an indictable offence it came with the heavy fine of £20 – the equivalent annual income for a very well paid schoolmaster at the time – and it is not apparent how the Catholics, such as the yeoman Thomas Beeston who maintained his recusancy for an unbroken twenty-two years, managed to pay. Punishment could include the fine, forfeiture of goods and imprisonment for up to a year. Revenue from fines averaged £6,000 during the 1620s but after an increase in the amount payable in 1632 they soared to over £20,000 per year.[807]

Support for the recusants of Clipstone undoubtedly came from the appointment of William Bishop by Rome in 1623 to oversee the interests of English Catholics. Bishop brought a progressive and forward-thinking attitude to the country that had previously been dominated by violent and direct political action during the Elizabethan period. He was supported in his work by a revived Jesuit mission begun under Henry Garnet and continued by Richard Blount and Thomas Fitzherbert. The Jesuits' success was encouraged by the foundation of a college in England which led to a steady increase in their numbers from around twelve in 1600 to almost two hundred in 1642. Overall the recusant population gradually increased from c 35,000 in 1603 to somewhere in the region of 60,000 in 1640, further backed up by a three-fold rise in the number of operative priests from about 250 to 750, often retained in the houses of the gentry.[808]

William Cavendish was a staunch royalist supporter during the English Civil War but subsequent to the disastrous defeat at Marston Moor in July 1644 he lived in exile until the Restoration. Although the war touched southern Nottinghamshire more greatly, on returning to the Midlands, Cavendish found that Clipstone Park had been virtually destroyed and his losses were estimated from this one estate alone at £20,000. His wife, Margaret, described the scene:

> '*The rest of the parks were totally defaced and destroyed, both*
> *wood, pales and deer, amongst which was also Clipston Park,*

of seven miles compass, wherein my lord had taken much delight formerly, it being rich of wood and containing the greatest and tallest timber-trees of all the woods he had; insomuch that only the pale-row was valued at £2,000. It was watered by a pleasant river that runs through it full of fish and otters; was well-stocked with deer, full of hares and had great store of partridges, pouts, pheasants etc., beside all sort of water-fowl, so that this park afforded all manner of sports for hunting, hawking, coursing, fishing, etc., for which my lord esteemed it very much. And although his patience and wisdom is such that I never perceived him sad or discontented at his own losses and misfortunes, yet when he beheld the ruins of that park, I observed him troubled, though he did little express it, only saying he had been in hopes it would not have been so defaced as he found it, there being not one timber-tree left for shelter. However, he patiently bore what could not be helped and gave present order for the cutting down of some wood that was left in a place near adjoining, to repale it and got from several friends deer to stock it.'[809]

Although the palace was now long gone, the survey of Richard Banks and the map by William Senior and then Margaret Cavendish's account in the 1660s all indicate that the deer park was preserved as a resource at Clipstone during the post-Mediaeval period well after the monarchy relinquished the estate. Game was seen as a military target during the English Civil War and parks were commonly broken up with many soldiers stating that '*they had fought for the deer*' and officers could not, or would not, prevent the taking of deer. Of approximately 1,100 deer in Sherwood Forest during the 1630s only 258 were recorded after the war. Additionally civilians sought to feed themselves in whatever ways they could after the breakdown in law and order and poaching of deer parks was rife. Parliament tried to sell off the entire forest stock during the Commonwealth to increase the revenue to pay the army but this scheme failed abysmally as so few people were interested in the sale and even a scaled-down plan to sell off just four forests (including Sherwood) was unsuccessful. The sale of royalist lands did provide an income during the 1650s and led to many parks being turned into closes and arable fields. As Emma

Griffin has written '*the preservation of deer parks was a low priority for new owners during these troubled times. Rioting, illegal plunder and land sales all tended in one direction – the destruction of deer, woodland and parks. It was just one of many problems which indicated the government was losing its grip.*'[810]

The specific reason for the destruction of Clipstone Park can be seen in a reference from 1653 when one Mr Farbane received permission to build a forge at Clipstone. This was probably a charcoal fuelled blast furnace constructed near Forge Bridge, to the north-east of village, on the River Maun. The 1766 estate map contains several references to Near Forge Close, Far Forge Close and Great Forge Close which were in the presumed vicinity of the furnace and it is still possible to find iron slag from the manufacturing process along the banks of the Maun in this locality. The blast furnace process of refining iron involved hammering out carbon impurities from pig iron under very high temperatures and required an ample source of both water and charcoal for power and as such the estate was an ideal location with access to both the River Maun and the trees of Clipstone Park. The Surveyor General of Woods, Robert Baskerville, was fined £800 for failing to prevent the offence of the felling of over one thousand trees at Clipstone and was recommended to be replaced in his post in 1655. At the same time a certain Mr Clark was accused of '*cutting down vast amounts of timber, with no due thought for the welfare of the forest or care of the deer there.*' Despite this the forge was still operational in 1658 and a slitting mill for rolling iron rods was sold to the Duke of Newcastle as late as 1689–90.[811]

Building timber was still at a premium in the late seventeenth century due to the losses incurred during the war, and a petition from the parishioners of Edwinstowe, Budby and Clipstone was issued in the late seventeenth century to Henry Cavendish, 2nd Duke of Newcastle, requesting help with the cost of repairs at St Mary's Church, Edwinstowe. The estimated costs of works were £300 (the average wage for a farm labourer was between 10 and 11 pence per day) and the petitioners requested help with £200 worth of timber from the woodland at Birklands and Bilhaugh. It is not possible to ascertain whether the bid was successful and record was not made of repairs during this period so perhaps the after-effects of the civil war depletion of trees in the area precluded the matter.[812]

The period of the sixteenth and seventeenth centuries was marked by tremendous upheavals in society from the shifting religious orthodoxies to social change linked to the doubling of the population in the century between 1530 and 1630, coupled with widespread agricultural adjustment towards enclosure which led to a lack of food and land resources for many. Overall wages began to plummet and a class tension began to manifest as the gap between rich and poor became a significant gulf. The civil war then traumatised a nation that lost approximately 190,000 people as battlefield casualties and to disease (plus an estimated 60,000 in Scotland and 616,000 in Ireland).[813] A factor in the cultural anxieties that were raised during the Early Modern period was the increased fear of the perceived threat from witches, demons and evil spirits. To our scientific, post-Enlightenment minds this may seem to be merely a superstitious folk tradition derived from ignorance; however the Early Modern psychological experience was essentially not one akin to our own. The household rather than family was the basic social unit and childhood was mercilessly brief with adolescence spent away from family either as a ward or apprentice. Privacy was simply not part of the life experience of the majority so that multiple people slept in a room together and there was no divided space as rooms were entered one from the other directly with no provision of corridors. The recurrent outbreaks of plague, widespread death in childbirth, harvest failures and infant mortality led to a very limited life expectancy in the mid-forties. Overarching all of this was religion which shaped all concepts of life, death and the after-life for every sector of society in a manner not apparent from our largely secularised viewpoint. Ultimately there is '*little evidence that the lives of early modern men and women resembled our own…Pre-modern conceptions of self and one's place in the world were not identical to our own…those who view the lives of early modern men and women through the lens of modernity ought to proceed with caution.*'[814] Analysis of court records of witchcraft trials has shown that the enormous socio-economic tensions inherent in society found a partial outlet in the tendency for slightly richer members of society to attempt to settle old scores through identifying witchcraft amongst their poorer, marginalised and vulnerable neighbours within the community. Whether or not the accusers genuinely believed that the accused had actually perpetrated witchcraft is irrelevant – the fear was instilled within society and scapegoats were routinely identified.[815]

The threat posed by the forces of evil were so real to the people of the time that even the scholarly king, James I, conducted his own interrogations of suspected witches, issued laws against conjuration and witchcraft and wrote a manual called the *Daemonologie* explaining how to identify and deal with the problem. Within his text James explained that evil spirits gained entrance to buildings which they sought to possess by '*being transformed in the likenesse of a little beast or foule, they will come and pearce through whatsoeuer house or Church, though all ordinarie passages be closed, by whatsoeuer open, the aire may enter in at.*' Effectively the vulnerable places in buildings were perceived to be wherever the air flowed in through windows, doors and chimneys. Although windows and doors could be closed there was still a fear of the insistent draughts that always assailed a portal, and of course it was physically impossible to stop up the passage of air in a functioning chimney. Consequently the ritual protection of these locations in the house became a common practice. There has been a tendency amongst sceptics of such practises to dismiss the evidence as mere doodles, accidents or carpenter's marks, however the study of ritual protection marks is slowly joining the archaeological mainstream with many county surveys leading to serious academic studies.

There were many forms of ritual protection in late Mediaeval and Early Modern buildings which included bottles buried below thresholds or hearths to deter witches, animals enclosed within the walls or floors to fight familiars, middens and deposits associated with chimneys full of worn out objects to act as decoys for evil spirits,[816] tear-shaped taper burns scorched onto timber framing to inoculate against malignant fires, and an array of symbols carved into the fabric including pentagrams, interlocking grids, ladders, knots, daisywheels, circles and very commonly double-V lettering.[817] The latter has been found in two post-Mediaeval cottages at Clipstone and can be rendered either as V-shapes interlocking or placed side-by-side and may also be inverted to create the letter M. These are Marian marks, carved to invoke the protection of Mary, the Mother of God – often referred to as the *Virgo Virginum* (Virgin of Virgins), hence the preference for double-V symbols.[818] The use of the letter M as a symbol of Mary was widespread in the Catholic world as can be seen from the flintwork crowned M's which adorn the fifteenth century church tower at St Martin's at Fincham and the contemporary rood screen at St James', Southrepps, both in Norfolk. Whilst it is admitted that there was a visible recusant presence in Clipstone during the early seventeenth century it does not necessarily follow that the Marian marks represent the covert continuity of Catholic beliefs. The pseudo-theological origins of the symbols may not have been readily apparent to all and the meaning of the marks may have been diluted and reinterpreted as simply bringing good luck or averting evil by the time that they were carved.

Historic building surveys of Arundel Cottage and Maun Cottage have revealed double-V ritual protection marks carved onto the overhead beams supporting the framing of the first floors. In the case of Arundel Cottage the beam probably dates to the 1761 construction of a dwelling against the north elevation of the relict palace boundary enclosure wall, and the ritual protection mark is opposite the location of a blocked up fireplace (Plate 12 A). At Maun Cottage the beam with the double-V symbol is again directly adjacent to a hearth on a beam that may date to the seventeenth century or earlier.[819] It is difficult to precisely date these marks as they could have been carved at any point after the construction of the floor frames. Detailed studies, such as those conducted in East Anglia by Matthew Champion and his team of volunteers and more recently in Sherwood Forest under the direction of Matthew Beresford, have shown that such symbols were current from the Mediaeval period well into the mid-nineteenth century in domestic buildings, and slightly later in agricultural structures.[820] An anonymous German illustration made c 1600 showing a nightmarish scene of a witches sabbat entitled 'Hort an new schrecklich abenthewr Von den vnholden vngehewr' (Listen to new terrifying adventures of the sinful monsters), shows a double-V apotropaic symbol on the left hand side of a chimney mantelpiece (Plate 12 C). Notably the symbol has been crossed out and therefore nullified so that the chimney is able to provide a means of access for a witch shown brandishing her broom at the top of the chimney as she is no longer deterred by the presence of the symbol.[821]

A more portable version of this ritual protection tradition comes from a late Mediaeval or Early Modern lead alloy token, featuring the characteristic interlocking double-Vs, uncovered by a metal detectorist at Clipstone in 2012 (Plate 12 B).[822] Such tokens were routinely thought to be trade tokens but the find of another similar example from Broxtowe in Nottinghamshire may point towards the widespread use of such items as personal protective talismans perhaps carried to ward off evil in a century that had seen such radical upheaval which touched every part of society.

The Age of the Antiquarians

The late seventeenth century marked the beginning of historical interest in Clipstone. Dr Robert Thoroton (1623–1678) was a Nottinghamshire physician who lived and worked at Car Colston, but is best remembered for writing *The Antiquities of Nottinghamshire* over a ten year period and published in 1677. He was the first to write of the Domesday survey of the manor, of the bacons carried from the palace to Northampton, and of the chaplain during John's reign. He also recorded the fire in the village in 1221, the land held by the Witheberd family, and the various changes in aristocratic land ownership. Thoroton was the first of a growing number of antiquarians to record the ruins of King John's Palace and Clipstone Park when he noted that "*there is scarcely any ruins left at all of the king's old house, except a piece of thick Stone Wall, and the Park is also cleared of the Gallant Oaks wherewith it was well furnished before the late Rebellion.*"[823] The rather emotive language reveals that Thoroton was a supporter of the royalist cause during the English Civil War although he took no active part in the fighting or politics. The antiquarian is best remembered today by the Thoroton Society of Nottinghamshire, founded in 1897, which acts as the principal academic study group for the history and archaeology of the county. The Society publishes an annual journal which has in the past included many articles relating to Clipstone.

Further damage was done to Clipstone Park in 1714, although in this instance it was a result of entirely natural causes referred to as a '*grate harakan*' in a letter of 1 February from the keeper Charles Palmer to Lord Edward Harley (husband of Henrietta Cavendish Holles who had inherited the estate in 1711). In a rather obsequious tone Palmer reported that the dog kennels had been destroyed by the high winds along with four miles of the park pale so that the deer had escaped and were being poached across the landscape by the local communities.[824]

Edward was later elevated to the position of 2nd Earl of Oxford, and after his death in 1741 Henrietta returned from their house at Wimpole, Cambridgeshire to her ancestral home at Welbeck and began a large programme of building work despite significant family debts. Much of the work was in the emerging Neo-Gothic style and included a hall modelled on that of Bolsover Castle. The construction disturbed the Countess to such an extent that she wrote to her friend Lady Mary Wortley Montagu advising her that she was having a new lodge built in the park so that she could live in peace from the building work at the house. An estimate prepared by Robert Birch in 1747 refers to stone being taken from a redundant building on the estate during the construction of Cavendish Lodge. It is tempting to link this to a reference in 1709–10 which mentions permission to use stone from the dilapidated Clipstone Hall in future construction work. Clipstone Hall was in itself probably made from stone robbed from the site of the King's Houses, therefore a transference of building materials from the Mediaeval royal palace to the seventeenth century hall to the eighteenth century lodge may have occurred.[825] Cavendish Lodge was drawn by Samuel Hieronymous Grimm in 1775, rendered in ink wash on paper, after the building had become a tenant farm on the Welbeck estate.

The 1766 estate map was made shortly after the marriage William Henry Cavendish-Bentick, 3rd Duke of Portland, to Lady Dorothy Cavendish, heiress of William Cavendish, 4th Duke of Devonshire.[826] The purpose of the map seems to have been part of a mechanism to better understand the nature of the enormous estate created by the recent marriage. The most significant change that can be seen is that the open fields of the previous century had all been completely enclosed. Gorsethorpe Lane had been extended beyond the Maun and led along the north-eastern boundary of the park in the direction of Warsop and may have been created to allow easier access beyond to Welbeck. More superficial alterations had been made within the village such as the enclosure called Greenwood Croft which had two dwellings in 1630, but had contracted to just one in 1766. Otherwise the road system and settlement appear remarkably untouched. Many of the buildings marked on the map must have been agricultural rather than domestic, and two rectangular structures to the east of Brammer Farmhouse may have been estate barns similar to one, dated 1541, standing adjacent to the Old Hall in Lowdham.[827]

The map shows buildings that still survive in the village, such as Rauceby, Maun Cottage and Brammer Farmhouse. The latter two buildings incorporated fabric from the former palace gatehouse. Brammer Farmhouse was still a relatively new structure in 1766, having been built only five years previously as a sturdy brick cottage with two rooms at ground floor. Each room was provided with a chimney stack against the east and west elevations capped off by a vernacular pantile roof. The building was constructed directly to the north of the surviving palace wall so that the latter formed the south elevation of the building. The cottage was later extended to the east in the 1830s and was tenanted by John Jepson from at least 1832. The seven enclosures created during the post-Mediaeval period around the nucleus of the old gatehouse may have been encouraged by the pre-existence of the surviving palace buildings, and by the time of George Sanderson's map of 1835 had been formalised into a tear-drop shape probably during the remodelling of the village under the 4th Duke of Portland.[828]

The first mention of the name of the ruin in Castlefield as King John's Palace occurred on John Chapman's map of Nottinghamshire of 1774 which depicted the nucleated village of Clipstone as well as the deer park, Parliament Oak, Clipstone Warren, Cavendish Lodge and the enclosed woodlands of Birklands and Bilhaugh to the north. The later eighteenth century marked a period of intense interest and activity by a number of antiquarians. Two years before Chapman published his map Francis Grose (1731–1791) published the earliest detailed view of King John's Palace in his in 1772 book *The Antiquities of England and Wales* (Plate 13 A). Grose was an antiquarian, soldier, herald and draughtsman and was himself portrayed by the famous caricaturist John Kay. He was a member of the Society of Antiquaries and a leading light in the mid-eighteenth century drive to begin to record Mediaeval buildings. Curiously Grose was the patron of Robert Burns' famous poem Tam O'Shanter which appeared in his 1790 publication the *Antiquities of Scotland*. Grose died, and was buried, in Ireland shortly after the publication of his final volume on the *Antiquities of Ireland*. Grose employed the local antiquarian, archaeologist and historian Major Hayman Rooke (1723–1806) to make the illustration of King John's Palace for the publication. Rooke left the army during the 1770s and was a close friend of William Cavendish-Bentinck, the 3rd Duke of Portland, so many of the sites that he recorded lay on Welbeck lands. The view of King John's Palace very much established the model for future illustrations of the ruin showing the building from a viewpoint looking north-east from the summit of the hill in Castlefield. A mounted rider looks on at a gentleman pointing with a stick towards the masonry and it is possible to see the arched niche, a round-headed doorway, a buttress to the south-west of the central door and the characteristic pinnacled profile of the ruin very much as it appears to this day. Rooke also made a late eighteenth century drawing of Clipstone Village, looking east from Gorsethorpe Lane, with a pollarded oak and the deer pale fence of Clipstone

Park to the right and the tofts and crofts of the village in the mid-ground crowned by a distant view of King John's Palace (Plate 14 B).

Samuel Hieronymous Grimm (1733–1794) made a sketch of the ruin in 1773 from much the same perspective as Rooke's illustration for Grose. Unlike Throsby's 1790 view (Plate 13 B), Grimm appears to have actually visited the site himself as he omits the figure with a stick standing against the south-west corner of the building that Throsby almost certainly copied from the Rooke drawing. Like many men involved with the church John Throsby (1740–1803), the parish clerk of St Martin's in Leicester, was a very keen antiquarian and his colleague John Nicholls described him as '*a man of strong natural genius, who, during the vicissitudes of a life remarkably chequered, rendered himself conspicuous as a draughtsman and topographer.*' As a local lad he spent much of his time researching and writing about his home town and county however in 1790 he arranged for the republication of Robert Thoroton's *Antiquities of Nottinghamshire* along with his own extensive textual additions and several illustrations. The detail of his Throsby's drawing is not as sharp as Rooke's – he showed the niche on the right hand side as having a pointed rather than rounded arch. He did include the spire of Edwinstowe church in the distance along with two cottages in the village of Clipstone – one of which may be a stylised representation of Maun Cottage, possibly made without visiting the site. Grimm, on the other hand, was born in Switzerland and moved to England in 1768 where he became the constant travelling companion of the rector of nearby Kirkby-in-Ashfield, the Reverend Sir Richard Kaye. Given this local connection, and the fact that Grimm's speciality was recording historic scenes and monuments it is likely that he did actually stand in Castlefield to make his sketch. In 1775 he also produced an ink wash on paper illustration of Clipstone looking east from a similar viewpoint that Rooke adopted around fifteen years later. This showed the village buildings prior to the remodelling of the settlement by the Duke of Portland in the early nineteenth century and the structures are broadly contemporary with the 1766 map (Plate 14 A).

A more unusual perspective of King John's Palace was made by the local architect William Stretton (1755–1828) circa 1810. Contrary to Rooke, Grimm and Throsby the view was shown looking north-west into the interior of the building rather than the more common depiction looking north-east. Stretton was notable for the rebuilding of Nottingham Exchange as well as restoration work at both St Peter's and St Mary's parish churches. He also acquired land at Lenton and excavated the site of the Cluniac priory where he found the Norman font which can now be seen at Holy Trinity Church.

Clipstone Remade

In 1832 William White described Clipstone as '*once the seat of Royalty, now one of the poorest and most decayed villages in Bassetlaw, though seated in the most picturesque part of the vale of the Maun…one of the wildest wastes of the forest, and a large portion of the remainder has been enclosed, and brought into a rich state of cultivation by the present owner and lord of the manor, the Duke of Portland, who formed, at an immense expense, the flood dike and sluices.*'[829] The flood meadows irrigation scheme led to radical change at Clipstone as a result of the 4th Duke of Portland's desire to improve the agriculture and living conditions of the estate. Stretching for an initial five and a half miles between Carr Bank Wood and the parish boundary between Edwinstowe and Ollerton, and later extended by an additional two miles, the scheme led to the creation of dykes fed from the River Maun which would release water via floodgates down a one in ten slope back to the riverbed. The purpose was to achieve an increased crop yield through greater agricultural fertility and by 1837 had cost a very substantial £39,296 1s 1d, much of which was paid out to returning soldiers from the Napoleonic Wars and to unemployed framework knitters.[830]

Construction work took place from 1810 until 1839 and caused a major shift in the character of Clipstone away from the semi-fossilised Mediaeval settlement to that of a planned model village operating on the modern principles of agriculture. The village plots to the north of Mansfield Road were heavily truncated and all of the dwellings except Rauceby were demolished to make way for a rationalised planned settlement. Test-pitting has demonstrated that the pre-nineteenth century levels have been completely scarped away leading to an almost total lack of evidence for the Mediaeval and post-Mediaeval settlement.[831]

Although the cottages that had developed to the south of Mansfield Road were left untouched, White reported that in Castlefield the foundations of the palace '*have formerly been very extensive, with several large vaults, but in 1810, a great part of these were dug up to be employed in a system of drainage, which the Duke of Portland then commenced upon his state here; but we understand that his Grace gave strict orders, that the venerable walls of this once royal pile should not be touched, yet in opposition to this edict, much demolition has taken place; and on our visit we observed under the ruins large heaps of stones which some churlish surveyor appeared to have broken for the purpose of repairing the roads, and which would have been so appropriated, had not his Grace on hearing of the dilapidation, forbidden their removal.*'[832] This explains why the archaeology recorded during the excavations over the last sixty years has been so very fragmentary as, after the initial demolition of the site in the fifteenth and sixteenth centuries, further piecemeal robbery occurred in the post-Mediaeval period until a catastrophic episode of foundation removal took away much evidence for the final surviving ground plan of the King's Houses. An archaeological evaluation in Castlefield during the summer of 2012 revealed the traces of a sandpit containing early nineteenth century pottery with a ramped exit that was probably made by labourers extracting aggregate for the extensive construction projects in the village at this time.[833] It is interesting to note that the Duke of Portland was resolutely opposed to the destruction of the site and we can but imagine his rage directed at the foreman in charge of the works.

As well as the demolition of much of the historic village and excavation of the palace foundations, change also came to the deer park which White reported: '*Amongst the numerous farms which his Grace retains in his owns hands, that of Clipston Park is now perhaps the most productive, though it was lately only a wild tract of cleared woodland, once famous for its large oaks, most of which were cut down during the civil wars, and the commonwealth.*'[834] Historic maps demonstrate that from the mid-eighteenth century areas of the parkland had begun to be enclosed, but the ambitious early nineteenth century changes to the estate finally ended the use of the land to stock deer which had been near continuous since the mid-twelfth century. At approximately the same time the Crown disposed of its last lands in Sherwood Forest – Birklands – by exchange with the Duke of Portland for the patronage of St Mary-le-Bonne, London in 1818.[835]

Perhaps drawn by the immense changes in the landscape, travellers and writers began to arrive at Clipstone during the nineteenth century and often left descriptions of what they witnessed. In 1813 John Hodgson and Francis Charles Laird described the former park as an area of waste and of the legendary Parliament Oak, which they speculated may have been the site of

Edward I's assembly, '*nothing now remains except part of its large trunk, scathed and denuded, with one solitary branch about ten feet from the ground, which annually puts forth a few leaves.*' However when they came to portray the scene at Castlefield Hodgson and Laird stated that '*the only part remaining of the palace, which stands in a large field close to the village, seems to have been the hall; and several of its Gothic windows are yet entire.*'[836] This suggests that more of the ruin was present than can be seen today. Rooke's eighteenth century antiquarian view of King John's Palace does show the round-headed south-western door, but this is emphatically a Romanesque rather than a Gothic architectural feature. However an illustration of the building published by Palmer and Crowquill in 1846 shows a pointed arched window high up in the north-east gable in a view of the ruin looking south-west.[837] Although this feature no longer survives, Palmer and Crowquill's drawing does serve as corroboration for Hodgson and Laird's identification of Gothic windows at King John's Palace. Although the building was originally a twelfth century Romanesque hall it must have been adapted for alternative uses from the mid-thirteenth century after the construction of Henry III's hall, and these new purposes may have led to a refenestration in a manner similar to Bishop William of Wykeham's remodelling of the twelfth century West Tower and Great Hall at Bishop's Waltham, Hampshire in the fourteenth century in which he ordered the removal of most of the original windows.[838] Palmer and Crowquill also reported that '*the traces of defence are to be followed as far as the edge of the moat pool*'[839] and it may be that they were able to see a continuation of the surviving stone palace enclosure wall further to the east of Arundel Cottage.

The Nottingham poet Robert Millhouse alluded to the former palace when he wrote of '*the mouldring ruins of a kingly dome*' in his 1827 collection *Sherwood Forest and Other Poems* and as the century progressed written descriptions of King John's palace tended to get steadily more romanticised such as Mary Roberts' imagined scene that '*this lone and melancholy spot was not always thus deserted: the broken-down walls encircled a spacious area, within which was all the life and business, the gladness and festivity of a palace; there was the great hall and the refectory, the chapel, where prayer was duly offered, the rooms of state, and apartments of various descriptions*[840]' and Christopher Thompson's account that '*village crones talk of long subterranean passages, and the dire sounds that have issued thence, like to the moan of captive knights and the shriek of pining ladies.*'[841]

The spiritual life of the village also changed during this period as the increasing population led to the provision for Anglican services in the village from 1841. This meant that for the first time the residents no longer had to trudge the two miles over to Edwinstowe to attend church. Rather surprisingly the venue for these services was the hexagonal dining room at Cavendish Lodge which was converted into a chapel used until 1897. After that, services were briefly held in the schoolroom at Archway House until the construction of the iron mission church on the edge of Castlefield in 1903. Meanwhile Clipstone Weslyan Chapel was also constructed to the south of Mansfield Road within the old palace enclosure. It was funded by private subscription in 1882 and lasted as a place of worship until November 1978 when it was converted into a private cottage.[842]

Hospitality was provided at the Dog and Duck, located on the east side of what had been Clipstone Dam, and was first referred to in White's 1832 trade directory. Abraham Staniland was the landlord at the time, but as the parish records from 1819 also list Abraham as a publican it is likely that the pub dates from c 1800 as the 1774 John Chapman map of Nottinghamshire does not show any structures on the site of the current building. Today the Dog and Duck is the only public house in Kings Clipstone, however another establishment used to be run from Maun Cottage as early as 1794 when James Cutts was listed as running a friendly society (a mutual insurance organisation) from a public house named The Gate.[843] The tradition of naming public houses after historic gates is still current within the surrounding area in the title of the 1970s White Gates Hotel which was named after one of the four entrances into Clipstone Park.[844]

Samuel Cutts inherited the tenancy of The Gate in 1818 and immediately transferred it to Joseph Watkinson of Ollerton for the sum of £250. Four years later Watkinson made a formal application at the cost of £20 to licence his property as a public house to be known as the Fox and Hounds[845] which is shown to be the same building as Maun Cottage on the Ordnance Survey map of 1885. In 1829 the resident at the property was named as Cornelius Amos,[846] listed as a victualler and joiner in White's directory of 1832. Six years later the estates of the Duke of Portland in Nottinghamshire and Derbyshire were surveyed in exacting detail and it is from this document that we can begin to understand something of the fabric and layout of the Fox and Hounds. The building was described as brick built with a tile roof although it was noted that the structure was in a bad state of repair. This seems to indicate that it may have been of some antiquity as the vast majority of the dwellings referred to during this period were newly constructed as part of the remodelling of the village and were therefore in very good condition. The house itself consisted of a back parlour two bedrooms and pantry; the complex also had a brewhouse, coal place, piggery and a hutch (presumably for keeping rabbits).[847]

Cornelius Amos was the son of a farmer and shopkeeper named Thomas Amos. He was born in 1795 and was therefore around the age of 34 when he was first named as tenant of the Fox and Hounds. He married his wife Mary (who hailed from Kirkby-in-Ashfield and was a full twenty years his senior) in 1813 and their son James was born at Mansfield in 1816. The description of Amos as a victualler and joiner in 1832 shows that he was a talented and resourceful man who was presumably brought up on his father's farm but, at some point in his early life, apprenticed as a joiner, only to move on to run the local public house. Given their age difference it is not surprising to discover that Cornelius was widowed by the time of the 1841 census. At this point the Fox and Hounds was also home to James Amos (1816–75) and his wife Sarah (1816–89) along with their new born daughter Elizabeth. Cornelius was also listed in the 1851 and 1861 censuses although by the mid-1850s he seems to have handed over the running of the public house to his son. Clearly the family were profiting, as the 1851 census also refers to a servant named Elizabeth North who came from Wellow and may have been recruited by Sarah Amos who grew up at nearby Ompton. It is not clear exactly when Cornelius died, but by 1871 James was head of the household.[848]

The kind of cheer that visitors might have expected to receive at Cornelius' hostelry was wonderfully and evocatively related in 1846 by two thoroughly eccentric authors – F. P. Palmer and A. Crowquill – depicting their summer walking holiday as they passed through Sherwood Forest:

> *'Cornelius Amos, of the "Fox and Dogs", with many apologies offered us his small neat chamber as a refuge for the night; and gratefully we accepted the favour. One difficulty he stated, — there was but one room for company down stairs, the contracted kitchen, devoted to evening visitors. Very soon, before we had quenched our thirst, — scarcely before we had taken our places, — in came the labouring men to their pipes and ale. At first we discomfited them; but we gave them the run of our hearts, and chatted homely things to them, and sang them worlds of song, and perpetrated certain curious amusements for their*

> *gratification, which will long be remembered in that simple dwelling.*
> *The landlord's son-in-law had a glorious voice, and, in modulated*
> *tenor, he delighted us in turn with store ditties — "Nothing to do", "The*
> *Bonny-Bunch of Roses", and "The Painful Plough". Our laughter*
> *and our ready purse made them "as happy as young cuckoos, with*
> *open mouths, and plenty to put in them", as one said to us. When*
> *we gave them, as the finale, "Mrs Hemans' Evening Hymn", with*
> *voices in unison, "Old John the labourer" crushed his deformed hat*
> *upon his grey head in a paroxysm of sentiment, and rushed home*
> *to his family, exclaiming as he stumbled over the threshold — "Well,*
> *well! ee' never heard the like on it — but that's grand!"*[849]

This incredibly colourful description of Palmer and Crowquill's visit to Clipstone is made all the more remarkable by the architectural and social history that can be extrapolated from it. It is incredibly rare to find such detailed primary sources relating to low status rural buildings, and perhaps it is the case that only a public house could receive such attention. It is clear that the chamber given to the travellers was in an upstairs room. This was perhaps one of the two bedrooms referred to in the Portland Estate survey which would usually have been given over to Cornelius and James Amos. The public space used by the villagers for their "*pipes and ale*" was specifically referred to as a "*kitchen*" and must have been the room used for food preparation by the Amos family which then became the venue for communal drinking during the evenings. Unlike our modern public houses it is likely that beer was dispensed straight from the barrels in the brewhouse into a large jug and thence into the topers pint pots. This room must have been part, or all, of the current open-plan living room at Maun Cottage today.[850]

Although the travellers were eventually given a very warm reception due to the merriment of their banter and songs it is noteworthy that the locals were initially suspicious of the outsiders. Presumably Clipstone received very few visitors, particularly those staging a walking holiday, so it may be that the Fox and Hounds was not normally required to offer accommodation leading to the possibility that Cornelius or James gave up a bedroom to the visitors. The reference to a number of folksongs which were performed during the evening by the visitors, locals and Amos' "*son-in-law*" offer an indication of how rural public houses brought the community together in such a shared experience.

Genealogical research has drawn a blank regarding Cornelius having had a daughter, so it may be that Palmer and Crowquill mistakenly identified James Amos who, by their account, had an exceptionally fine singing voice. One of the songs that James sang – *The Bonny-Bunch of Roses* has a lengthy pedigree. It was first published in 1881 but was clearly a popular song four decades earlier when it was performed at the Fox and Hounds. Thematically it is a dialogue between Napoleon II and his mother mourning the defeat of the French at Waterloo at the hands of the *'bonny bunch of roses'* representing England, Ireland and Scotland and is therefore ultimately a patriotic song born out of the Napoleonic Wars. The song is still performed and recorded on the folk music circuit, most notably by The Chieftains, Fairport Convention and the Oysterband.[851]

James Amos eventually took over the running of the Fox and Hounds, probably at some point during the early 1850s, until he died on 21 April 1875. His wife Sarah and their youngest daughter Fanny maintained the pub for another fourteen years until Sarah's death, in 1889, when the Fox and Hounds closed its doors for the last time.[852]

Next door to Maun Cottage, at Brammer Farmhouse, Robert Jepson inherited the tenancy in 1844, but he was fatally injured by a runaway horse in 1859. His wife Elizabeth then continued to raise their twelve children whilst running the property as a village shop until at least 1876. The estate landlord at the time was the 5th Duke of Portland, William John Cavendish-Scott-Bentinck who, despite a promising early career in the military and serving as MP for Kings Lynn, suffered debilitating ill-health including memory loss and sciatica. As his life progressed he became increasingly more eccentric and he withdrew completely from public life. All of his business was handled by post, only his valet was allowed to directly communicate with him and an estate worker was sacked for repeatedly saluting him. During the day he would wear two overcoats, a very tall hat, and an extremely high collar, and he carried a very large umbrella behind which he would hide himself if someone addressed him. When he went out on his estate at night a servant carried a lantern 40 yards ahead of him. He retreated into only four or five rooms in Welbeck Abbey and left the rest to decay. However, he is possibly best remembered for the creation of the underground rooms complete with fifteen miles of tunnels, one of which was wide enough for two carriages to pass. There was also an observatory, a library, a billiard room and a ballroom capable of holding two thousand guests (not that any were ever invited). All of the rooms were painted pink. Nevertheless, the Duke took pity on his tenant Elizabeth Jepson and her large family as he provided for the construction of a large brick oven in the garden, allowed her children gleaning rights to collect leftover crops from the fields after harvesting, and even provided a horse and cart for her deliveries, bins for flour, chickens, a cow and the rights to collect timber and gorse on the estate. The indomitable spirit of Elizabeth Jepson is readily apparent in being able to bring up such a large number of children as a single mother, but it is also worth considering the care and attention paid towards her difficult circumstances by the Welbeck Estate.[853]

Elizabeth's daughter Hannah inherited the tenancy of the cottage and ran the village shop along with her farmer husband James Brammer, who probably gave the building its current name. James later purchased a horse and cart from the Welbeck estate and began a haulage business which was later extended by his son-in-law and eventually continued into the late twentieth century as John Bradley and Sons. The Brammers were again provided for by their landlords in 1895 when an extension intended to provide accommodation for James and Hannah's three children was built to the west and south of Brammer Farmhouse at the instigation of the nephew of the 5th Duke, Sir William John Arthur Charles James Cavendish-Bentinck. It is likely that Brammer Farmhouse and Arundel Cottage were divided into the two buildings that exist today in 1895, as the 1916 Ordnance Survey map was the first to show a clear property boundary dividing the two cottages.[854]

The stories of Maun Cottage, Brammer Farmhouse and Arundel Cottage help to articulate how and why the final upstanding remains of the palace gatehouse have been entirely masked within later fabric and were essentially lost to history until the early twenty-first century. Clipstone was radically altered during the nineteenth century and it is perhaps fitting that during the final decade Alfred Stapleton made the first serious and comprehensive study of the village and its relationship with the now almost invisible royal palace and associated Mediaeval landscape. Stapleton worked from Nottingham University College which opened in June 1881 and contained the Nottingham Free Library. Now part of Nottingham Trent University, the college was constructed in Ancaster stone at a cost of £75,000 by the Corporation of Nottingham. Stapleton immersed himself in this library during the late 1880s with the single-minded objective of writing the very first book about the history of Clipstone. Previously writers had included small sections on the village in their publications, but Stapleton was the first to try and gather all of the references together to create a chronology of events from 1086 down to 1886. Although Stapleton visited the parish of Clipstone just twice and only had access to published documents, he provided a remarkably complete and detailed account of the events which took place in the village, especially during the Mediaeval period, and his book *A History of the Lordship of King's Clipstone or Clipstone in Sherwood, Nottinghamshire* is still a very valuable source.

The Modern Era

A year after the publication of Stapleton's book the railway finally came to Clipstone. Although the nearest station was Edwinstowe, construction of the Lancashire, Derbyshire and East Coast Railway, begun in 1891 and opened in August 1897, was laid just to the north of Clipstone. It ran the length of the Maun Valley, once again transforming the appearance of the northern quarter of the former deer park and open fields. An act of Parliament passed in 1911 gave permission for the Mansfield Railway to run between Kirkby-in-Ashfield and Clipstone Junction, to the north-east of the village. In its latter stretches this second railway ran along the valley of the Vicar Water, through the old deer launds and coneygarth to the south-west of the palace. It was completed in June 1916[855] by which time two other new changes had been made to the landscape through the foundations of Clipstone Colliery and an army training camp.

The stories of the local colliery and the military camp have been extensively told in an excellent publication by local historian Pauline Marples[856] and in the text of *A Celebration of Kings Clipstone*.[857] It is not the place of this book to repeat that information, but it is worth taking a moment to mention how those developments affected the landscape as the installation of both infrastructures had a dramatic effect on the former woodlands and deer park. Mining operations began one and a half miles to the south-west of Kings Clipstone under the aegis of the Bolsover Mining Company in 1912. Work was suspended in 1914 by the outbreak of the First Wold War and the development of Clipstone Army Camp which trained new recruits. The landscape around the southern edge of the former park was transformed again with entire streets of barracks, an iron mission church, a hospital, practice trenches in what had been Clipstone Shrogges, and firing ranges which were dug into the hills to the west of the Vicar Water pond. Clipstone Camp opened in May 1915 and was originally intended to accommodate 14,000 men, although this was soon revised to house a maximum of 30,000. Clipstone Drive, which passes from the site of the White Gate in the south-west to Cavendish Lodge in the north-east of the former deer park, was used as a thoroughfare by the military traffic, and the camp hospital was located on the western side of this road. Later in time Clipstone Drive was often used for speed trials by motorcycle manufacturer George Brough. Born in Basford, Nottingham, Brough was best known for the manufacture of the iconic Brough Superior, a motorcycle made famous for being the model that T. E. Lawrence was riding when he was killed in a Dorset road accident in May 1935. Brough's own bike 'Old Bill' was raced on Clipstone Drive in 1923, and the redoubtable seventy-two year old George returned to ride it one last time at Clipstone in 1962.

Eventually Clipstone Colliery became fully operational in 1922 when the Tophead seam was reached. The village of New Clipstone was laid out on top of the former army camp immediately to the south-west of the colliery, to provide accommodation for the miners and their families. The village of King's Clipstone was powered by electricity for the first time in 1925 using power generated from the colliery.[858] The colliery, camp and village were located in what had once been Fless-greave Wood on the south-eastern edge of Clipstone Park.

Clipstone's surviving pithead structures include the 61 metre tall headstocks which are reputedly the tallest in-situ pair in Europe and third tallest in the world. Completed in 1953 to the designs of architects Young and Purves of Manchester the headstocks were constructed by Head Wrightson Colliery Engineering of Thornaby-on-Tees and Sheffield, whilst the winding engines were manufactured by Markham and Company in Chesterfield. The headgear and winder house were given Grade II listed building status in 2000 as an early example of the Koepe system and, whilst they were not amongst the first built, they are the earliest in-situ example of this type left in the United Kingdom. The colliery survived the British Coal closures of the 1980s, closed briefly in 1993–4 and reopened under the management of RJB Mining (now UK Coal) until its final closure in April 2003. A sculpture known as the Golden Hand was commissioned by the Sustrans National Cycle Route. The cycle route passes along the old route of the Mansfield Railway, and the Golden Hand was placed in the Vicar Water Country Park on land formed from parts of the old pit tips from Clipstone Colliery. This controversial sculpture is said to reflect New Clipstone's mining heritage and potential for economic revival.

At the turn of twentieth century the Brammer family of Kings Clipstone were photographed outside the front door of their farmhouse. Emma Brammer (the daughter of James and Hannah), shown wearing a black dress, had been schooled at Archway Lodge during her childhood. This was another of the philanthropic foundations of the 4th Duke of Portland, built as an architectural mimic of the fourteenth century Worksop Priory gatehouse in 1844. Emma married John Bradley in 1915 and eventually the tenancy of Brammer Farm passed to their daughter Hannah and her husband Roy Wood. Next door the tenancy of Maun Cottage was taken over by William and Ann Gill in 1914 and it was presumably Ann and her children who can be seen standing outside the west door of the building in a photograph taken at a similar time to that of Emma Bradley (Plate 15 A and B). The Gills set up their own shop after the closure of the Brammer shop run next door and it is indicative of a community working together rather than against themselves that, after the Gills retired in 1928, the Bradleys again re-opened their shop at Brammer Farmhouse until early 1947.[859]

Following the death of William Cavendish-Bentinck, the 6th Duke of Portland, in 1943 the landowners of Clipstone reached a financial crisis arising from the tremendous increase in the inheritance tax brought about by the 'People's Budget' introduced to Parliament by David Lloyd George in 1909. This was a complete land valuation and a 20% tax on increases in value when land changed hands. Many old landed families could no longer afford to maintain their estates due to the consistently failing agricultural economy. In March 1945 an advertisement was published in *The Times* after the decision was made to sell off large portions of the Welbeck Estate in order to manage the financial difficulties. This was by no means an isolated incident as the following year the Sackville-West family, who had owned Knole in Kent since 1603, sold the property to the National Trust. The entire 4,941 acre Clipstone estate was put up for auction and sold in 108 lots for a total of £118,080. For the first time since the Norman Conquest the estate farmers were again the landowners.

Hannah Bradley's brother Fred, and his wife Molly, moved in to Maun Cottage after the Gills and ran Brammer Farm from there. Fred bought the farm in 1945 and further enlarged his landholding via the additional purchase of nearby Waterfield Farm which included the ownership of Castlefield and King John's Palace. The Bradleys allowed the previous tenant of Waterfield Farm, Ernest Belfield, to remain there until 1955 and Fred then ran his substantial landholding until retirement in 1981 when it was split between his sons. Martin Bradley and his wife Mickie Bradley still live and work at Waterfield to this day and have proved to be the most conscientious custodians of King John's Palace who openly admit to considering themselves less as landowners and more to be the guardians of the palace for future generations.

It has been during the period of the Bradley family's tenure at Castlefield that the vast majority of archaeological and historical work has been carried out. Pevsner, Rahtz and Colvin undertook their research in the 1950s, and this was followed up by the first of David Crook's articles during the 1970s. The next significant piece of work was undertaken by the village community who brought together local authors John Severn, Joy and Felicity Shaw Browne, Thomas Kirton, Mickie Bradley, John Danbury, Jane Bealby and Ivy Redfern in 1998 as a collaboration to produce the Millennium commemoration book *A Celebration of Kings Clipstone – 1000 Years of History*. Around the time of David Crook's second article on Clipstone Peel in 2005, Nottinghamshire County Council began to take an interest in the site which led to the first geophysical survey of Castlefield and a considered attempt to arrest the decay of King John's Palace.

Early photographs of the ruin show a stark profile in which a very large hole had appeared in the north-west end of the longitudinal wall that was rather miraculously spanned by a sliver of masonry apparently held intact by mere prayer (Plate 16 A). Following an archaeological watching brief by Richard Sheppard of Trent and Peak Archaeological Trust (now Trent and Peak Archaeology), remedial repairs were undertaken to the monument by Cranes of West Bridgford in 1991. These works involved the introduction of a concrete pad laid on top of the existing foundations which supported a rather ungainly, yet entirely necessary, pre-cast masonry wall that held up the surviving Mediaeval rubble core. This proved to be only a temporary and localised fix as the process of decay to the rest of the original stonework began to accelerate exponentially due to structural undermining caused by rising groundwater salts.[850] Visually more dramatic were the areas of overhanging masonry coupled with deep voids in the wall core, and it was a fall of stones in 2007 that precipitated the cooperation between landowners, local authority and English Heritage (now Historic England) which led to the complete stone conservation of the entire structure in 2009 by Paul Mendham Stonemasons (Plate 16 B).

The preservation of King John's Palace seemed to give a new lease of life to the interest shown towards the site by a very wide range of groups and this was in no small part down to two very exuberant events known as the Picnic at the Palace that saw thousands of people enjoying Castlefield during the summers of 2010 and 2011. A second geophysical survey of the entire field was carried out in 2010 and the following year Channel 4's Time Team filmed an episode based on the King's Houses during their penultimate series. The past four years have seen an increasingly large amount of fieldwalking, topographical and geophysical surveys, test-pitting and archaeological evaluations at sites including Castlefield, the village gardens and St Edwin's Chapel undertaken by Mercian Archaeological Services, and historic standing building surveys and documentary analysis by the author of this book.

Three miles to the south-west of King John's Palace, on the edge of Clipstone Park, the ownership of the land around the flight of fourteenth century fishponds known as Spa Ponds (which were created during the controversial fourteenth century development of Clipstone Peel) has recently passed to a local charity known as the Forest Town Nature Conservation Group. This band of local community volunteers is energetically restoring the water and woodlands as a public resource to be enjoyed by all. The work of the group exhibits a remarkable and historic transition in landownership across ten centuries from kings to dukes to farmers and back to community. And that is a story that may well have made that fourteenth century activist, Robert de Clipstone, smile very broadly indeed.

Epilogue

During the Mediaeval period the King's Houses witnessed many types of events including tournaments, a parliament, choral concert and wedding, the arrival of a papal envoy and a Scottish king, the transference of the Great Seal of England, and a local community standing up to the monarchy after the loss of their common rights. The modern era has continued in offering a plethora of occasions to celebrate the continued existence of King John's Palace incorporating television programmes, community excavations, country walks, picnics, beer festivals and nativity plays. The ownership of the palace has passed from kings to dukes to farmers, and is now in a situation where it can be celebrated and enjoyed by a variety of communities from near and far.

Over the last fifteen years the royal Mediaeval palace in the heart of Sherwood Forest has gone from being one of the most obscure archaeological sites in Britain, that was regrettably misunderstood and overlooked, to one whose history has been widely researched through a number of disciplines. The work has also been variously disseminated through archaeological reports, academic journals, books, local newspapers, popular and specialist magazines, television programmes, social media, lectures, conferences, workshops, guided tours and open days. The place of this book is to round up the sum of knowledge and research as it stands at the date of publication in the summer of 2016. However that is not, and should never be, the end of the story. Clipstone still has many secrets to reveal.

The ground plan of the palace has only been notionally established through a comparison between historic mapping, geophysical survey and previously published excavations alongside a very detailed analysis of original historical documents which describe the site during the thirteenth and fourteenth centuries. Only one largely complete ground plan of a Mediaeval royal palace – Clarendon – has been established archaeologically, but it should now be accepted that there is a potential plan which has been determined for Clipstone based on a very careful interrogation of data and comparison with other standing buildings of applicable status. Whilst this is a valuable addition it is only the beginning and the site should now be more widely tested archaeologically to pin down the specific locations of the built environment alongside the material culture, environmental evidence and zooarchaeology.

Beyond the palace, the archaeology of the Mediaeval village, park pale, deer leaps, coneygarth, fishponds and woodland are awaiting developed survey and excavation. Perhaps most crucially, the site of Clipstone Peel has never been looked at using any archaeological technique and along with its surviving masonry, soilmarks identified from aerial photography, earthworks and flight of fishponds, is ripe for a comprehensive study.

Archaeological projects at palace sites should never be entered into lightly without detailed written schemes of investigation supported by research frameworks which have been established based on discussion and agreement with the landowners, local planning authority, Historic England, local community and relevant experts in the field of both the local history and archaeology, as well as experts in Mediaeval palaces and high status landscapes. The proper context for research into sites such as the King's Houses is against the background of other similar sites as well as overarching research into the entire Mediaeval period, and it is recommended that all future studies of the site make use of as wide a group of specialists as is available both regionally and nationally.

It is hoped and encouraged that both the recent and ongoing archaeological work will be adequately and fully published. The publication schedule must involve a regular and prompt production of annual interim reports, complete with plans, sections, technical and general photographs, trench descriptions, specialist assessments and discussion of findings. Alongside this there is a clear responsibility to produce separate local archaeological journal summaries, grey literature reports, published articles and eventually a monograph. Even more importantly this work must be accessible to all communities of interest through both hard copy and electronic versions downloadable online via information sharing platforms. It should go without saying that any work undertaken has to be completely funded from inception, throughout fieldwork, assessment and analysis stages and right up to the moment of publication. Sadly, such rigorous and complete procedures have not always been adopted by researchers working on palace sites. The conclusions of Graham Keevill's study *Medieval Palaces – An Archaeology* list a catalogue of nationally and internationally important archaeological sites which have undergone very extensive and important fieldwork stretching back into the 1950s that tragically remains unpublished. It would not only be a great catastrophe if such a pattern was repeated at Clipstone – it would also be an appalling derogation of professional duty. This passage should not just be considered as a bald criticism of such practices, but must be taken as a serious plea to not repeat the mistakes of the past alongside a genuine encouragement towards the full completion of publication for all outstanding projects.

A further recommendation is that the extent of the scheduled ancient monument in Castlefield should be comprehensively reconsidered and overhauled. Currently the designation is limited to a very small area surrounding the immediate environs of the ruin of King John's Palace. This scheduling was arbitrarily drawn, prior to a fuller understanding of the limits of the archaeology that has now been established. An earlier reconsideration of the boundary could have helped to prevent or moderate local development, which has taken place within the north-east sector of the palace enclosure, for which no suitable archaeological mitigation was imposed. This protection is particularly needed due to the revelation from documentary analysis, backed up by the stray find in 2014 of a very high quality architectural fragment, that the major buildings of the palace extended from the standing ruin of King John's Palace in a north-easterly direction. Perhaps this outdated scheduling and lack of mitigation could have been avoided if the historic environment records for the site were also kept up to date with modern studies so that researchers could immediately pinpoint the extent and importance of the palace.

The greatest encouragement that the site of the King's Houses can remain safe and fully appreciated into the future is through widespread public engagement which enables people to experience, understand and love the site for themselves. Any monument which remains off limits is one that will slip into neglect and disrepair. Fortunately King John's Palace is a highly visible and well regarded landmark that local communities have taken to their hearts. Beyond the region, the building has come to be discussed and valued by a worldwide audience through both traditional publications and mainstream media alongside the all-embracing power of the internet. The archaeology and history of King's Clipstone has never been more accessible than it is in 2016, and it is greatly desired that such a phenomenon will only increase through proactive, community-driven and highly responsible research in the future.

Appendix 1

Dates of the Plantegent Visits to Clipstone

Henry II

(Compiled from Eyton, R.W., 1878, *Court, Household and Itinerary of King Henry II*)

August 1181

February 1185

Additional data:

1164 – 6d was also paid for a tun of wine to be transported from London to Clipstone – and is indicative of a possible lost royal visit (Stapleton 1890)

1178–9 – A reference to payment to Hugo de St Mauro of £4 15s 3d for horses and beasts for the king's use may also be an oblique reference to a royal visit (Stapleton 1890)

Richard I

(Compiled from Stapleton, A., *A History of the Lordship of King's Clipstone or Clipstone in Sherwood, Nottinghamshire*)

29 March 1194

2–3 April 1194

John

(Compiled from Hardy, T. D., 1835, *Rotuli Litterarum Patentium in Turri Londinensi Asservati*)

19 March 1200

20 November 1200

6 March 1201

10–11 March 1205

2 December 1210

26–27 March 1215

29 March 1215

Henry III

(Compiled from Craib, T., 1923, *'The Itinerary of Henry III, 1216–1272'*, edited and annotated by S. Brindle and S. Priestley (English Heritage, no date.))

21 July 1244 (According to Crook 1976)

13 December 1251

12 January 1252

3 August 1255

Edward I
(Compiled from Gough, H., 1900, *Itinerary of Edward I 1277–1285* Vol. I; Gough, H., 1900, *Itinerary of Edward I* 1286–1307 Vol. II)
5 September 1279
5 Aug 1280
21–24 January 1284
20 September 1290
12 October–13 November 1290
4–5 December 1300

Edward II
(Compiled from Hartshorne, C. H., 1861, *The Itinerary of King Edward the Second*)
16–17 September 1307
20–21 September 1307
23–27 September 1307
29 October 1315
31 October–26 November 1315
20 December 1315
23 December 1315–25 January 1316
27 February–10 March 1316
12–14 March 1316
9–10 December 1316
12–23 December 1316
1–17 January 1317
18–20 August 1318
27 August–15 September 1318
1–3 February 1320

Edward III
(Compiled from Ormrod, W. M., 2013, *Edward III*)
17 May 1327
28 August 1327
12–15 November 1327
27–29 November 1327
9–14 January 1328
13 March 1328
22–26 July 1328
25 August 1328
28–31 August 1328
29 August–4 September 1330
22–23 September 1330
25 – 27 July 1331

2–5 August 1331
9–10 October 1332
7–11 July 1334
11 April–2 May 1335
19–25 May 1337
10–11 September 1343
4–5 December 1345
7–15 December 1345
20–24 September 1350
1 September 1354
25 July–10 August 1363

Richard II
(Compiled from Saul, N., 1999, *Richard II*)
2–8 September 1387
16 March 1396

Appendix 2

List of the Keepers and Chaplains of Clipstone

Manor

Known Dates	Name	Notes
1184 – 5	Humphrey de Busei	Paid 66s
1189	Humphrey de Busei	Paid 60s
1204–1207	Geoffrey de Gors	
1207–1215	Philip Minekan	
1215	Brian de Insula	
1220	Brian de Insula	
1221	Brian de Insula	Ordered to view burned properties in the village
1223	Brian de Insula	Allow the Sherriff building wood to repair fire damaged King's Chamber
1225	Hugh de Nevill	Ordered to give manor to Brian de Insula
1225	Brian de Insula	A second term of office
1235–6	Roger de Essex	
1236	Warner Engayne	
1244–5	Roger de Essex	
1247	Warner Engayne	
1246–7	Robert le Vavassur	
1255–6	Roger Lovetot	
1313	Thomas de Merk	
1319–20	Humphrey de Warden	Also keeper of the park
1322	Thomas de Merk	
1323–4	Humphrey de Warden & Richard de Ikene	Joint keepers
1324–5	Richard de Winfathing & Richard de Ikene	Joint keepers
1328–9	Robert de Clipstone	Formerly Keeper of the Pale only. Keeper of Manor and Park until his death in 1339
1339–40	Robert de Mauley	Keeper of Manor and Park

1358–9	Richard de la Vache	£10 12s 11d per annum. Also keeper of park in 1363.
1368	Robert Morton	
1372–3	Nicholas Dabrichecourt	King's shieldbearer, keeper of park and palace
1376–7	Nicholas Dabrichecourt	Letters Patent issued
1444	Geoffrey de Kniveton	Also keeper of Bestwood, Sherriff in 1446–7
1485	Simon Digby	
1520	William West	Groom of the Privy Chamber
1528	Sir John Byron	
1568	Thomas Markham	Standard Bearer of the Gentleman Pensioners
1591	Thomas Markham	With underkeeper Paul Dawe

Park

Known Dates	Name	Notes
1184–5	Ranulph and Herbert	Paid 4s
1189	Ranulph and Herbert	Paid 4s
1205	Ivon de Fontibus and Richard de Lexington	
1318–20	Roger Dobman	Assisted by three park keepers
1319–20	Humphrey de Warden	Also keeper of the palace
1320–1	Thomas de Mark	Keeper of the Pale
1321–3	Roger de Warsop	Probably until keepership of Robert de Clipstone
1327–8	Robert de Clipstone	Keeper of the Pale
1328–9	Robert de Clipstone	Keeper of Manor and Park until his death in 1339
1339–40	Robert de Mauley	Keeper of Manor and Park
1363	Richard de la Vache	Also keeper of manor in 1358–9
1366–7	Robert de Moreton	Also keeper of park and lodge at Bestwood, but apparently not of the palace
1372–3	Nicholas Dabrichecourt	King's shieldbearer, again keeper of park and palace
1376–7	Nicholas Dabrichecourt	Letters Patent issued
1445	Ralph Cromwell	
1485	Simon Digby	
1520	William West	Groom of the Privy Chamber

1524	Thomas Manners	Lord Roos
1603	Roger, Earl of Rutland	
1653	John Lupton	

Chaplains

Known Dates	Name	Notes
1201	Anonymous	Paid 20s St Nicholas 6th December – Ascension 18th May and again for Ascension 18th May – St Michael 29th September
1215	Anonymous	Ordered to say masses in the chantry to Henry II
1265–6	Two anonymous chaplains at Clipstone & Walter Chaplain of the Chapel of Birchland	Paid 100s. Walter was presumably at St Edwin's Chapel
1313	Anonymous	Paid his wages arrears
1318	Nicholas de Nottingham	Fined 1d for taking a load of branches from the woods
1327	Henry de Wytherton	2 marks + 40s for the chantry chapel
1339–40	Henry de Wytheton	5 marks per annum
1355–6	Robert Rotor	100s per annum
1365	John Davy of Shillewell	100s per annum
1383–4	John Davy of Colwick	100s per annum
1486	Richard Scoley	Chaplain during the reign of Edward IV, paid 100s per annum as chaplain at the chantry of Clipstone and of St Edwin's Chapel

Appendix 3

A note on the creation of the ground plan of the King's Houses

At the point of publication of this book in the summer of 2016 there is only a single coherent ground plan of a royal Mediaeval palace in existence, that of Clarendon in Wiltshire. The available published sources for both geophysical survey and archaeological evaluation at Clipstone have so far not yielded any indication of a similar level of archaeological preservation below ground. This is almost certainly a result of the extensive quarrying of the site between the late fifteenth and early nineteenth centuries.

The ground plan that has been produced for this publication is a tentative composite drawn from many strands which have been selectively interrogated and then reinterpreted. The excavated evidence is extremely limited but a cross-comparison of Rahtz 1960; Sheppard 1991; Wessex Archaeology 2011; and Gaunt, Wright, Crossley & Budge 2015 alongside layering the geophysical data from magnetic, resistivity and ground penetrating radar surveys published by Nottinghamshire County Council and Wessex Archaeology has produced some anomalies principally for the area immediately surrounding King John's Palace. Standing building surveys – Wright 2004, Wright 2013 and Wright 2016 – have pointed towards the identification of King John's Palace as a twelfth century hall and the location of the thirteenth century the great gate. Further evidence for the specific locations, relationships between buildings and some dimensions have been gleaned from documentary sources, principally Turner 1851 for the thirteenth century evidence and Richard Reeves' translations of the fourteenth century accounts held at the National Archives. Where dimensions for the archival references to buildings are unknown comparison with contemporary buildings have informed calculations. In certain cases, such as the possible pentice, chapel and tower, a combination of fieldwork and documentary research has led to tentative attribution to archaeological features.

Background mapping of the semi-fossilsed landscape – 1630 and 1766 estate maps
Great Gate and King John's Palace – standing building survey

Robert de Mauley's Chamber – documentary evidence for dimensions from data held by the National Archives

King's Long Stable, Great Chamber, all kitchens and relative courtyard sizes – comparison with excavated evidence at Clarendon alongside National Archives data

Great Hall – comparison with thirteenth century halls at Winchester, Clarendon and Nottingham alongside National Archives data

Queen's Hall – comparison with thirteenth century halls at Wallington, Stokesay Castle and Bisham Abbey alongside National Archives data

Chambers adjacent to the Great Hall – comparison with chambers at Dartington Hall alongside National Archives data

King and Queen's Chambers – comparison with late thirteenth century double chambers at Ludlow Castle alongside National Archives data

Pentice, chapel and tower – combination of Rahtz 1960, Wessex 2011 and accounts held by the National Archives.

Excavated and geophysical anomalies – combination of Rahtz 1960; Sheppard 1991; Gaunt 2011, Wessex Archaeology 2011; and Gaunt, Wright, Crossley & Budge 2015

Rosamund's Chamber – National Archives data

Earliest boundary ditch – Rahtz 1960, Wessex Archaeology 2011

Second boundary ditch – Gaunt 2011, Gaunt, Wright, Crossley & Budge 2015

The wider landscape features such as the open fields, Great Pond and roads comes from a comparison between the 1630 and 1766 maps and the identification of the demesne land from Challis 2013

It should be noted that several buildings known to have existed from the documentary sources – the Knight's Chamber, Earl of March's Chamber, Lionel's Chamber and the Treasurer's Chamber cannot be pinpointed from the information provided in the fourteenth century accounts. It is also likely that there were many other essential ancillary structures such as barns, granaries, wine cellar and a brewhouse at the King's Houses which have altogether vanished from the documentary record. Consequently this ground plan is a tentative attempt to rationalise a variety of published and archival evidence as it stands in the middle of 2016 and will be subject to change as and when further research occurs.

Appendix 4

Plantagenet Family Networks

The extended family network of the Plantagenets is extraordinarily complicated. So complicated, in fact, that it was not possible to incorporate a practically functioning diagram of the family across three and a half centuries within A Palace For Our Kings.

Consequently, readers of the book are welcome to download (for free) a number of family trees relating to many of the individuals mentioned in the text. The diagrams are available from: http://www.triskelepublishing.com/a-palace-for-our-kings/family-trees/

These diagrams were created via the excellent online family tree-maker – www.familyecho.com – which comes as a highly recommended tool.

The tree has been broken down into six elements:

The Angevin and Plantagenet monarchy
The French connections of the Plantagenets
Scottish Kings
The Mortimers and the Yorkists
Lancastrians
De Burgh family
Post-Mediaeval owners of Clipstone

Acknowledgments

So very many people have been involved in such a wide-ranging manner of ways in the research at Clipstone. It would feel insufficient to do anything less than to name every single person that I have encountered in supportive, advisory, professional, curatorial or funding capacities, so please indulge me this opportunity to thank each and every one of those people for helping to contribute in so many ways to the creation of this book...

First and foremost in this group of individuals are undoubtedly Mickie and Martin Bradley who first welcomed me to King John's Palace in the early months of 2004 and have become a hugely important and valued part of my life ever since. Without the Bradleys there would be no book, but, more importantly, without the Bradleys there would not be the drive and determination that so many of us have caught directly from them, to visit, research and help to conserve this nationally important monument.

My wife, Michelle-Louise Wright, has put up with so much in my obsession with Clipstone over the last twelve years. The times where I have disappeared for weeks on end during fieldwork, the 5am starts for lectures and workshops, the vast amounts of money spent on books or research trips, my bright-eyed enthusiasms for minute nuances of history that perhaps only I in the entire world am actually interested in, the evenings, weekends and holidays spent on this book that perhaps could have been spent with her. For all of these things, for assistance in editing the text and so much more, I thank her; she has borne all of it with a calm and utterly understanding patience.

Shlomo and Lorraine Dowen first made themselves known through the interest that they paid to the history of their local area through online social media; that interest flourished into a friendship and friendship developed into a very positive and uplifting collaboration which has led directly to the creation of this book. Without their unflinching and creative support during the summer of 2015 I would not have managed a single word of this text. They, along with their son Josh, were also good enough to offer an honest and robust edit to the final publication. I wish them and the Forest Town Nature Conservation Group every success in their future endeavours to manage the ecology and continue the historical research at Spa Ponds and the site of Clipstone Peel.

I have been fortunate to have met so many of the local community in Sherwood Forest who have been so generous with their support, including time as volunteers, or by allowing me to intrude on their privacy to conduct fieldwork on their land or in their buildings: Jodie Govan, Denise Cooper, Rose at Maun Cottage, Stuart Reddish and Lynda Mallet, Richard Smith (thanks for the ginger and privot, brother!), Mark Fretwell (the gift of the Rahtz article meant so much), David and Daryl Maguire (for allowing a man to drink when he was thirsty), Paul Bobrucki, Tim Priestley, Philip Nixon, Tim King, and Stephen Parkhouse.

The publishing, conservation, archaeological and historical community who have had input or caused inspiration at Kings Clipstone are very numerous indeed: Richard Reeves, Tom Beaumont James, Emma Cheshire and Faber & Faber, Simon Armitage, David Crook, Derek Adlam, Gareth Hughes, Jason Mordan, David Littlewood, Pauline

Marples, Tim Allen, Terry Girdler, John Humble, Kate Fearn, Mary South and the Friends of Clarendon Palace, Mark Stafford, Paul Mendham, Kathryn Warner, Matthew Champion, Sarah Speight, Philip Dixon, Matt Beresford, Richard Sheppard, Hugh Shannon, Mat Hurford, Anja Rohde, Lauren McIntyre, Mick Aston, Jim Mower, Alex Rowson, Naomi Brennan and Wessex Archaeology, Christine Rawson, Kate Ravilious, Carly Hilts, Jon Kaneko-James, Cathy Block, Mike Bishop, Ursilla Spence, Andy Gaunt, Emily Gillott, Sean Crossley, Virginia Baddeley, David Budge, Ali Bush, Peter Masters, David Hoskins, Barbara Cast, John Beckett, Chris King, Keith Challis, the Thoroton Society of Nottinghamshire, Daryl Garton, CBA East Midlands, Jenny Page, Sarah Seaton, Andrew Nicholson, Neil Guy, the Castle Studies Group, Andrew Herrett and Philip Davis.

My colleagues (and former colleagues) at the Museum of London Archaeology have often appeared bemused at my apparent need to open my mouth to divulge massively obscure details of my research on a site that they have never once seen, but I like to think that they have put up with my musings with very good grace: Nathalie Cohen, David Sorapure, Andrew Westman, Julian Bowsher Greg Laban, Azizul Karim (who has saved my bacon with drawings more times than I can count), Lara Band, Amy Smith, plus Tracy Wellman and Sue Cawood whom we can also thank for the typesetting, graphic design and front cover of the book.

Finally, my family and friends who have offered advice, encouragement, books, technical and funding assistance or simply a place to sleep during one of my research trips up to the Midlands: Margaret and John Wright, Dave and Veronica Scott, Christopher Meir, Christina Wild, Richie Hudson, Ed and Tony Brenton, Daisy Alice Crook and family, Graham Johnson and Rachel Pillsbury, Magnus Halldorsson and Maggi's Mum.

Illustration Credits

All photographs, illustrations, maps and plans created by the author except for the following:

Fig 2 See Appendix 3; PLATE 2: British Library Board Royal 14 C. VII, f.9.; PLATE 4B: Tim King; PLATE 6 A: Portable Antiquities Scheme https://finds.org.uk/database/artefacts/record/id/432345; PLATE 6 B, C & D: David and Anthony James; PLATE 7A & B: Mark Fretwell; PLATE 8, 9, 10 & 11: A private collection; PLATE 12 B: Portable Antiquities Scheme https://finds.org.uk/database/artefacts/record/id/480187; PLATE 12 C: Trustees of the British Museum 1880,0710.1582; PLATE 13 A: Grose, F., 1772, The Antiquities of England and Wales. Hooper. London, Nottingham City Council; PLATE 13 B: Throsby, J., 1790 (ed.) & Thoroton, R., 1677, *History of Nottinghamshire Vol. 3* (reprinted 1972). Nottingham City Council; PLATE 14 A British Library Board Add.15543, f164, online gallery; PLATE 14 B: Major Hayman Rooke; PLATE 15 A & B: private archive of Michelle Bradley; PLATE 16 A: private archive of Michelle Bradley

204

Bibliography

Primary Sources

Hampshire Record Office
Reg Edyngdom, 21M65 A1/9 fo.17

National Archives
E 101/542/24 – Particulars of the account of Robert Rotour of works at Clipston (Notts) (1348–9)

E 101/460/18 – Particulars of the account of William de Emeley of works at Clipston and Beskewod (1360–3)

E 101/460/19 – Roll of Richard de Clifford, surveyor of the same (1360–3)

E 101/460/20 – Particulars of the account of the said William (1367–75)

E 101/460/21 – Roll of the said Richard (1367–75)

E 101/135/20 – PARTICULAR FORESTS: NORTH OF TRENT: Particulars of the account of William Danyell for repairs on Clipston manor house and park (1394–5)

E 364/77 – Exchequer: Pipe Office: Foreign Accounts Rolls (1435–1446)

Fine Roll C 60/49, 36 HENRY III (1251–1252)

Nottinghamshire Archives
NA C/QDLv/3/1,2 – BASSETLAW HUNDRED   Licensee: George PINDAR   Place: Laxton   Date of Sessions: 14 Sept 1822

Private Collection
Anonymous, 1766, Estate map of Clipstone
Senior, W., 1630 Estate map of Clipstone

University of Nottingham Manuscripts and Special Collections
Pl C 1/43 – Letter from Charles Palmer, Clipston[e] Park, Nottinghamshire to [E. Harley] Lord Harley [later 2nd Earl of Oxford], St James's Street, London; 1 Feb. 1714/15

Pl E12/6/8/3/4 – Copy agreement to surrender the Fox and Hounds public house in Clipstone, Nottinghamshire, to the 4th Duke of Portland; 27 Nov. 1829

PI E12/1/1/1 – Survey of the estates of the Dukes of Portland in Nottinghamshire and Derbyshire; 1822–1842

Secondary Sources

Almond, R., 2003 (reprinted 2011), *Medieval Hunting*. The History Press. Stroud.
Armitage, S., 2007, *Sir Gawain and the Green Knight*. Faber & Faber. London.
Ashley, M., 1972 (reprinted 1984), *The Life and Times of King John*. Book Club

Associates. London.

Aston, M. & Gerrard, C., 2013, *Interpreting the English Village*. Windgatherer. Oxford.

Barber, R., 2014, *Edward III and the Triumph of England*. Penguin. London.

Barley, M. W., 1986, 'Sherwood Forest' in Skelton, R. A. & Harvey, P. D. A (eds.) *Local maps and plans from medieval England*. Clarendon Press. Oxford.

Benedictow, O. J., 2004, *The Black Death, 1346–1353: The Complete History*. Boydell & Brewer. Martlesham.

Bernhardt, J. W., 1993, *Itinerant Kingship and Royal Monasteries in Early Medieval Germany c 936–1075.* Cambridge University Press.

Birmingham Post, 2013, 'Rich List 2013: No.30 – William Parente (£200m)' in *Birmingham Post*, 28 January 2013

Biggs, D., 2000, 'The Appellant and the clerk: the assault on Richard II's friends in government, 1387–9' in Dodd, G. (ed.), *The Reign of Richard II*. Tempus. Stroud.

Bingham, C., 1973, *The Life and Times of Edward II*. Book Club Associates. London.

Bossy, J., 1983, 'The English Catholic Community 1603–1625' in Smith, A. G. R., *The Reign of James VI and I*. Macmillan Press Ltd. London & Basingstoke.

Boulton, H. E. (ed), 1964, *The Sherwood Forest Book*. Thoroton Society Record Series XXIII. Nottingham.

Bradley, M. & Severn, J., 2002, 'King's Houses – King Johns Palace' in *A Celebration of Kings Clipstone – 1000 Years of History*. Tuxford

Bradley, M., 2002, 'Clipstone Hall' in *A Celebration of Kings Clipstone – 1000 Years of History.* Tuxford.

Bradley, M, 2002, 'Seventeenth Century Clipstone' in *A Celebration of Kings Clipstone – 1000 Years of History*. Tuxford

Carlton, C., 1992, *The Experience of the British Civil Wars*. Routledge. London.

Cavendish, Margaret, *The Life of William Cavendish*, ed. C.H. Firth (2nd revised edition, 1906). University of Nottingham. King's Meadow Campus East Midlands Collection Not 468.V38 CAV

Cawthorne, N., 2010, *A Brief History of Robin Hood: The True History Behind the Legend*. Robinson. London.

Challis, K., (ed.), 2014, 'Archaeology in Nottinghamshire' in *Transactions of the Thoroton Society* Vol. 118. Nottingham.

Challis, K. (ed.), 2013, 'Archaeology in Nottinghamshire' in *Transactions of the Thoroton Society* Vol. 117. Nottingham.

Champion, M., 2015, *Medieval Graffiti – The Lost Voices of England's Churches*. Ebury Press London.

Champion, M., 2015, 'Magic on the Walls: Ritual Protection Marks in the Medieval Church' in Hutton, R. (ed), 2015, *Physical Evidence for Ritual Acts, Sorcery and Witchcraft in Christian Britain*. Palgrave Macmillan. Basingstoke.

Chapman, J., 1774 (reprinted 2003), *Map of Nottinghamshire*. Nottinghamshire County Council.

Chaucer, G., 'The Book of the Duchess' in Stone, B. (ed.), 1983, *Love Visions: The Book of the Duchess, The House of Fame, The Parliament of Birds, The Legend of Good Women*. London. Harmondsworth.

Clay, R. M., 1914 *The Hermits and Anchorites of England*. Methuen. London.

Cockerill, S., 2014, *Eleanor of Castile: The Shadow Queen*. Amberley. Stroud.

Cokayne, G. E., 1912, *The Complete Peerage, Volume* II, St. Catherine Press. London.

Colvin, H.M., 1986, 'Royal gardens in medieval England' in MacDoughall, E. (ed.) *Medieval Gardens*. Dumbarton Oaks Research Library and Collection, Washington.

Colvin, H. M., Brown, R. A. & Taylor A. J., 1963, *The History of the King's Works Vol. 2: The Middle Ages*. Her Majesties Stationary Office. London.

Cook, G. H., 1947, *Mediaeval Chantries and Chantry Chapels*. Phoenix House. London.

Copnall, H. H., 1915, *Notes and Extracts from the NottinghamshireCounty Records of the Seventeenth Century*. Nottingham

Costain, T. B., 1973, *The Pageant of England 1272–1377: The Three Edwards*. Tandem. London.

Craib, T., 1923, 'The Itinerary of Henry III 1216–1272', edited and annotated by S. Brindle and S. Priestley (English Heritage, no date.)

Crook, D., 2008, 'Jordan Castle and the Foliot family of Grimston, 1225–1330' in *Transactions of the Thoroton Society* Vol. 112. Nottingham.

Crook, D., 2005, 'Clipstone Peel: Fortification and politics from Bannockburn to the Treaty of Leake 1314–18' in Prestwich, M., Britnell, R. & Frame, R. (eds), *Thirteenth Century England 10 – Proceedings of the Durham Conference 2003*. Boydell Press. Woodbridge.

Crook, D., 2002, 'The foundation of Bestwood Lodge, 1284' in *Transactions of the Thoroton Society* Vol. 106. Nottingham

Crook, D., 1976, 'Clipstone Park and Peel' in *Transactions of the Thoroton Society of Nottinghamshire*. Vol. 80. Nottingham

Crouch, D., 1997, 'The Culture of Death in the Anglo-Norman World' in Hollister, C. W., *Anglo-Norman Political Culture and the Twelfth-century Renaissance: Proceedings of the Borchard Conference on Anglo-Norman History, 1995*. Boydell & Brewer. Woodbridge.

Curry, A., 2000, 'Richard II and the war with France' in Dodd, G. (ed.), *The Reign of Richard II*. Tempus. Stroud.

Danbury, J., 2002, 'The Water-Meadows Irrigation Scheme' in *A Celebration of Kings Clipstone – 1000 Years of History*. Tuxford.

Danbury, J., 2002, 'Railways Associated with Clipstone' in *A Celebration of Kings Clipstone – 1000 Years of History*. Tuxford.

Danbury, J., 2002, 'Clipstone Army Camp' in *A Celebration of Kings Clipstone – 1000 Years of History*. Tuxford.

Danbury, J., 2002, 'Clipstone Colliery and Village' in *A Celebration of King's Clipstone – 1000 Years of History*. Tuxford.

Davis, J.P., *The Gothic King – A Biography of Henry III*. Peter Owen. Chicago.

Deputy Keeper of the Records (ed.), 1922, Calendar of the Close Rolls of Richard II Vol. IV AD1389–92. London.

Deputy Keeper of the Records (ed.), 1898, *Calendar of the Close Rolls of Edward III* Vol. II AD1330–33. London.

Deputy Keeper of the Records (ed.), 1898, *Calendar of the Close Rolls of Edward II* Vol. IV AD1323–27. London.

Deputy Keeper of the Records (ed.), 1895, *Calendar of the Close Rolls of Edward II* Vol. III AD1318–23. London.

Deputy Keeper of the Records (ed.), 1893, *Calendar of the Close Rolls of Edward II* Vol. II AD1313–18. London.

Dodd, G., 2000, 'Richard II and the transformation of Parliament' in Dodd, G., (ed.), *The Reign of Richard II*. Tempus. Stroud.

Doubleday, W. E., 1943, 'Notts villages: Blyth' in *The Nottinghamshire Guardian*

Drage, C., 1990, *Nottingham Castle – A Place Full Royal*. Nottingham.

Dyer, C., 2001, *Everyday Life in Medieval England*. A & C Black. Hambledon & London.

Easton, T., 2015, 'Apotropaic Symbols and Other Measures for Protecting Buildings against Misfortune' in Hutton, R. (ed), 2015, *Physical Evidence for Ritual Acts, Sorcery and Witchcraft in Christian Britain.* Palgrave Macmillan. Basingstoke.

English Heritage, 2011 *Introduction to Heritage Assets – Animal Management*. Swindon.

Eyton, R.W., 1878, *Court Household and Itinerary of King Henry II*. Holborn, London.

Fisher, J. L., 1968, *A medieval farming glossary of Latin and English words, taken mainly from Essex records*, National Council for Social Service. London

Gardner, A., 2011, *English Medieval Sculpture*. Cambridge University Press.

Gasquet, F. A., 1908, *The Black Death of 1348 and 1349*. G. Bell. London.

Gaunt, A., Wright, J., Crossley, S. & Budge, D., 2015, *Excavation of the Medieval Boundary Ditch of King John's Palace, Kings Clipstone, Sherwood Forest, Nottinghamshire*. Unpublished report.

Gaunt, A. & Wright, 2013–14, 'A palace for our kings' – A decade of research into a royal residence in the heart of Sherwood Forest at Kings Clipstone, Nottinghamshire' in *The Castle Studies Group Journal* No. 27

Gaunt, A. & Wright, J., 2013, 'A romantic royal retreat, and an idealised forest in miniature: The designed landscape of medieval Clipstone, at the heart of Sherwood Forest' in *Transactions of the Thoroton Society* Vol. 117. Nottingham.

Gaunt, A, 2011, *Clipstone Park and the King's Houses: Reconstructing and interpreting a medieval landscape through non-invasive techniques*. Unpublished MA thesis in Landscape Archaeology, GIS and Virtual Environments, University of Birmingham.

Giles, J. A., 1852, *Matthew Paris's English History from the Year 1235 to 1273 Vol. 1*. G. Bohn. London.

Gillingham, J., 2000, *Richard I*. Yale.

Gillingham., J., 1978, *Richard the Lionheart*. Book Club Associates. London.

Given-Wilson, C. (ed.), 1993, *Chronicles of the Revolution 1397–1400*. Manchester

University Press.

Gough, H., 1900, *Itinerary of Edward I 1277–1285* Vol. I. Paisley. London

Gough, H., 1900, *Itinerary of Edward I* 1286–1307 Vol. II. Paisley. London

Gregory, A., 2014, *The Queen's House and Bell Tower: Statement of Significance.* Unpublished report.

Griffin, E., 2008, *Blood Sport: Hunting in Britain since 1066.* Yale.

Grose, F., 1772, The Antiquities of England and Wales. Hooper. London.

Gummer, B., 2014, *The Scourging Angel: The Black Death in the British Isles.* Random House. London.

Hanawalt, B., 1979, *Crime and Conflict in English Communities 1300–1348.* London and Cambridge, Massachusetts.

Hardy, T. D., 1835, *Rotuli Litterarum Patentium in Turri Londinensi Asservati.* London.

Harries, S., 2011, *Nikolaus Pevsner: The Life.* Chatto & Windus. London.

Hartshorne, C. H., 1861, *The Itinerary of King Edward the Second.*

Haskins, G. L., 1938, 'Francis Accursius: A New Document' in *Speculum* Vol. 13. doi:10.2307/2848831.

Hayman, R., 2014, *The Green Man.* Shire. Oxford.

Hewlings, R., 2008, 'Sir Howard Colvin: Architectural historian whose biographical dictionaries laid a foundation for all other scholars in his field' in *The Independant* Tuesday 01 January 2008

Hodgson, J. & Laird, C. F., 1813, *The Beauties of England.* Volume 12. J. Harris London.

Horne, S., 2013, *Thynghowe and Birklands.* Nottinghamshire.

Howard, D. R., 1987 (reprinted 1989), *Chaucer: His Life, His Works, His World.* Ballentine. New York.

Hutton, R. (ed), 2015, Physical Evidence for Ritual Acts, Sorcery and Witchcraft in Christian Britain. Palgrave Macmillan. Basingstoke.

Ingram, J. (trans.), 1823 (reprinted 1993), *The Saxon Chronicle.* Studio Editions. London.

James, A., 2012 *Metal detecting finds from the grounds of King John's Palace at King's Clipstone, Mansfield, Nottinghamshire.* Unpublished report.

James, T. B., 2010, *Clarendon: Landscape, Palace and Mansion.* Salisbury and South Wiltshire Museum.

James, T.B. & Gerrard, C., 2007, *Clarendon: Landscape of Kings.* Windgatherer. Oxford.

James, T. B., 1999, *The Black Death in Hampshire*, Hampshire County Council.

James, T.B., 1990, *The Palaces of Medieval England.* Seaby. London.

Jeffries, F. (ed.), 'The Record Commision, No. X – King's Remembrancer's Records' in *The Gentleman's Magazine*, April 1938. London.

Johnson, P., 1973, *The Life and Times of Edward III.* Book Club Associates. London.

Keevill, G. D., 2000, *Medieval Palaces – an archaeology.* Tempus. Stroud.

King, A. & Penman, M. A., 2007, *England and Scotland in the Fourteenth Century: New Perspectives.* Boydell & Brewer.Woodbridge.

King, C., (ed.), 2015, 'Archaeology in Nottinghamshire' in *Transactions of the Thoroton Society* Vol. 119. Nottingham.

Kirton, T., 2001, 'Clipstone Forest and Shrogges' in *A Celebration of Kings Clipstone – 1000 Years of History*. Tuxford.

Lavelle, J. (ed.), 1854 (reprinted 1992), *Le Chasse de Gaston Phoebus, Comte de Foix*. Lacour, Nimes.

Liddiard, R., 2005, *Castles in Context – Power, Symbolism and Landscape, 1066 to 1500*. Windgatherer. Oxford.

Lofts, N., 1977, *Queens of England*. Doubleday. New York.

Marples, P., 2013, *Clipstone Camp and the Mansfield Area in World War One*. Forest Town Heritage Group.

Marples, P., 2005, *Forest Town: The Village That Grew Out Of Coal*. Forest Town Heritage Group.

Mastoris. S. and Groves. S., 1997, "Sherwood Forest in 1609 : A Crown Survey by Richard Bankes", *Thoroton Society Record Series XL* (for 1992 & 1993)

McHardy, A. K., 2000, 'Richard II: a personal portrait' in Dodd, G. (ed.), *The Reign of Richard II*. Tempus.

Mills, A. D., 1993, *A Dictionary of English Place Names*. Oxford University Press.

Mordan, J., 2004, *Timber-frame Buildings of Nottinghamshire*. Nottinghamshire County Council.

Morris, M., 2009, *A Great and Terrible King – Edward I and the Forging of Britain*. Windmill. London

Morris, J. (ed.), 1977, *Domesday Book: Nottinghamshire*. Phillimore. Chichester.

Mortimer, I., 2015, 'Was Edward really killed?' in Letters, *BBC History Magazine*, April 2015

Mortimer, I., 2008, *The Fears of Henry IV The Life of England's Self-Made King*. Vintage. London.

Mortimer, I., 2005, 'The Death of Edward II in Berkeley Castle' in *English Historical Review*, CXX

Myers, A. R., 2013, *English Historical Documents 4: 1327–1485*. Psychology Press. Hove.

O'Connor, T. & Sykes, N., 2010, *Extinction and invasions: a social history of British fauna*. Oxbow. Oxford.

Ormrod, W. M., 2013, *Edward III*. Yale.

Oxford University Press, 1994, *The Concise Dictionary of National Biography*

Palmer, F. P. & Crowquill, A., 1846, The *Wanderings of a Pen and Pencil*. Jeremiah How.

Palmer-Brown, C. & Munford, W., 2004, 'Romano-British Life in North Nottinghamshire: Fresh evidence from Raymoth Lane, Worksop' in *Transactions of the Thoroton Society* Vol. 108. Nottingham.

Parker-Pearson, M., 1993, *Bronze Age Britain*. Batsford. London.

Pearsall, D., 1992, *The Life of Geoffrey Chaucer*. Blackwell. Oxford.

Peltzer, J., 2013, 'Marriages of the English earls: A new perspective' in *Thirteenth*

Century England XIV: Proceedings of the Aberystwyth and Lampeter Conference, 2011 Volume 14 of Thirteenth Century England Series

Phillips, S., 2011, *Edward II*. Yale.

Pevsner, N. & Williamson, E., 1979 (2nd ed.), *The Buildings of England: Nottinghamshire*. Yale.

Pevsner, N., 1951, *The Buildings of England: Nottinghamshire*. Penguin. Harmondsworth.

Platt, C., 1978, *Medieval England: A Social History and Archaeology from the Conquest to 1600AD*. London

Public Record Office, 1910, *Calendar of the Close Rolls, Edward III, Vol. 12. 1364–136*. London.

Rackham, O., 1980, *The History of the Countryside*. Phoenix. London.

Rahtz, P., 2001, *Living Archaeology*. Tempus. Stroud.

Rahtz, P., 1969, *Excavations at King John's Hunting Lodge, Writtle, Essex, 1955–7*. Medieval Archaeology Monograph Series 3. London.

Rahtz, P. & Colvin, H. M., 1960, 'King John's Palace, Clipstone, Nottinghamshire' in *Transactions of the Thoroton Society* Vol. 64. Nottingham.

Redmonds, G., King, T. & Hey, D., 2011, *Surnames, DNA and Family History*. Oxford University Press.

Richardson, A., 2007, 'The king's chief delights': A landscape approach to the royal parks of post-Conquest England' in Liddiard, R. (ed.), 2007, *The Medieval Park: New Perspectives*. Windgatherer. Oxford.

Riley, H. T. (trans.), 1853, *The annals of Roger de Hoveden: Comprising the history of England and of other countries of Europe from A.D. 732 to A.D. 1201. Translated from the Latin, with notes and illus*. London

Roberts, M., 1844, *Ruins and Old Trees, Associated with Memorable Events in English History*. Harvey & Darton. London.

Rowley, T., 1988, *The High Middle Ages 1200–1550*. Paladin. London

Salzman, L. F., 1952 (reprinted 1997), *Building in England down to 1540*. Oxford University Press.

Sanderson, G., 1835 (reprinted 2001), *Twenty miles around Mansfield*. Nottinghamshire County Council.

Saul, N., 1999, *Richard II*. Yale.

Sayles, G. O. (ed.), 1988, *The Functions of the Medieval Parliament of England*. Bloomsbury. London.

Scullard, H. H., 1979 (reprinted 1997), Roman Britain – Outpost of the Empire. Thames & Hudson. London.

Shapiro, J., 2010, *Contested Will*. Faber & Faber. London.

Sharpe, J., 2001, *Witchcraft in early modern England*. Pearson. Harlow.

Sharpe, K., 1992, *The Personal Rule of Charles I*. Yale University Press.

Shaw Browne, J., 2002, 'The ancient forest of Rumwood in Sherwood' in *A Celebration of Kings Clipstone – 1000 Years of History*. Tuxford.

Sheppard, R., 2015, *A small archaeological investigation at King John's Palace, Clipstone, Nottinghamshire, 1991*. Unpublished report.

Speight, S., 2004, 'Religion in the bailey: charters, chapels and the clergy' in *Chateau Gaillard: études de castellologie médiévale*. Caen.

Spencer, A. M., 2013, *Nobility and Kingship in Medieval England: The Earls and Edward I, 1272–1307* Volume 91 of Cambridge Studies in Medieval Life and Thought: Fourth Series. Cambridge University Press

Stapleton, A., *A History of the Lordship of King's Clipstone or Clipstone in Sherwood, Nottinghamshire*. Mansfield.

Steane, J., 2014, *The Archaeology of Medieval England and Wales*. Routledge. London.

Steane, J., 2001, *The Archaeology of Power*. Tempus. Stroud.

Steane, J., 1993 (reprinted 1999), *The Archaeology of the Medieval English Monarchy*. Routledge. London.

Stocker, D., 1991, *St Mary's Guildhall, Lincoln – The survey and excavation of a medieval building complex*. City of Lincoln Archaeological Unit.

Sykes, N., 2007a, 'Animal bones and animal parks' in Liddiard, R. (ed.), 2007, *The Medieval*

Park: New Perspectives. Windgatherer. Oxford.

Sykes, N., 2007b, 'Taking sides: the social life of venison in medieval England' in A. Pluskowski, *Breaking and shaping beastly bodies: animals as material culture in the Middle Ages*. Oxbow. Oxford.

Taylor, A. J., 1984, *The Welsh Castles of Edward I*. Bloomsbury. London.

Thompson, C., 1850 'Clipstone Castle and St. Edwin's Chapel' in *Sherwood Gatherer*. January Searle.

Throsby, J., 1790 (ed.) & Thoroton, R., 1677, *History of Nottinghamshire Vol. 3* (reprinted 1972). Nottingham.

Trent & Peak Archaeological Trust, 1991, *King John's Palace, Clipstone*. Unpublished excavation archive.

Turner, T. H., 1851, *Some account of domestic architecture in England, from the conquest to the end of the thirteenth century*. J.H. & J. Parker. Oxford.

Tweedale-Meeby, K., 1947, *Nottinghamshire County Records in the Eighteenth Century*. Nottingham.

Vincent, N. C., 2015, 'King John's Diary & Itinerary', *The Magna Carta Project*. University of East Anglia.

Warner, K., 2014, *Edward II – The Unconventional King*. Amberley. Stroud.

Warren, H. L., 1991, *Henry II*. Methuen. London.

Welch, M., 1992, *Anglo-Saxon England*. Batsford. London.

Wessex Archaeology, 2011, *King John's Palace, Clipstone, Nottinghamshire – archaeological evaluation and assessment of results*. Unpublished report.

White, F., 1844, *History, gazetteer & directory of the county of Nottinghamshire*. Nottingham

White, W., 1832, *History, Gazetteer and Directory of Nottinghamshire*. Nottingham.

Wood, M., 1986, *Domesday: A Search for the Roots of England*. BBC. Chatham.

Wood, M., 1965 (reprinted 1983). *The English Mediaeval House*. Bracken. London.

Wright, J., 2016, *Maun Cottage, Mansfield Road, Kings Clipstone, Nottinghamshire – an historic standing building survey*. Unpublished report.

Wright, J., 2015, *'The instruments of darkness tell us truths': Ritual Protection Marks and Witchcraft at Knole, Kent*. Gresham College.

Wright, J., 2014, *Merton Priory boundary wall – an historic standing building survey*. Unpublished report.

Wright, J., 2013, Brammer Farmhouse and Arundel Cottage, Mansfield Road, Kings Clipstone, Nottinghamshire, NG21 – a standing building survey report. Unpublished report.

Wright, J., 2009 *Strelley Hall, Strelley, Nottinghamshire – Archaeological Investigations*. Unpublished report.

Wright, J., 2008, *Castles of Nottinghamshire*. Nottinghamshire County Council.

Wright, J, 2007 Unpublished archive of King's Clipstone masonry survey (Held by Nottinghamshire County Council)

Wright, J. & Mordan, J., 2005, *A Condition Survey of King John's Palace, Kings Clipstone, Nottinghamshire*. Unpublished report.

Wright, J., 2004, 'A Survey of King John's Palace, Kings Clipstone, Nottinghamshire' in *Transactions of the Thoroton Society of Nottinghamshire*. Vol. 108. Nottingham.

Notes

Chapter One: The King's Houses

[1] Brown, R.A., 1963, *English Medieval Castles*, p17

[2] *Oxford English Dictionary*, 2015

[3] Hoad, T.F., 1993, *Concise Oxford Dictionary of English Etymology*, p331

[4] Steane, J., 2001, *The Archaeology of Power*, pp21–24

[5] Speight, S., 2004, 'Religion in the bailey: charters, chapels and the clergy' in *Chateau Gaillard: études de castellologie médiévale*. Caen.

[6] Steane, 2001, 37–9

[7] Ibid, 79

[8] Ibid, 276

[9] Keevill, G.D., 2000, *Medieval Palaces – an archaeology*, p14

[10] Ibid, 166

[11] Davis, J.P., *The Gothic King – A Biography of Henry III*, pp213–4

[12] Steane, 2001, 104

[13] Steane, J., 1993, The Archaeology of the Medieval English Monarchy, p84

[14] Keevill, 2000, 18

[15] Warren, H.L., 1991, *Henry II*, pp390–3

[16] Steane, 1993, 79–80

[17] Griffin, E., 2008, *Blood Sport: Hunting in Britain since 1066*, pp28–30 & pp43–44

[18] James, T. B., 1990, *The Palaces of Medieval England*, p18

[19] Wright, J., 2013, *Brammer Farmhouse and Arundel Cottage – standing building survey report*, pp30–1

[20] Rowley, T., 1988, *The High Middles Ages 1200–1550*, pp50–1

[21] Wright, J., 2008, *Castles of Nottinghamshire*, p28

[22] Crook, D., 2005, 'Clipstone Peel: Fortification and politics from Bannockburn to the Treaty of Leake 1314–18' in Prestwich, M., Britnell, R. & Frame, R. (eds), *Thirteenth Century England 10 – Proceedings of the Durham Conference 2003*. Woodbridge. Boydell Press, pp187–95

[23] Keevil, 2000, 13

[24] Steane, 1993, 87

[25] James, 1990, 17

[26] Steane, 2001, 97–8, 109

[27] James, 1990, 20–1; Steane 1993, 184–5

[28] Ormrod, M. W., *Edward III*, 2013, p128

[29] Stapleton, A., 1890, *A History of the Lordship of King's Clipstone or Clipstone in Sherwood, Nottinghamshire*, pp14–16

[30] Steane, 1999, 88

[31] Steane, 1999, 123–4

[32] Steane, 2001, 26–7

[33]   Bernhardt, J.W., 1993, *Itinerant Kingship and Royal Monasteries in Early Medieval Germany c 936–1075*, p47

[34]   Crook, D., 1976, 'Clipstone Park and Peel' in *Transactions of the Thoroton Society of Nottinghamshire*. Vol. 80, p40–1

[35]   James, 1990, 40

[36]   Steane, 1993, 126–9

[37]   James, 1990, 125

[38]   Ibid, 16

[39]   Steane,1993, 88

[40]   James, 1990, 93

[41]   Eyton, R.W., 1878, *Court Household and Itinerary of King Henry II;* p241; 261

[42]   Stapleton, 1890, 35–6; 49

[43]   Ormrod, 2013, 617

[44]   Stapleton, 1890, 40–1

[45]   Given-Wilson, C. (ed.), 1993, *Chronicles of the Revolution 1397–1400*, p.241

[46]   James, T.B. & Gerrard, C., 2007, Clarendon: Landscape of Kings, p.90

[47]   Stapleton, 1890, 22–3

[48]   Fine Roll C 60/46, 33 HENRY III (1248–1249)

[49]   Keevill, 2000, 142

[50]   James & Gerrard, 2007, 89

[51]   James, 1990, 89

[52]   Ormrod, 2013, 316

[53]   James, 1990, 97

[54]   Ibid, 110

[55]   James, A., 2012, *Metal detecting finds from the grounds of King John's Palace at King's Clipstone, Mansfield, Nottinghamshire*

[56]   James & Gerrard, 2007, 49

Chapter Two: Early History of Clipstone

[57]   Gaunt, A., Wright, J., Crossley, S. & Budge, D., 2015, *Excavation of the Medieval Boundary Ditch of King John's Palace, Kings Clipstone, Sherwood Forest, Nottinghamshire*, pp101–5

[58]   Nottinghamshire Historic Environment Record 5965, 5909 and 6819

[59]   Parker-Pearson, M., 1993, *Bronze Age Britain*, pp103–8

[60]   Pastscape Monument No. 1430560

[61]   Scullard, H. H., 1979 (reprinted 1997), Roman Britain – Outpost of the Empire, p113

[62]   Throsby, J., 1790 (ed.) & Thoroton, R., 1677, *History of Nottinghamshire* Vol. 3 (reprinted 1972)

[63]   Rahtz, P. & Colvin, H. M., 1960, 'King John's Palace, Clipstone, Nottinghamshire' in *Transactions of the Thoroton Society* Vol. 64, p29

64   Wessex Archaeology, 2011, *King John's Palace, Clipstone, Nottinghamshire – archaeological evaluation and assessment of results,* p19

65   Palmer-Brown, C. & Munford, W., 2004, 'Romano-British Life in North Nottinghamshire: Fresh evidence from Raymoth Lane, Worksop' in *Transactions of the Thoroton Society* Vol. 108, pp37–51

66   Portable Antiquities Scheme DENO-AF76A7, DENO-E31EC0, DENO-907885; Wessex Archaeology, 2011, 20

67   Wessex Archaeology, 2011, 19–20

68   Portable Antiquities Scheme DENO-907885

69   Nottinghamshire Historic Environment Record 5965

70   Portable Antiquities Scheme DENO-6FFD50

71   Wessex Archaeology, 2011, 19

72   Stapleton, 1890, 3–4

73   Morris, J. (ed.), 1977, *Domesday Book: Nottinghamshire*, p285

74   Mills, A. D., 1993, A Dictionary of English Place Names, p.83

75   Horne, S., 2013, *Thynghowe and Birklands,* pp22–6

76   Welch, M., 1992, Anglo-Saxon England, pp120–1

77   Wood, M., 1986, *Domesday: A Search for the Roots of England*, pp149–50

78   Trent & Peak Archaeological Trust, 1991, King John's Palace, Clipstone. Unpublished excavation archive.

79   Challis, K., (ed.), 2014, 'Archaeology in Nottinghamshire' in *Transactions of the Thoroton Society* Vol. 118. Nottingham.

80   York Minster Library, Magnum Resistrum Album, Ms

81   Ingram, J. (trans.), 1823 (reprinted 1993), *The Saxon Chronicle*, pp196

82   Morris, 1977, 285

83   Gaunt, A. & Wright, J., 2013, 'A romantic royal retreat, and an idealised forest in miniature: The designed landscape of medieval Clipstone, at the heart of Sherwood Forest' in *Transactions of the Thoroton Society* Vol. 117, pp44–5

84   Wood, 1986, 18–25

85   Ibid, 164–5

86   Ibid, 213

87   Crook, 1976, 36

88   Wood, 1986, 26

89   Ibid, 27; 167

90   Ibid, 174–5

91   Stapleton, 1890, 7

92   Griffin, 2008, 16–17

93   Warren, 1991, 393

94   Griffin, 208, 25–8

95   Ibid, 20

96   Crook, D., 2008, 'Jordan Castle and the Foliot family of Grimston, 1225–1330' in *Transactions of the Thoroton Society* Vol. 112, pp146–7

[97] Griffin, 2008, 28
[98] Crook, 2008, 147
[99] Griffin, 2008, 34–6
[100] Crook, 2008, 147
[101] Griffin, 2008, 38–40
[102] Gaunt & Wright, 2013, 40
[103] Warren, 1991, 394–5

Chapter Three: Development of Park and Palace: 1164–1199

[104] Rahtz & Colvin, 1960, 22
[105] Bradley & Severn, 2002, 29
[106] Stapleton, 1890, 11
[107] Ibid
[108] Keevill, 2000, 23
[109] Ibid, 25
[110] Steane, 2001, 275
[111] Rahtz & Colvin, 1960, 34
[112] Rahtz, P., 1969, *Excavations at King John's Hunting Lodge, Writtle, Essex, 1955–7*
[113] Stapleton, 1890, 12
[114] Colvin, H. M., Brown, R. A. & Taylor A. J., 1963, *The History of the King's Works Vol. 2: The Middle Ages*, p920
[115] Mickie Bradley, landowner of Castlefield, pers. Comm.
[116] James, 1990, 52–5
[117] E 101/542/24
[118] Stocker, D., 1991, *St Mary's Guildhall, Lincoln – The survey and excavation of a medieval building complex*, 40–1
[119] Ibid, 38–9
[120] Ibid, 17–32
[121] Ibid, 37–8; 40
[122] Warren, 1991, 117–8
[123] Ibid, 125–36
[124] Ibid, 136–43
[125] Ibid, 142–3
[126] James, 1990, 50; 55
[127] Brown, 1954, 120
[128] Stapleton, 1890, 15
[129] Rahtz & Colvin, 1960, 27
[130] Keevill, 2000, 51
[131] Ibid, 34
[132] Sheppard, R., 1991, *A small archaeological investigation at King John's Palace, Clipstone, Nottinghamshire, 1991*, p8

[133] Grose, F., 1772, *The Antiquities of England and Wales*

[134] Stocker, 1991, 27

[135] Rahtz & Colvin, 1960, plate 2c

[136] Ibid, 36

[137] Wessex Archaeology, 2011, 12

[138] Rahtz & Colvin, 1960, 29–30

[139] Ibid, 43

[140] James, 1990, 48

[141] Steane, 2001, 93

[142] Ibid, 111–2

[143] Wessex Archaeology, 2011, 19

[144] Rahtz & Colvin, 1960, 34

[145] Ibid, 34

[146] Keevill, 2000, 72

[147] Wessex Archaeology, 2011, Fig 3

[148] Rahtz & Colvin, 1960, 36

[149] Warren, 1991, 604–5

[150] Ibid, 393

[151] Stapleton, 1890, 15

[152] King, C., (ed.), 2015, 'Archaeology in Nottinghamshire' in *Transactions of the Thoroton Society* Vol. 118. Nottingham.

[153] Rahtz & Colvin, 1960, 30

[154] Wessex, 2011, 11

[155] Rahtz & Colvin, 1960, 30

[156] Wessex Archaeology, 2011, Fig 3

[157] Crook, 1976, p35

[158] Stapleton, 1890, 16

[159] Gillingham, J., 1978, *Richard the Lionheart*, p236

[160] Ibid, 230–1

[161] Drage, C., 1989, Nottingham Castle: A place full royal, p42

[162] Riley, H. T. (trans.), 1853, *The annals of Roger de Hoveden : Comprising the history of England and of other countries of Europe from A.D. 732 to A.D. 1201,* p316

[163] Ibid, 316

[164] Gillingham, 1978, 66; 69

[165] Ibid, 227

[166] Gillingham, J., 2000, *Richard I*, p272

[167] Challis, K., (ed.), 2014, 'Archaeology in Nottinghamshire' in *Transactions of the Thoroton Society* Vol. 118. Nottingham.

[168] Stapleton, 1890, 17

[169] Gillingham, 2000, 272

[170] Gillingham, 1978, 242

Chapter Four: Politics and Palace Expansion: 1199–1307

[171] Ashley, M., 1972 (reprinted 1984), *The Life and Times of King John*, pp204–11

[172] Crook, 1976, 35

[173] Nottinghamshire Historic Environment Record L8565

[174] E 101/460/18; E101/460/19

[175] E 101/460/20; E 101/460/21

[176] Gaunt, A, 2011, *Clipstone Park and the King's Houses: Reconstructing and interpreting a medieval landscape through non-invasive techniques*, p20

[177] Stapleton, 1890, 26

[178] Stapleton, 1890, 58–9

[179] Cook, G. H., 1947, *Mediaeval Chantries and Chantry Chapels*, p17

[180] Crouch, D., 1997, 'The Culture of Death in the Anglo-Norman World' in Hollister, C. W., *Anglo-Norman Political Culture and the Twelfth-century Renaissance: Proceedings of the Borchard Conference on Anglo-Norman History, 1995,* p177

[181] Stapleton, 1890, 22–4

[182] Stapleton, 1890, 27

[183] Vincent, N. C., 2015, 'King John's Diary & Itinerary', *The Magna Carta Project*

[184] Seaton, S., 2015, 'King John, Nottingham Castle and the Magna Carta' in *Nottingham Evening Post* June 15 2015; Shaw Browne, J., 2002, 'The ancient forest of Rumwood in Sherwood' in *A Celebration of Kings Clipstone – 1000 Years of History* p17

[185] Ashley, 1972, 114–5

[186] Jeffries, F. (ed.), 'The Record Commision, No. X – King's Remembrancer's Records' in *The Gentleman's Magazine*, April 1938, p358

[187] Almond, 2003, 87

[188] Griffin, 2008, 29

[189] Steane, 1993, 147

[190] Ibid, 152

[191] Wood, M., 1965 (reprinted 1983), *The English Mediaeval House*, p10

[192] Throsby, 1790, 340–2

[193] Stapleton, 1890, 28

[194] Rahtz, 1960, 23

[195] Stapleton, 1890, 29

[196] Crook, 2008, 147–8

[197] Keevill, 2000, 77

[198] Ibid, 78

[199] Rahtz, 1960, 30

[200] Wessex Archaeology, 2011, 11

[201] Crook, 2008, 147–8

[202] Ibid, 149

[203] Rahtz, 1960, 23

[204] Giles, J. A., 1852, *Matthew Paris's English History from the Year 1235 to 1273 Vol. 1*, pp138–9

[205] Salzman, L. F., 1952 (reprinted 1997), *Building in England down to 1540*, p174

[206] Steane, 1993, 99

[207] Turner, T. H., 1851, *Some account of domestic architecture in England, from the conquest to the end of the thirteenth century*, 235

[208] Davis, 2013, pp137–8

[209] Doubleday, W. E., 1943, 'Notts villages: Blyth' in *The Nottinghamshire Guardian*

[210] Turner, 1851, 205

[211] E 101/460/18; E101/460/19

[212] James, 1990, 14; 44; 62

[213] James, 1990, 82

[214] Steane 2001, 105

[215] James, 1990, 69

[216] Salzman, 1952, 174

[217] James, 1990, 21

[218] James, 1990, 84; Steane 2001, 106–7

[219] James & Gerrard, 2007, 71

[220] E 101/542/24

[221] Steane, 2001, 100

[222] Wood 1965, 247; Steane 2001, 101

[223] Wood, 1965, 248; Keevill, 2000, 144

[224] Steane2001, 102

[225] James, 2012

[226] Steane 2001, 102

[227] Keevill, 2000, 144–5

[228] Ibid, 147–51

[229] James & Gerrard 2007, 89

[230] Colvin, Brown & Taylor, 1963, 920

[231] Steane, 1993, 185

[232] James, 1990, 67–8

[233] Steane, 2001, 116; Steane 1999, 184

[234] Steane, 2001, 117

[235] Davis, 2013, 143–9

[236] Turner, 1851, 235–6

[237] James & Gerrard 2007, 79

[238] Rahtz, 1960, 36; Wessex Archaeology 2011, 19–20; Challis 2013, 15

[239] James & Gerrad 2007, 95

[240] Wessex Archaeology 2011, 13–15; 17–18

[241] Ibid, 19

[242] Colvin, Brown & Taylor, 1963, 125

[243] Sassin Allen, A., 2015, Church Orientation in the Landscape: a Perspective from

Medieval Wales in *Archaeological Journal* Vol. 172

[244] P.R.O., 1910, *Calendar of the Close Rolls, Edward III, Vol. 12. 1364–136*

[245] Keevill, 2000, 122

[246] Fine Roll C 60/49, 36 HENRY III (1251–1252)

[247] Steane 1999, 101

[248] Turner, 1851, 235–6

[249] Steane, 1993, 116

[250] Turner, 1851, 235–6

[251] James & Gerrard 2007, 74

[252] Steane 2001, 94–6

[253] E 101/542/24

[254] Mordan, J., 2004, *Timber-frame Buildings of Nottinghamshire*, p22

[255] Turner, 1851, 235–6

[256] Keevill, 2000, 82

[257] Turner, 1851, 235–6

[258] Turner, 1851, 235–6

[259] E 101/460/18; E101/460/19

[260] Turner, 1851, 262

[261] James & Gerrad 2007, 82–3; 90

[262] James, T. B., 2010, *Clarendon: Landscape, Palace and Mansion*, pp32–3

[263] Keevill, 2000, 106

[264] Davis, 2013, 186–7

[265] James, 1990, 78, Steane 1999, 81

[266] Ibid, 96

[267] Davis, 2013, 151–8

[268] James, 1990, 65; 68–90

[269] Ibid, 72; 90

[270] Rahtz 1960, 30

[271] Gaunt 2011, 31–2

[272] Wessex Archaeology 2011, 12–3

[273] Kevill, 2000, 56

[274] Rahtz 1960, 26

[275] James, 1990, 12

[276] Drage 1990, 110

[277] Wessex Archaeology 2011, 21

[278] King, 2015

[279] Keevill, 2000, 50

[280] Steane 2001, 255

[281] Gaunt & Wright 2013–14, 246

[282] James & Gerrad 2007, 92

[283] James, 1990, 143

[284] Ibid, 87

285 Steane, 2001, 256

286 Steane 1999, 136; James & Gerrad 2007, 90

287 Steane 2001, 257–8

288 Wright, J., 2016, *Maun Cottage, Mansfield Road, Kings Clipstone, Nottinghamshire – an historic standing building survey*

289 Wright, 2013, 16–17

290 Ibid, 25–31

291 Wright, J., 2014, Merton Priory boundary wall – an historic standing building survey

292 Wright, 2013, 25–31

293 Wright 2016

294 Gaunt & Wright, 2013–14, 239

295 Ibid, 239

296 Shaw Browne, 2002, 10

297 James, 1990, 69

298 Steane 1993, 147

299 Morris, M., 2009, *A Great and Terrible King – Edward I and the Forging of Britain*, pp159–172

300 Ibid, 173

301 Almond, 2003, 87

302 Morris, 2009, 174

303 Lofts, N., 1977, *Queens of England*, pp 48–50

304 Rahtz 1956, 23

305 E 101/542/24; E 101/460/18; E101/460/19

306 James, 1990, 92–4

307 Liddiard, R., 2005, *Castles in Context – Power, Symbolism and Landscape, 1066 to 1500*, pp97–8

308 Wood, 1965, 69–70

309 Morris, 2009, 177–88

310 Rahtz 1960, 23

311 Colvin, Brown & Taylor, 1963, 920

312 Steane, 2001, 268–70

313 Armitage, S., 2007, *Sir Gawain and the Green Knight*, p42, lines 820–823

314 E 101/542/24

315 E 101/135/20

316 E 101/460/18; E 101/460/19

317 James & Gerrard 2007, 69; 76; pers. comm. Mary South, July 2015

318 Steane 2001, 269

319 Murray, A., 2006, *All the Kings' Horses: A Celebration of Royal Horses from 1066 to the Present Day*, p14

320 Steane 1993, 124–5

321 Murray, 2006, 14–15

[322] Ibid, 15

[323] Morris, 2009, 190

[324] Almond, 2003, 87

[325] Morris, 2009, 221–3

[326] Ibid, 225

[327] Ibid, 227

[328] Ibid, 228

[329] Stapleton, 1890, 33

[330] Ibid

[331] Ibid

[332] Haskins, G. L., 1938, 'Francis Accursius: A New Document' in *Speculum* Vol. 13, pp 76–77. doi:10.2307/2848831.

[333] Stapleton, 1890, 34

[334] Sayles, G. O. (ed.), 1988, *The Functions of the Medieval Parliament of England*, p202

[335] Peltzer, J., 2013, 'Marriages of the English earls: A new perspective' in *Thirteenth Century England XIV: Proceedings of the Aberystwyth and Lampeter Conference, 2011*, p68

[336] Crook 2008, 152

[337] Spencer, A. M., 2013, *Nobility and Kingship in Medieval England: The Earls and Edward I, 1272–1307,* pp 217–219

[338] Bradley & Servern, 2002, 33

[339] Stapleton, 1890, 35

[340] Ibid

[341] Sayles, 1988, xii

[342] King, A. & Penman, M. A., 2007, England and Scotland in the Fourteenth Century: New Perspectives. pp175–6

[343] Morris, 2009, 235–7

[344] Cockerill, S., 2014, Eleanor of Castile: The Shadow Queen

[345] Ibid

[346] Morris, 2009, 240; 249

[347] Rohde, A., 'Coinage' in Gaunt, A., Wright, J., Crossley, S. & Budge, D., 2015, *Excavation of the Medieval Boundary Ditch of King John's Palace, Kings Clipstone, Sherwood Forest, Nottinghamshire*, pp97–100

[348] Taylor, A. J., 1984, *The Welsh Castles of Edward I*, p27

[349] E 101/460/18

[350] *Warner, K., 2014, Edward II – The Unconventional King, p17; 30*

Chapter Five: A Century of Turbulence: 1307–1399

[351] Bingham, C., 1973, *The Life and Times of Edward II*, p197

[352] Warner, 2014, 243;

353 Phillips, S., 2011, *Edward II,* pp560–565

354 Mortimer, I., 2005, 'The Death of Edward II in Berkeley Castle' in *English Historical Review*, CXX, pp1175–1214

355 Warner, 2014, 248–262

356 Phillips, 2011, 577–606

357 Mortimer, I., 2015, 'Was Edward really killed?' in Letters, *BBC History Magazine*, April 2015

358 Warner, 2014, 14

359 Ibid, 15

360 Costain, T. B., 1973, *The Pageant of England 1272–1377: The Three Edwards*, p128; p466

361 Almond, 2003, 120

362 Steane, 1993, 147

363 Wessex Archaeology 2011, 21

364 Warner, 2014, 30–32; Phillips, 2011, 126–8

365 Phillips, 2011, 152 n143

366 Ibid, 174–5

367 Ibid, 190–1

368 Crook, 1976, 40

369 Phillips, 2011, 252–3

370 Ibid

371 Deputy Keeper of the Records (ed.), 1893, *Calendar of the Close Rolls of Edward II* Vol. II AD1313–18, p257

372 Platt, C., 1978, *Medieval England: A Social History and Archaeology from the Conquest to 1600AD*, p91

373 Wright, 2008, 28

374 Hanawalt, B., 1979, Crime and Conflict in English Communities 1300–1348, pp261–73

375 Crook 2005, n12

376 Ibid, n52

377 Phillips, 2011, 244–7; 264–5

378 Crook, 1976, 40

379 Phillips, 2011, 271–2

380 James 2012

381 James, 1990, 172–3

382 Stapleton, 1890, 38

383 Steane 2001, 263

384 Warner, 2014, 98

385 Crook, 1976, 40–1

386 Stapleton, 1890, 38

387 Warner, 2014, 98

388 Phillips, 2011, 279; Warner, 2014, 98

[389] Warner, 2014, 98

[390] Ibid, 98–9

[391] Phillips, 2011, 265–8

[392] Crook 2005

[393] Warner, 2014, 105; Phillips, 2011, 279

[394] Warner, 2014, 105

[395] Crook 2005

[396] Warner, 2014, 104–5

[397] Stapleton, 1890, 40

[398] Warner, 2014, 107

[399] Stapleton, 1890, 39; Warner, 2014, 106–7

[400] Stapleton, 1890, 40–1

[401] Steane, 1993, 156

[402] Barber, R., 2014, *Edward III and the Triumph of England*, p49

[403] Crook 2005

[404] Ibid

[405] Permission was sought to reproduce a detail of Clipstone Park from the c 1400 Sherwood Forest Map in this publication. It is currently held at Belvoir Castle but sadly the Duke and Duchess of Rutland declined the request citing '*owner's prerogative*' as their reason. Readers curious as to the appearance of this source are referred to Barley, M. W., 1986, 'Sherwood Forest' in Skelton, R. A. & Harvey, P. D. A (eds.) *Local maps and plans from medieval England*. Clarendon Press. Alternatively conducting an image search in an internet search engine for "Clipstone Park" may also produce a ready illustration of the detail.

[406] Crook, 1976, 40; Crook 2005

[407] E 101/460/18; E101/460/19

[408] Crook, 1976, 40; Crook 2005

[409] Crook 2005

[410] Crook, 1976, 41

[411] Fisher, J. L., 1968, *A medieval farming glossary of Latin and English words, taken mainly from Essex records.* I am indebted to Dr Mary South of the Friends of Clarendon Palace for pointing me towards this identification.

[412] Crook 2005

[413] Crook, 1976, 43

[414] Ibid, 38–9

[415] Warner, 2014, 124

[416] Crook 2005

[417] Ibid

[418] Warner, 2014, 132–3

[419] Deputy Keeper of the Records (ed.), 1895, *Calendar of the Close Rolls of Edward II* Vol. III AD1318–23, p270; p666; Deputy Keeper of the Records (ed.), 1893, *Calendar of the Close Rolls of Edward II* Vol. II AD1313–18, p435

[420] Crook, 1976, 41

[421] Warner, 2014, 141–57

[422] Crook, 1976, 41

[423] Ormrod, 2013, 64–6

[424] Ibid, 66

[425] Barber, 2014, 49

[426] Stapleton, 1890, 45

[427] James, 1990, 108

[428] Steane, 1993, 157–9; James, 1990, 109

[429] Barber, 2014, 50

[430] James & Gerrard, 2007, 68

[431] Crook 1976; Crook 2005

[432] Shaw Browne, 2002, p10

[433] Stapleton, 1890, 45–6

[434] Crook 1976, 39

[435] Ibid, 44

[436] Ibid, 41

[437] Rahtz 1956, 24

[438] E 101/460/18 & E 101/460/19

[439] Warner, 2014, 236

[440] Ormrod, 2011, 74

[441] Barber, 2014, 62

[442] Ormrod, 2011, 88–9; 613

[443] Deputy Keeper of the Records (ed.), 1898, *Calendar of the Close Rolls of Edward III* Vol. II AD1330–33, p113; 264

[444] Crook 1976, 39; 43

[445] Ormrod, 2011, 316

[446] Steane 1993, 83

[447] Ibid, 165–6

[448] Barber, 2014, 104–7

[449] Ormrod, 2011, 175

[450] Ibid, 128

[451] Cokayne, G. E., 1912, *The Complete Peerage, Volume* II, pp. 44–5

[452] Barber, 2014, 155–6

[453] Ormrod, 2011, 268

[454] Portable Antiquities Sceme DENO-4C6163

[455] Steane 1993, 124–5

[456] James, A., 2012 *Metal detecting finds from the grounds of King John's Palace at King's Clipstone, Mansfield, Nottinghamshire*

[457] Steane, 1993, 125; Steane, 2001, 261; 266–7

[458] Wessex Archaeology 2011, 21

[459] Steane 2001, 265

[460] Benedictow, O. J., 2004, *The Black Death, 1346–1353: The Complete History,* pp46–8; 71–2

[461] James, T. B., 1999, *The Black Death in Hampshire*, p1

[462] Gummer, B., 2014, *The Scourging Angel: The Black Death in the British Isles,* p47

[463] 21M65/A1/9 fo.17

[464] E 101/542/24

[465] Benedictow, 2004, pp139 40

[466] Gummer, 2014, 201

[467] Ibid, 220

[468] Gasquet, F. A., 1908, *The Black Death of 1348 and 1349*, p173

[469] Gummer, 2014, 55

[470] E 101/542/24

[471] James, 1999, 17–18

[472] Johnson, P., 1973, *The Life and Times of Edward III*, p154; James, 1999, 11

[473] Steane, J., 2014, *The Archaeology of Medieval England and Wales*, p233; Gardner, A., 2011, *English Medieval Sculpture*, pp299–300; Myers, A. R., 2013, *English Historical Documents 4: 1327–1485*, 942–3

[474] Johnson, 1973, 152

[475] Dyer, 2000, 13

[476] Platt, 1978, 129

[477] E 101/542/24; E 101/460/18; E101/460/19; E 101/460/20; E 101/460/21; E 101/135/20

[478] Ibid

[479] E 101/542/24

[480] Salzman 1952,251–2

[481] Ibid, 254

[482] E 101/460/18; E101/460/19

[483] James & Gerrard 2007, 73

[484] E 101/460/20; E 101/460/21

[485] E 101/460/18; E101/460/19

[486] E 101/460/18; E101/460/19

[487] E 101/460/20; E 101/460/21

[488] Colvin Brown & Taylor, 1963, 918–921

[489] Hewlings, R., 2008, 'Sir Howard Colvin' in *The Independent* Tuesday 1 January 2008

[490] Rahtz, 1960, 22

[491] Pevsner, N, 1951, *The Buildings of England: Nottinghamshire*, p52

[492] Stapleton, 1890, 10

[493] White, W., 1832, *History, Gazetteer and Directory of Nottinghamshire*, pp417–8; White, F., 1844, *History, Gazetteer and Directory of Nottinghamshire*, pp625–6

[494] Throsby, J., 1790, 173

[495] Harries, S., 2011, *Nikolaus Pevsner: The Life*, p410

[496] Pevsner, 1952, 11

[497] Harries, 2011, 412

[498] Ibid, 401

[499] Pevsner, 1951, 52

[500] White, 1832, 418

[501] Pevsner, 1951, 52

[502] Rahtz, 1960, 29

[503] Gaunt & Wright 2013–14, 237

[504] Rahtz 2001, 36–62

[505] E 101/542/24

[506] Wright 2013; Wright 2016

[507] E 101/542/24

[508] Ibid

[509] E 101/460/18; E101/460/19

[510] Challis, K., (ed.), 2014, 'Archaeology in Nottinghamshire' in *Transactions of the Thoroton Society* Vol. 118. Nottingham

[511] E 101/542/24

[512] Salzman, 1952, pp99–100

[513] Wood 1983, 289

[514] Armitage, 2007, p41; line 798

[515] E 101/460/18; E101/460/19

[516] E 101/542/24; E 101/460/18; E101/460/19

[517] E 101/135/20

[518] Gregory, A., 2014, *The Queen's House and Bell Tower: Statement of Significance*

[519] E 101/542/24

[520] E 101/542/24

[521] E 101/460/18; E101/460/19

[522] James, 1990, 62

[523] Ormrod, 2013, 44; 220; 291; 403

[524] Pearsall, D., 1992, *The Life of Geoffrey Chaucer*, p38

[525] Ibid, 34

[526] Ibid, 39

[527] Ibid 41

[528] Ibid, 47–9

[529] Howard, D. R., 1989, *Chaucer: His Life, His Works, His World*, pp454–8

[530] Ibid, 52–3; 57–8

[531] James, 2012

[532] Wessex Archaeology, 2011, 20

[533] Howard, 1989, 53

[534] Ibid, 54–6

[535] Ormrod, 2013, 462–3

[536] Ormrod, 2013, 461–2

[537] E 101/460/18; E101/460/19

[538] Mortimer, I., 2008, *The Fears of Henry IV: The Life of England's Self-Made King*, p63

[539] Curry, A., 2000, 'Richard II and the war with France' in Dodd, G. (ed.), *The Reign of Richard II*, p45

[540] McHardy, A. K., 2000, 'Richard II: a personal portrait' in Dodd (ed.), p24

[541] Mortimer, 2008, 68

[542] Biggs, D., 2000, 'The Appellant and the clerk: the assault on Richard II's friends in government, 1387–9' in Dodd (ed.), 67; Dodd, G., 2000, 'Richard II and the transformation of Parliament' in Dodd (ed), 71; Mortimer, 2008, 69; Saul, N., 1999, *Richard II*, 171–2

[543] Saul, 1999, 171–2

[544] Ibid, 173

[545] Ibid, 175

[546] Mortimer, 2008, 69

[547] Biggs, 2000, 62

[548] Dodd, 2000, 72; 82

[549] McHardy, 2000, 21

[550] Ibid, 19–21

[551] Ibid, 24

[552] Steane, 1993, 147

[553] Griffin, 2008, 62

[554] Almond, 2011, 93

[555] Ibid, 94–5

[556] Lavelle, 1854 (1992)

[557] Armitage, 2009, 44; lines 887–893

[558] Ibid, 48, 993–4

[559] Given-Wilson, 1993, 241

[560] Mortimer, 2008, 70–74

[561] Deputy Keeper of the Records (ed.), 1922, Calendar of the Close Rolls of Richard II Vol. IV AD1389–92, p365

[562] Stapleton, 1890, 52

[563] Crook 1976, 44 n1

[564] Saul, 1999, 472

[565] E 101/135/20

[566] Ibid

[567] Redmonds, G., King, T. & Hey, D., 2011, *Surnames, DNA and Family History*, p127

[568] Saul, 1999, 227–9

[569] Curry, 2000, 35–6

[570] Saul, 1999, 473

[571] Federico, 2000, 52–4

[572] Armitage, 2009, 18; lines 309–315
[573] Federico, 2000, 51; 55
[574] Armitage, 2009, 7; 33; 43; 44; 46; 49; 50; 67; 94

Chapter Six: Beyond the Palace

[575] Griffin 2007, 21
[576] Barley 1986
[577] Stapleton, 1890, 55–6
[578] Rowley 1988, 177
[579] Crook 1976, 38; E 101/135/20
[580] James & Gerrard, 2007, 50; Rowley 1988, 172
[581] Crook, 1976, 35
[582] Ibid, 35
[583] Gaunt & Wright 2013, 48
[584] Crook, 1976, 43
[585] Boulton 1964
[586] Gaunt 2011
[587] Ibid
[588] Ibid
[589] Ibid
[590] James & Gerrard 2007, 47
[591] Gaunt & Wright 2013, 46
[592] James & Gerrard, 2007, 45
[593] Griffin 2007, 65
[594] James & Gerrard 2007, 50
[595] Steane 2001, 273
[596] Rowley 1988, 171; Steane, 2001, 273
[597] Gaunt & Wright 2013, 46–47, James & Gerrard, 2007, 46
[598] E 101/135/20
[599] E 101/460/18; E101/460/19; E 101/460/20; E 101/460/21; E 101/542/24; E 101/135/20
[600] Stapleton, 1890, 75; Gaunt 2011
[601] Shaw-Browne, 2001, 8–10
[602] Crook 1976, 36
[603] Crook, 1976, 36–8
[604] Griffin, 2007, 12; 15
[605] Ibid, 55
[606] Sykes 2007a, 51–5
[607] Ibid, 44
[608] Griffin 2007, 22
[609] Armitage, 2007, 58' lines 1158–1172

[610] Griffin 2007, 52–5

[611] Pearsall, 1992, 57–8

[612] Chaucer, G., 'The Book of the Duchess' in Stone, B. (ed.), 1983, *Love Visions: The Book of the Duchess, The House of Fame, The Parliament of Birds, The Legend of Good Women*, pp31–2; lines 344–86

[613] James & Gerrard 2007, 61

[614] Armitage, 2007, 68–9; 73–5; 79–80; 87

[615] Almond, 2003, 87

[616] Griffin 2007, 63

[617] Kirton, T., 2001, 'Clipstone Forest and Shrogges' in *A Celebration of Kings Clipstone – 1000 Years of History*, p24

[618] James & Gerrard 2007, 62; Griffin 2007, 64

[619] Rackham, O., 1980, *The History of the Countryside*, p181

[620] Shaw Browne, 2001, 11

[621] Griffin 2007, 29

[622] James & Gerrard 2007, 61–2; Griffin, 2007, 54–5

[623] Griffin, 2007, 21

[624] Steane 1999, 151

[625] Wessex Archaeology 2011, 21

[626] Steane 1999, 151

[627] Drage 1990, 134–7

[628] Wright 2009, 33

[629] James & Gerrard 2007, 86–7

[630] Sykes 2007b, 149–60

[631] Armitage, 2007, 64; lines 1330–1336

[632] Steane 1999, 152

[633] Armitage, 2007, 65; lines 1355; 1359

[634] Ibid, 65; lines 1362–5

[635] Griffin, 2007, 31

[636] Wessex Archaeology, 2011, 21

[637] Griffin, 2007, 30–1

[638] Steane 1999, 117

[639] James & Gerrard 2007, 71–3

[640] Steane 1999, 117

[641] James, 1990, 84

[642] Ibid, 57

[643] Steane 1999, 118

[644] Ibid, 120

[645] James & Gerrard 2007, 71; Steane 2001, 106–7

[646] James, 1990, 84; 94–5

[647] Steane, 2001, 107

[648] Gaunt & Wright 2013, 44

649 Wessex Archaeology, 2011, 13
650 Gaunt & Wright 2013–14, 246
651 Crook, 1976, 42–3
652 James, 1990, 50; Steane, 1999, 139
653 Rowley 1988, 64–8
654 Wessex Archaeology 2011, 9; 13
655 Keevill, 2000, 56
656 Rahtz 1960, 22
657 Ibid, 23
658 Stapleton, 1890, 28
659 Ibid
660 Crook 1976, 42
661 E 101/542/24
662 E 101/460/18; E 101/460/19
663 James & Gerrard 2007, 87
664 Rowley 1988, 64
665 Gaunt & Wright 2013, 44
666 Keevill, 2000, 134–5
667 Rowley 1988, 183–4
668 Griffin, 2007, 59
669 E 101/542/24
670 Gaunt & Wright 2013, 48
671 E 101/460/18 & E 101/460/19
672 Stapleton 1890, 25
673 Wessex Archaeology, 2011, 31
674 Rowley, 1988, 183–4
675 Steane 1999, 140
676 James & Gerrard 2007, 59; 87
677 Steane 2001, 262
678 James & Gerrard 2007, 59
679 Rowley, 1988, 149
680 Dyer, 2000, 20
681 Gaunt & Wright 2013, 46; 48
682 Kirton, 2001, 20
683 Rowley, 1988, 149
684 James & Gerrard 2007, 55; Kirton, 2001, 22
685 Rowley, 1988, 150
686 Celebration 2002, 11
687 Rowley, 1988, 153
688 Kirton, 2002, 24
689 Ibid
690 Crook, 1976, 38

[691] Barley 1986
[692] Gaunt & Wright 2013, 48
[693] Ibid, 49
[694] Crook 1976, 42
[695] Richardson, 2007, 30
[696] Armitage, 2007, 40; lines 764–772
[697] Ibid, 41; lines 787–9
[698] Ibid, 100; lines 2185–6
[699] Hayman, R., 2014, *The Green Man*, pp10–3; 22
[700] James & Gerrard 2007, 69
[701] Ibid, 47
[702] Keevill, 2000, 134–5
[703] James & Gerrard 2007, 45, 53–4
[704] Gaunt 2011, 44

Chapter Seven: The People of the Palace

[705] Hoad, 1993, 341
[706] Dyer, C., 2001, *Everyday Life in Medieval England*, p134
[707] Aston, M. & Gerrard, C., 2013, *Interpreting the English Village*, pp196–7
[708] James, 1990, 14
[709] Shaw Browne, 2002, 41
[710] Throsby, J., 1790, 173
[711] Ibid
[712] Gaunt & Wright 2013, 42
[713] Stapleton, 1890, 29
[714] Aston & Gerrard, 2013, 200
[715] Ibid, 253
[716] Rowley 1988, 76–7
[717] Ibid, 78
[718] Gaunt 2011, 39
[719] Aston & Gerrard, 2013, 202–3
[720] Rowley 1988, 95
[721] Ibid, 96–7
[722] Dyer, 2000, 137; 144–5
[723] Ibid, 139–41
[724] Ibid, 144–8
[725] Ibid, 148; 155; 161
[726] Shaw Browne 2002, 11
[727] Mordan 2004, 7
[728] Ibid, 13–5
[729] Ibid, 9; 16

730 Ibid; 19–21
731 Ibid; 10
732 Aston & Gerrard, 2013, 209
733 Ibid, 211–14
734 Rowley 1988, 120–1
735 Aston & Gerrard, 2013, 197
736 Rowley 1988, 121–3; 129–31
737 Ibid, 131
738 Aston & Gerrard, 2013, 248
739 Ibid, 249
740 Challis 2013, 15
741 Ibid, 14
742 Rowley, 1988, 138
743 Gaunt & Wright 2013, 42; Shaw Browne 2002, 39
744 Rowley, 1988, 137–8
745 Aston & Gerrard, 2013, 246; 248
746 Aston & Gerrard, 2013, 214–15
747 Stapleton 1890, 8
748 James & Gerrard 2007, 86
749 Crook 1976, 36
750 Dyer, 2000, 134
751 Rowley, 1988, 132–3; 141
752 Ibid, 138
753 Ibid, 135–6
754 Ibid, 142
755 Ibid 143–5
756 Stapleton, 1890, 21
757 Crook 1976, 39
758 Griffin 2007, 32–33
759 Steane, 2001, 273; Griffin, 2007, 45
760 Kirton, 2002, 24
761 Griffin, 2007, 45; 58
762 Ibid, 14; 21–2; 31; 43
763 Ibid, 40–1
764 Cawthorne, N., 2010, *A Brief History of Robin Hood: The True History Behind the Legend*, p31
765 Stapleton, 1890, 18–19
766 Cawthorne, 2010, 35–7
767 Ibid, 64–5
768 Ibid, 38; 41;133; 135–6
769 Dyer, 2001, 3

Chapter Eight: The Decline of the Palace: 1399–1568

[770] Steane 1999, 83

[771] James, 1990, 114–15; 128; 136; 138

[772] Steane 1999, 83

[773] Stapleton, 1890, 53

[774] James, 1990, 138–9

[775] Ibid, 140; 143

[776] Wessex Archaeology 2011, 20

[777] Sheppard, 2015, 9

[778] E 364/77

[779] Rahtz, 1960, 36

[780] Wessex Archaeology, 2011, 8

[781] James, 1990, 144

[782] Stapleton, 1890, 58

[783] James, 1990, 148–64

[784] Steane, 1999, 81

[785] Rowley 1988, 46–7

[786] Keevill, 2000, 157; Rowley 1988, 48

[787] Rowley 1988, 48

[788] James & Gerrad 2007, 96; James 1990, 170

[789] Stapleton, 1890, 60

[790] Bradley & Severn, 2002, 36

[791] Clay, R. M., 1914 *The Hermits and Anchorites of England*, p28

[792] Rahtz, 1960, 36

[793] Wessex Archaeology 2011, 10–11

[794] Ibid, 17

[795] Challis 2013, 15

[796] Bradley & Severn, 2002, 36

Chapter Nine: Dukes, Antiquarians, Farmers and Community: 1568–2016

[797] Pevsner, 1979; Birmingham Post, 2013, 'Rich List 2013: No.30 – William Parente (£200m)' in *Birmingham Post*, 28 January 2013

[798] Mastoris. S. and Groves. S., 1997, "Sherwood Forest in 1609 : A Crown survey by Richard Bankes", *Thoroton Society Record Series XL* (for 1992 & 1993)

[799] Oxford University Press, 1994, *The Concise Dictionary of National Biography*, p504

[800] Mordan 2004, 30

[801] P1 E12/1/1/1

[802] Bradley, M., 2002, 'Clipstone Hall' in *A Celebration of Kings Clipstone – 1000 Years of History*, p68

803 Copnall, H. H., 1915, *Notes and Extracts from the Nottinghamshire County Records of the Seventeenth Century*, pp149–56

804 Crook 1976, 43

805 Copnall, 1915, 149–56

806 Sharpe, K., 1992, *The Personal Rule of Charles I*, p303

807 Bossy, J., 1983, 'The English Catholic Community 1603–1625' in Smith, A. G. R., *The Reign of James VI and I*, pp91–105

808 Cavendish, Margaret, The Life of William Cavendish, ed. C.H. Firth (2nd revised edition, 1906) [King's Meadow Campus East Midlands Collection Not 468.V38 CAV]

809 Griffin 2007, 100–3

810 Stapleton, 1890, 70–3; Bradley, M, 2002, 'Seventeenth Century Clipstone' in *A Celebration of Kings Clipstone – 1000 Years of History*, pp60–6

811 Petition of the inhabitants of Edwinstowe, Clipstone and Budby to Henry Cavendish, 2nd Duke of Newcastle upon Tyne, [no date, 1681–1691] Pw 1/284

812 Carlton, C., 1992, *The Experience of the British Civil Wars*, p211

813 Shapiro, J., 2010, *Contested Will*, pp306–9

814 Sharpe, J., 2001, *Witchcraft in early modern England,* p.37

815 Hutton, R. (ed), 2015, *Physical Evidence for Ritual Acts, Sorcery and Witchcraft in Christian Britain*. See especially: Hoggard, B., 'Witch Bottles: Their Contents, Contexts and Uses' pp91–105; Swann, J., 'Shoes Concealed in Buildings' pp118–130 and Easton, T., 'Spiritual Middens' pp147–163

816 Champion, M., 2015, 'Magic on the Walls: Ritual Protection Marks in the Medieval Church' in Hutton, R. (ed), 2015, *Physical Evidence for Ritual Acts, Sorcery and Witchcraft in Christian Britain*, pp15–38

817 Easton, T., 2015, 'Apotropaic Symbols and Other Measures for Protecting Buildings against Misfortune' in Hutton, R. (ed), 2015, *Physical Evidence for Ritual Acts, Sorcery and Witchcraft in Christian Britain*

818 Wright 2016

819 Champion, M., 2015, *Medieval Graffiti – The Lost Voices of England's Churches*, 197–210

820 Wright, J., 2015, *'The instruments of darkness tell us truths': Ritual Protection Marks and Witchcraft at Knole, Kent,* p21

821 Portable Antiquities Scheme DENO-AFFB41

822 Throsby (ed.), 1796, 340–2

823 Pl C 1/43, University of Nottingham Manuscripts and Special Collections. I am indebted to Josh Dowen and Lucy Veale for bring this document to my attention.

824 Shaw Browne, 2002, 57–8

825 Oxford University Press, 1994, 215

826 Mordan 2004, 25

827 Wright, 2013

828 White, 1832, 420

829 Danbury, J., 'The Water-Meadows Irrigation Scheme' in *A Celebration of Kings Clipstone – 1000 Years of History*, pp105–6

830 Challis 2013, 15

831 White, 1832, 421

832 Gaunt, Wright, Crossley & Budge, 2015, 66–7

833 Ibid, 420

834 Shaw Browne, 2002, 16

835 Hodgson, J. & Laird, C. F., 1813, *The Beauties of England*. Volume 12, pp385–386

836 Palmer, F. P. & Crowquill, A., 1846, The *Wanderings of a Pen and Pencil*, p353

837 Keevill, 2000, 36

838 Palmer & Crowquill, 1846, 352

839 Roberts, M., 1844, *Ruins and Old Trees, Associated with Memorable Events in English History*

840 Thompson, C., 1850 'Clipstone Castle and St. Edwin's Chapel' in *Sherwood Gatherer*.

841 Danbury, J., 2002, 'Christianity in Clipstone' in A Celebration of Kings Clipstone – 1000 Years of History, pp147; 149

842 Tweedale-Meeby, K., 1947, *Nottinghamshire County Records in the Eighteenth Century*, p351

843 Wright 2016

844 NA C/QDLv/3/1,2

845 Pl E12/6/8/3/4

846 PI E12/1/1/1

847 Wright 2016

848 Palmer * Crowquill, 1846, 352

849 Wright 2016

850 ibid

851 ibid

852 Wright 2013

853 ibid

854 Danbury, J., 2002, 'Railways Associated with Clipstone' in *A Celebration of Kings Clipstone – 1000 Years of History*, pp205–210

855 Marples, P., 2013, *Clipstone Camp and the Mansfield Area in World War One*; Marples, P., 2005, *Forest Town: The Village That Grew Out Of Coal*

856 Danbury, J., 2002, 'Clipstone Army Camp' in *A Celebration of Kings Clipstone – 1000 Years of History*; Danbury, J., 2002, 'Clipstone Colliery and Village' in *A Celebration of King's Clipstone – 1000 Years of History*

857 Danbury, 2002, 217

858 Wright 2013, Wright 2016

859 Wright, J., 2004, 'A Survey of King John's Palace, King's Clipstone, Nottinghamshire' in *Transactions of the Thoroton Society of Nottinghamshire* Vol. 108, pp111–3

Index